QMW Library

23 1099849 9

BR 750 BAR

D1333421

34855
24. 11. 50.

OXFORD HISTORICAL SERIES

Editors
F. M. POWICKE B. H. SUMNER

BRITISH SERIES

NOTE

This Series comprises carefully selected studies which have been submitted, or are based upon theses submitted, for higher degrees in this University. In 1948 a new General Series was added to a British Series. The British Series is a collection of works which advance knowledge of the structural development, whether political, ecclesiastical, or economic, of British Society. The General Series comprises works on any aspect of non-British history, and also works on British history which lie outside the scope of the British Series.

BRITISH SERIES

GENERAL SERIES

DURHAM JURISDICTIONAL PECULIARS

BY

FRANK BARLOW

OXFORD UNIVERSITY PRESS
LONDON: GEOFFREY CUMBERLEGE
1950

WESTFIELD COLLEGE
LIBRARY
UNIVERSITY OF LONDON

Oxford University Press, Amen House, London E.C. 4

GLASGOW NEW YORK TORONTO MELBOURNE WELLINGTON
BOMBAY CALCUTTA MADRAS CAPE TOWN

Geoffrey Cumberlege, Publisher to the University

PRINTED IN GREAT BRITAIN

PREFACE

THIS essay was begun in the first year of the war both as an intellectual distraction and as a token render to a university which paid me a salary but imposed no duties; and the work was resumed after five years' military service as a familiar task amid the bewildering exigencies of a profession that had become strange. It is a technical study. I must confess that I was interested in disentangling a complicated story, in tracing the evolution of a few connected ecclesiastical peculiars through their different phases, in an ordinary detective problem. Yet I could not fail to see, and I hope in some measure to have conveyed the view, that the development of these irregularities in the ecclesiastical system illuminates at every stage the nature of the polity in which they were formed, and that in using a microscope on a fragment a deeper knowledge of the whole can be obtained.

My thanks are due to those friends and colleagues who read the essay in its various drafts and encouraged me to persevere, especially to Sir F. M. Powicke, who also gave me valuable help while reading the proofs; and I am much obliged to the University College of the South West of England, Exeter, on the staff of which I have the honour to be, for its generous grant of £50 towards the cost of publishing the book.

F. B.

EXETER
1949

CONTENTS

INTRODUCTION

THE parliamentary legislation of the nineteenth century which reformed the organization of the Church of England secured the abolition of most of those geographical irregularities in the diocesan and archidiaconal system, those jurisdictional franchises and outliers, which are known as peculiars. By this necessary reform institutions of great interest to the ecclesiastical historian were destroyed, for the peculiars pointed both to the antiquity of the organization in which they were embedded and to the vicissitudes in the evolution of that system.[1] The history of the English bishoprics is intricate and often obscure. In origin they recall vanished folks and submerged kingdoms; but their medieval shape was due to the interplay of many forces. Among these influences—weaker, it is true, than the impact of the fortune of kings or the disruption of foreign invasions, yet of some importance—were those strains within the fabric of society itself, the pull of different loyalties, the cohesion of dynastic and public estates, the pressure of needs in no way, or but superficially, religious. Such tensions distorted and displaced the diocesan boundaries. The map of a thirteenth-century bishopric is adorned by curious aberrations; and it may be fancied that the lines of other cartographers show through the palimpsest.

In the evolution of peculiars can be seen the shifting

[1] For bibliographies of historical literature concerned with the subjects dealt with in this essay, see Dom David Knowles, *The Monastic Order* (1940), ch. xxxii and xxxiv; J.-F. Lemarignier, 'Étude sur les privilèges d'exemption et de juridiction ecclésiastique des abbayes normandes depuis les origines jusqu'en 1140', *Archives de la France monastique* (1937), pp. xxvi–xxxiii. For *Eigenkirchentum*, see the works of Ulrich Stutz, e.g. the easily accessible 'The Proprietary Church as an Element of Medieval Germanic Ecclesiastical Law', in *Studies in Medieval History: Medieval Germany 911–1250*, ed. Geoff. Barraclough (1938), ii. 35–70. For Anglo-Saxon and Norman conditions, see Heinrich Böhmer, *Kirche und Staat in England und in der Normandie im xi. und xii. Jahrhundert* (Leipzig, 1889), and 'Das Eigenkirchentum in England' in *Texte und Forschungen zur englischen Kulturgeschichte, Festgabe für Felix Liebermann zum 20 Juli 1921* (Halle, 1921); F. M. Stenton, *Anglo-Saxon England* (1943), pp. 148–56; and R. R. Darlington, 'Ecclesiastical reform in the late O.E. period', *E.H.R.* li, 385, and *Vita Wulfstani of Wm. of Malmsbury*, R. Hist. Soc. (Camden Ser.), xl (1928). For a study of some English exemptions, see Dom David Knowles, op. cit., and 'Essays in Monastic History: vi—Parish Organization', in *Downside Review*, vol. 51, pp. 501–22.

attitude of society towards the possessions and organization of the Christian Church in western Europe after the dissolution of the Roman Empire. In England, where the destruction of Roman culture was almost complete and Christianity was introduced anew into a barbarian society, three main influences affected the growth of ecclesiastical institutions: the mission impulses from Rome and from Ireland and the ideas and habits of the Anglo-Saxons.

From Rome came to England, through Italian, African, and Greek, the classical tradition of an urban and territorial Church; but the papal agents found no convenient civil administrative framework that could be taken over; and their adoption of the petty Germanic kingdoms as ecclesiastical units was a compromise which connected the episcopal sees with few ancient centres of government and produced dioceses which by their nature could be only imperfectly defined. Moreover, the strong Celtic influence, which persisted, especially in the north of England, long after its formal discomfiture, weakened the Roman impetus to discipline and order. In England, therefore, the provincial and diocesan system was congenitally infirm; but, as it was flexible and associated with living political institutions, it was more fitted than some of the archaic territorialized Churches to pass unbroken through the cataclysms which periodically shook western Europe. Even so it barely survived the disruptive influence of the Germanic conception of ownership, which substituted a rival pattern formed by the relationship between churches and their owners; and by the late Anglo-Saxon period English dioceses were disintegrating. The bishops had never had much independent spiritual jurisdiction; they had almost ceased to hold diocesan synods or to visit the parish churches of their bishoprics; and naturally they had failed to subdivide their sees into smaller administrative areas.

The private ownership of churches was an unescapable result of the barbarization of society. According to the new ideas a church was something that could be owned, bought and sold, disposed of in any way provided that the purpose of the endowment was unimpeded. A church could not properly be turned into a cowshed; but its revenues could be divided between the sons of its late owner so long as they maintained the services. Such churches were called in Latin documents *ecclesiae propriae*—proprietary churches, or, to use the convenient German word, *Eigenkirchen*. Moreover, the private ownership of churches involved a private relationship between the giver and the recipient of the ecclesiastical appointment, which inevitably assumed forms similar to those prevalent in lay society. The priest in a proprietary church was the man of the lord. In Domesday Book the village priest is often classified with the *villani*; but similar ideas prevailed even when the priest had a higher social status, as can be seen from the king's relations with his bishops and abbots. And a lord's men, whether they were household dependants or enfeoffed with land, were subject to his jurisdiction.

Developments of this kind had a profound effect on diocesan organization. Bishops ceased to have control over their diocesan parishes as such; their authority was confined to those churches which they themselves owned through either their episcopal or private estates. And the bishop enjoyed this power over his proprietary churches whether they were situated in his own diocese or within that of another. Dioceses were dissolving. Apart from ancient tradition only one factor preserved them from complete dissolution: the duty incumbent on every parish priest to obtain the chrism, or holy oil, annually on Maundy Thursday from his local diocesan. The maintenance of this formal link was probably the work of national legislation of *c.* 925, doubtless aimed at safeguarding one of the residuary public sources of episcopal revenue.[1] It was a law of considerable importance, for it hindered a bishop who had estates and churches in the diocese of another from attaching those estates radically to his own bishopric. The link could, of course, be broken; but it maintained a principle, and preserved the conception

[1] Böhmer, *Das Eigenkirchentum*, p. 333. The principle was maintained intact throughout the Middle Ages. Cf. letter of Archbishop Arundel of Canterbury in 1409, 'Cum curati omnes et singuli nostre iurisdiccionis predicte ut subditi immediati nostre sancte Cantuariensis ecclesie ab ipsa ecclesia tanquam a maiori et matrice ecclesia eorundem et nullatenus alibi oleum at crisma benedicta singulis annis ut iusticia exigit petere et percipere teneantur', Irene Josephine Churchill, *Canterbury Administration* (S.P.C.K., 1933), p. 129.

of a fixed territorial diocese such as had been expressed by the councils of Theodore of Tarsus.

The effects of the Norman Conquest were ambivalent. On one hand, *Eigenkirchentum* was as widespread in Normandy as in England, and even harsher in its effect on the status of the parish clergy. Hence there was no interference with the private ownership of churches in England; the system was, indeed, developed more stringently, so that the owner's share of the revenues was increased and the parish priests were, to use Böhmer's word, proletarianized. On the other hand, the reorganization of the constitution of the Church was vigorously undertaken on the reformed Norman model: the hierarchical system was redefined; the fundamental rights of a bishop in his diocese were re-stated; territorial archdeaconries and rural deaneries were introduced;[1] diocesan synods and the visitation of churches were made obligatory; and by the erection of separate ecclesiastical courts the ordinary was given an instrument by which he could enforce his discipline. No contradiction was seen at the time. Indeed, Archbishop Lanfranc, the architect of the new order, was equally the champion of the customary rights of the church of Canterbury. Under the influence of his reorganization he allowed the priests of his proprietary churches situated outside Kent to attend the synods of the local ordinary for their Christian edification, although reserving his jurisdiction over them; but when the archdeacons of the diocese of Chichester took money from the clerks at the synods Lanfranc indignantly withdrew this small concession, and recalled his priests entirely from the control of the local ordinary except in the matter of chrism.[2]

---

[1] The organization of the archdeaconries and rural deaneries naturally took some time. The diocese of Durham had its two archdeacons, who were to take their names from the cathedral church and from the county of Northumberland, by 1128 (see Appendix). According to A. Hamilton Thompson, 'Diocesan Organization in the Middle Ages: Archdeacons and Rural Deans', Raleigh Lecture on History, 1943, *Proc. of the Brit. Academy*, vol. xxix, fixed local titles for archdeaconries were not usual in England before the second half of the twelfth century and for rural deaneries before the thirteenth.

[2] *Eadmeri historia novorum in Anglia*, ed. Martin Rule (Rolls Ser., 1884), pp. 21–2. Letter of Lanfranc to Stigand, bishop of Chichester. Cf. 'Sicut namque ea quae antiquitus usque ad nostra tempora antecessores nostri habuerunt sollerti vigilantia cupimus illibata servare, ita aliis debita aliqua, quod absit, usurpatione nolumus denegare', p. 22. For the later history of the Canterbury peculiars, see I. J. Churchill, op. cit., pp. 62 seqq.

Eigenkirchentum remained for ever strong in English ecclesiastical life. But the Norman Conquest, by re-establishing the bishop as the local ordinary, provided a rival force; and in the inter-reaction of the conception of private ownership with the idea of the authority and status of a bishop, and especially with the view of a territorial administration and constitution of the Church, compromise solutions must eventually be produced. Lay ownership of churches will in time be attacked, reduced, and transformed into the right of advowson. Ecclesiastical *ecclesiae propriae* may share the same fate; but they were in a stronger position. Rights which become obnoxious to reformers when in lay hands may yet be owned by ecclesiastical persons and corporations without offence. This is understandable. For a layman to have proprietary rights in ecclesiastical matters was wrong; but those same rights, deriving from exactly the same conditions of society, when exercised by ecclesiastics appeared quite different. Some merely took their place among the many rights which a reformed Church was claiming for its members. A bishop's control over his proprietary churches was, for instance, largely engulfed in the right to control all his diocesan parishes which was now put forward. Even when the old did not fit quite neatly into the new system the retention of these traditional rights by ecclesiastics, when remodelled according to the fashion of the age, was seldom wrong in itself. It might be contrary to discipline or to common practice; but it might be tolerated as special custom. Hence ecclesiastical *ecclesiae propriae* will be transformed, but less radically, and may change into lawful irregularities in the diocesan administration, forming independent quasi-bishoprics, detached portions of another diocese, or peculiars and franchises of varying competence.

The origin of many ecclesiastical immunities lies, then, in the perpetuation of a primitive Germanic conception of ownership. Its survival into an age hostile to it was helped, and its application rendered less offensive, by what came to be known as the appropriation or incorporation of a church. As a church was considered not as an entity—in scholastic terms, a substance of inseparable duties—but as an accidental collection of transferable and useful rights, it could be freely partitioned, broken up, indeed, into as many particular rights as there were means of exploiting the church. Owners, therefore, were not hindered from diverting the revenues of their churches to other pious uses, and, if the owner was an ecclesiastical corporation, such as a monastery, then the parish church could be entirely or partly absorbed within the property of the corporation, provided that the cure of souls was maintained in the parish. By this process the owner not only possessed the church as fully as possible, but also destroyed functions which the local ordinary was resuming or claiming in respect of churches in lay hands. If monks served the church it was never vacant, and the bishop was unable to institute a priest or have him inducted into corporal possession of the church.[1] Even when stipendiary priests were appointed—the more usual practice—the insignificance of their role and their lack of a benefice caused the bishop to take less interest in his rights over them. Appropriation of parish churches began as early as the end of the eleventh century. Later the process was regulated and defined: the appropriator who owned the tithe and the glebe was considered the parson, and the priest in charge was transformed, largely through episcopal pressure, into a vicar with a permanent position and a fixed and competent revenue. Appropriation was only one of several methods of exploiting the ownership of a church; but it was that of most importance in the development of peculiars, because it created the strongest possible link between the owner and the church and disintegrated the parish.

The jurisdictional bond which existed between the lord and the priests of his proprietary churches was also strongly affected by the reforms which followed the Norman Conquest of England. William I had to arrest his half-brother

---

[1] For the serving of parishes by monks, see Dom U. Berlière, 'L'exercice du ministère paroissial par les moines dans le haut moyen-âge', in *Revue Bénédictine*, xxxix (1927), pp. 227–50. There is no evidence for the serving of parish churches by Durham monks; but while St. Godric was at Finchale in the second quarter of the twelfth century monks rode out regularly to hold services in the church of St. John the Baptist, which Godric had built, and which the local inhabitants attended [Reginald, *Libellus de vita et miraculis S. Godrici*, ed. J. Stevenson (Surtees Soc., vol. 20), *passim*, and cf. cap. cix]. This hermitage developed into a cell; but that was not inevitable. In any case the cells may not always have maintained secular chaplains in the twelfth century.

as earl of Kent; and this new immunity spread down in time
to the village priest. But if reform weakened the hold of lay
proprietors over the persons of their priests, it had unequal
effects on ecclesiastical owners. Episcopal jurisdiction was,
of course, strengthened. The specific ecclesiastical jurisdiction of the bishop was re-introduced by the reformers; and
the development of the feudal honorial courts must have
helped by analogy to preserve much of the old ideas. Ecclesiastical proprietors other than bishops were less fortunate.
Monasteries, for instance, had no inherent right of jurisdiction under the new dispensation; but the traditional rights
of the proprietary abbot over his priests must have been
supported to some extent by feudal ideas: just as courts for
his lay tenants were after 1066 maintained or evolved, so, it
may be imagined, the priests in the convent's churches would
still form a class of suitor. They must have been invested
with their temporalities, have taken the oath of fidelity, and
answered for some types of misdeeds in the court of the
monastery.[1] The twelfth-century formula runs that the
priests were to answer to the monastery for their benefices,
and to the diocesan for the cure of souls. This was a denial
of ecclesiastical jurisdiction proper to the proprietor; but it
at least recognized the tenurial bond and its implications.

Eigenkirchentum in its various manifestations provided a
fertile soil for the growth of peculiars. It supplied a private,
as opposed to a diocesan, grouping of churches, and it contained private jurisdictional and tenurial links, which, when
in ecclesiastical hands, appeared often proper and reasonable.
But it would seem that *Eigenkirchentum*, especially if the
owner of the churches was not a bishop, was not normally
sufficient of itself to produce a peculiar. Otherwise ecclesiastical parish franchises, numerous as they were, would have

---

[1] Even in the early thirteenth century investiture of the convent's rectors took
place in the chapter of Durham. In 1221 a monk giving evidence about the priory's
right of advowson said that he had been present in the chapter of the convent at
Durham when the rectors of Howden, Brantingham, Kirkby Sigston, Walkington,
and the proctor of the rector of Welton had received their charters of investiture
and had sworn fealty to the monks (*jurare fidelitatem, facere eis fidelitatem*),
Feodarium prioratus Dunelmensis, ed. Rev. Wm. Greenwell (Surtees Soc., vol. 58)
(henceforth *F.P.D.*), pp. 299–300. This is analogous to the way in which bishops
were enfeoffed in the royal court. The ceremonies represent residuary proprietary
rights.

been even more common in the Middle Ages. When, after the Norman Conquest, bishops resumed their ancient canonical rights, began to organize their dioceses in an orderly manner, and subdivided their bishoprics into archdeaconries and rural deaneries, it became increasingly necessary for the owners of parish churches to advance special and valid reasons why their possessions should not submit to the normal administrative system. Episcopal owners, like Lanfranc, could rely on the ancient customs of England. Archbishop Anselm consulted the last representative of the Old-English episcopacy, Wulfstan of Worcester, on the subject, and the reply was unequivocally in favour of a bishop's rights over his proprietary churches within an alien diocese.[1] The principle persisted throughout the Middle Ages.[2] Episcopal estates, therefore, which fell outside the diocese were almost bound to develop into a detached portion of the bishopric or remain as a peculiar.[3] The position of monasteries and other ecclesiastical corporations was, however, different. No doubt individual bishops would be tender to the possessions of their favourite monasteries within their sees; but with the increase in legal knowledge and a growing uniformity of custom, some title to franchise became advisable. The touchstone became possession of the episcopal customs.

A bishop's church, like a parish church, was no irreducible

---

[1] *Eadmeri historia*, pp. 45–6 and 361–2.

[2] In 1390 Robert Braybrooke, bishop of London, gave Walter Skirlaw, bishop of Durham, jurisdiction over the latter's subjects within the diocese of London, *Scriptores tres*, ed. Jas. Raine (Surtees Soc., vol. 9), p. clix. In 1318 Richard Newport, bishop of London, had granted a similar courtesy privilege to Walter Stapledon, bishop of Exeter, *The Register of Walter de Stapledon*, ed. F. C. Hingeston-Randolph (1892), p. 274.

[3] The archbishops of York, for example, possessed the peculiars of Hexham in the diocese of Durham and Churchdown (Glos.) in the diocese of Worcester. For the history of the former, see *A History of Northumberland*, vol. iii; for the latter, see A. Hamilton Thompson, 'The Jurisdiction of the Archbishops of York in Gloucestershire', *Trans. of the Bristol and Glos. Arch. Soc.*, vol. xliii. It is interesting to find that the priors of St. Oswald's in the peculiar of Churchdown prejudiced the archbishops' rights in the later thirteenth century by going to Worcester instead of to Southwell for the ingredients of chrism, and that when the franchisal jurisdiction was attacked by the archbishops of Canterbury and the bishops of Worcester, York could find no adequate documentary evidence to justify it. The peculiar was able, however, to withstand the most determined attacks because the royal dignity was involved (ibid., pp. 143 seqq.).

entity. According to the ideas of the time it could be split into transferable fragments. Hence *episcopalia* could be alienated to other ecclesiastics, if not always to laymen, without any impropriety, and were in fact not infrequently so alienated. By 1066 Anglo-Saxon bishops had lost most of their rights except that of the provision of chrism; but the vanished rights are perhaps to be regarded more as lapsed or in abeyance than as formally alienated. It is doubtful whether there are genuine Anglo-Saxon grants of *episcopalia* as such to immunists, and the authority of prescription, although exploited, for instance, by Lanfranc and Anselm in respect of the rights of the church of Canterbury, had hardly in that period the legal precision it later acquired. With the re-establishment of the position of the ordinary and of an ecclesiastical administration after the Conquest, bishops resumed or assumed valuable rights: the holding of synods, dispensation of coercive justice, visitation of churches, and, perhaps a later development, the right to call on the clergy of the diocese for financial aid on analogy with the feudal *auxilia*. All these *episcopalia* were financial rights: at the synod the clergy paid *synodalia*, on visitation *procuratio* or *hospitium*, and the synodal courts produced fines and amercements. And these rights could be acquired by a person other than the *ordinarius loci* by genuine episcopal grant, either of grace or under pressure, by gift from an earlier possessor— a cheap act of piety when the benefactor was a layman with condemned rights—by prescription, or by usurpation.

Possession of some or all of the episcopal customs naturally produced an immunity of varying degree. If all the *episcopalia*, including those inseparable from the bishop's order—ordination, institution of incumbents, consecration, provision of holy oil—were alienated, to another bishop, or to any bishop of the grantee's choice, then a gap had been made in the diocese. If, however, the bishop alienated only those customs which did not touch his order—synodals, procuration fees, justice, or aids—then a franchise was created, but the diocese was maintained intact. Naturally for the lawful possession of such episcopal rights a title was advisable wherever the diocesan bishop was conscious of his rights and intent on maintaining them. Immemorial custom and peaceful possession were often sufficient in the greater part of the twelfth century; but episcopal charters of alienation could usually be produced by the immunist, although these were perforce of varying degrees of authenticity.

The duties of which the bishop was deprived by the alienation of the episcopal customs which did not touch his order were those which, after the eleventh century, he normally delegated and later abandoned to his archdeacons. Hence a franchise dependent on possession of the episcopal customs, and without the greater privileges involving the intrusion of an alien bishop, normally tended to be equated with an archdeaconry. Clearly, then, the organization of bishoprics into territorial archdeaconries and the growing power of archdeacons had disturbing effects on immunities. On the one hand, this change removed the bishop from direct concern with the franchise, for the rights claimed by the immunist were largely those now devolved on the archdeacon. The immunist became only another of the episcopal subordinates; and, although this complicated the administration of the diocese, it was part of the accepted scheme. There is little reason to think that bishops were hostile to franchises as such. They were often immunists themselves in another diocese,[1] and their proprietary churches within their own diocese were usually separately administered.[2] On the other hand, the archdeacon became directly concerned with the immunity; and, with the growth of his powers as an ordinary, the peculiars were franchises within his territory. It was his jurisdiction and revenue more than those of the bishop that the immunist was decreasing. Hence in the twelfth and thirteenth centuries the franchisal authority probably found in the archdeacon his most active opponent.

These, then, are the general conditions behind the development of ecclesiastical peculiars, and some aspects of them have been studied with considerable intensity. The process, however, by which Germanic conceptions of ownership and of *beneficia*, together with alienations of episcopal customs, led to the establishment of various kinds of fran-

---

[1] See above, p. xiv, n. 3.
[2] For the position in the diocese of Canterbury, see I. J. Churchill, op. cit., pp. 83 seqq.

chises, and, especially, the history of this process in the twelfth century, have not been studied so fully. Nor is it an easy task. The development takes place in a period not rich in sources, and is often concealed by abundant forgery. Again, not only does the terminology of grant and charter take new forms, but the terminology inevitably assumes a different meaning and significance according to the period of its interpretation. An eleventh-century charter exhibited in the thirteenth century is bound to mean something different from the original intention of the grantor. Hence the development of a franchise is not merely a mechanical process depending on grants and forgeries and the acceptance of these; it is an organic process inseparable from and depending on changes in the society which surrounds it. Nor is the growth spontaneous and undirected. Men forge the charters, wield the jurisdiction, and argue in the courts. Medieval anonymity must not make us forget that policies and administrations are the works of men.

Studies of individual peculiars, tracing aspects in the development of each, are, therefore, required before safe generalizations can be made. An attempt is made here to write the history of franchises claimed or won in respect of churches possessed by the monastery of Durham. Benedictine monks were introduced into the church of Durham by Bishop William of Saint-Calais in 1083. Within about a quarter of a century the convent had established its claim to a share of the endowments of the see, and thus obtained churches in the dioceses of Durham and York. During the same period the kings of Scotland granted it large estates with their churches in Lothian within the diocese of St. Andrews. A few churches were also acquired in the diocese of Lincoln.

It will be seen that the choice of Durham as the subject for this investigation offers certain advantages: the convent possessed churches in different dioceses and under different conditions. The various groups, therefore, act as mutual controls. There is, however, one disadvantage: the history of the franchises in most cases does not begin earlier than 1083; but this is to some extent mitigated by the backwardness of conditions in the Border area.

Each of the groups of churches developed differently. The convent obtained franchises in the dioceses of Durham and York, failed in St. Andrews, and apparently made no claims in the diocese of Lincoln. The histories of the Durham, York, and St. Andrews franchises are described here in that order. The essay is a study in origins, and in each case the story is abandoned as soon as development within the medieval framework appears to have ceased. This occurs in the thirteenth and fourteenth centuries.[1]

---

[1] There is a wealth of manuscript material, imperfectly catalogued, in the archives of the Dean and Chapter of Durham concerning the monastery's archdeaconries in the later Middle Ages. Little attempt has been made here to use this material, as it appears mainly to illustrate the administration of the franchises after the period of development was over; but doubtless there are documents to be discovered which might help to produce a firmer outline to the earlier period. It is to be hoped that a useful calendar of the Durham D. & C. archives will eventually be produced.

THE MAPS

AN ATTEMPT has been made to show all the parish churches which belonged to the prior and convent of Durham in the twelfth and thirteenth centuries within the area represented, and those dependent chapels to which reference is made in the text and notes. The status of the church, as indicated by the symbol employed, is generally that which obtained in the second half of the thirteenth century; but a conservative attitude has been adopted towards the promotion of chapels to parochial status, in order that the more primitive organization should not be unnecessarily obscured.

THE CONVENT'S CHURCHES IN THE TWELFTH CENTURY IN DURHAM, NORTHUMBRIA, YORKSHIRE, AND SCOTLAND[1]

1196[2]	1157[3]	1146[4]	1196[2]	1157[3]	1146[4]
DURHAM			Ellingham	+	
†*Elvet	+	+	*South Charlton*		
Croxdale			Bedlington	+	+
Witton Gilbert			*Camboise*	+	?
Finchale					
Pittington	+		BEYOND TEES		
†*Dalton-le-Dale	+		†Northallerton	+	+
†*Monk Hesleden	+		†Brompton	+	+
Castle Eden			*Deighton*	+	+
Hardwick			High Worsall	+	+
Merrington	+		Kirkby Sigston	+	+
Bishop Middleham	+		Hemingbrough	+	+
chapels			Skipwith	+	+
†*Aycliffe	+		†*Howden	+	+
Ketton			*Eastrington*	+	+
Heighington			†*Brantingham	+	+
Staindrop	+	+	*Ellerker*	+	+
†Billingham	+		*Blacktoft*	?	?
Wolviston			*Hunsley*	?	?
*Jarrow	+		*'Middelhil'*	?	?
Wallsend			†*Welton.	+	+
Heworth			†*Walkington	+	+
Shields	+		York, All Saints	+	+
†*Monkwearmouth	+		York, St. Peter-the-		
Hilton	+		Little	+	+
NORTHUMBRIA			†York, St. Trinity	+	
†*Norham	+	+	Holtby	+	+
Cornhill	+	+			
*Holy Island	+	+	BEYOND TWEED		
Lowick	+	+	Coldingham	desunt	+
Ancroft	+	+	Old Cambus		
Kyloe	+	+	Lamberton		
Tweedmouth	+	+	Berwick		+
Fenham			Fishwick		+
Branxton			Edrom		
Edlingham			*chapels*		
Bolton			Swinton		+
Bywell St. Peter			Ednam		+
			Stichill		+

[1] These three lists of churches (with chapels in italic type), arranged in vertical columns, are taken from papal confirmations of the convent's possessions. As it appears that the inventories were compiled in ever-increasing detail the schedules are an unsafe guide to the date of the foundation or acquisition of a dependent chapel. The phrase 'and chapel(s)' sometimes anticipates the listing of chapels by name. Churches mentioned in the forged foundation charters are marked * ('Ego Willelmus', *F.P.D.*, p. xli) and † ('Notum sit omnibus', ibid., p. lv).

[2] Privilege of Pope Celestine III, Dr. Walther Holtzmann, *Papsturkunden in England* (Berlin, 1930, 1935), ii, no. 278. [3] Privilege of Pope Adrian IV, ibid., no. 94.

[4] Privilege of Pope Eugenius III, ibid., no. 51.

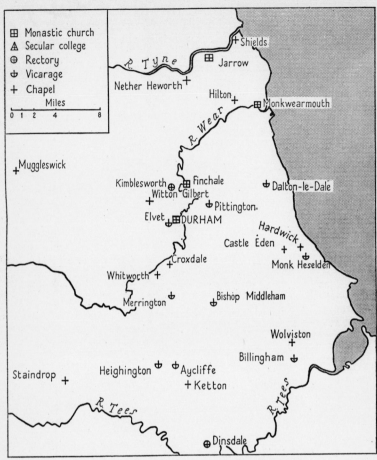

ARCHDEACONRY OF DURHAM

(The convent's churches)

Map legend:

- ⊞ Monastic church
- △ Secular college
- ⊕ Rectory
- ♱ Vicarage
- + Chapel

Miles
0 1 2 4 8

Shields
R. Tyne
Jarrow
Nether Heworth
Hilton
Monkwearmouth

Muggleswick
R. Wear
Kimblesworth
Finchale
Witton Gilbert
Dalton-le-Dale
Pittington
Elvet DURHAM
Hardwick
Castle Eden
Croxdale
Monk Heseldeñ
Whitworth
Merrington
Bishop Middleham
Wolviston
Staindrop
Heighington
Aycliffe
Billingham
Ketton
R. Tees
R. Tees
Dinsdale

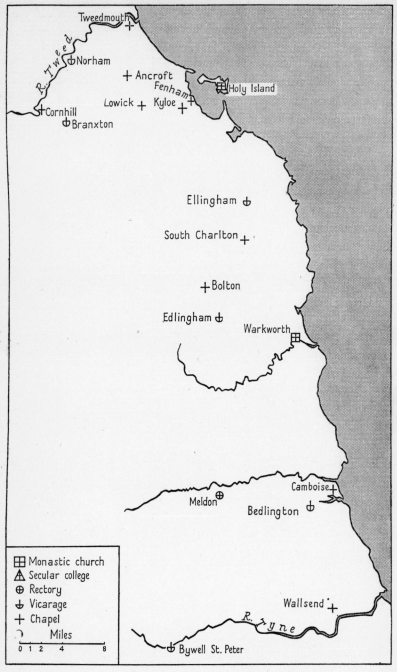

Tweedmouth

R. Tweed

✠ Norham

✠ Ancroft

Fenham

Lowick ✠ Kyloe

✠ Cornhill

✠ Branxton

⊞ Holy Island

Ellingham ⚓

South Charlton ✠

✠ Bolton

Edlingham ⚓

Warkworth ⊞

Camboise ✠

Meldon ⊕

Bedlington ⚓

Wallsend ✠

⊞ Monastic church
⚠ Secular college
⊕ Rectory
⚓ Vicarage
✠ Chapel
⌒ Miles

0 1 2   4   8

R. Tyne

⚓ Bywell St. Peter

ARCHDEACONRY OF NORTHUMBERLAND
(The convent's churches)

THE DURHAM FRANCHISE

§ 1. *The Norman Constitution of the Church of Durham*

FEW churches have a more romantic history than St.
Cuthbert's, Durham. The see of Lindisfarne, associated
with the earliest Scottish Christianity in Northumbria, became indissolubly linked with the fate of its sixth bishop, St.
Cuthbert († 687), whose incorrupted body became its most
precious possession. Where went the body, there went the
church; and the celebrated wanderings during the periods
of Scandinavian invasion came to a fitting close with the
settlement on the fortress rock of Durham in 995. By the
Norman Conquest the heroic period was over, and in 1083
the second Norman bishop, William of Saint-Calais (1081–
96), made the first reform in the constitution of the church.
He replaced the secular canons, or clerks of St. Cuthbert—
descendants of the Lindisfarne monks—by Benedictine
monks from the Vale of Evesham who had newly resettled
Benedict Biscop's old foundations at Jarrow and Monkwearmouth, and thus restored the spirit of Northumbrian
Christianity, and created another example of that English
custom, the monastic cathedral.

For our knowledge of the changes made at Durham and
of the organization of the church at the turn of the eleventh
century we are largely dependent on the chronicle of the
Durham monk Symeon[1] and on a series of forged charters.
Symeon was one of the earliest monks, and his narrative is
of great authority. He was intelligent and accurate, but not
always free from bias. He represents the pure monastic
spirit, and when there is disagreement between the views of
the bishop and of the monks Symeon is partisan. He was,
for instance, a staunch supporter of the monastic scheme of
maintaining or re-establishing a division of the church's
estates, so that the priory should have a separate endowment;

---

[1] The edition used is *Symeonis monachi opera omnia,* ed. Thos. Arnold (Rolls
Ser., 1882–5). The often-quoted *Historia Dunelmensis ecclesiae* is henceforth referred
to as *Symeonis H.D.E.*

and his presentation of the past loses its objectivity when it concerns the administration of Durham's territorial possessions. The forged charters are a superb set of documents concerning William of Saint-Calais's foundation. A bull of Pope Gregory VII, charters of King William I, Archbishops Lanfranc of Canterbury and Thomas I of York, and of Bishop William himself, sometimes in different versions, compose a series of outstanding importance.[1] It has been proved that these instruments were forged in the early twelfth century; but this does not deprive them of historical value. The very fact that it was necessary to create such charters throws much light on the situation; and from a careful analysis of the contents it is possible to discover not only the true wishes of those concerned with the reforms at Durham, but also the frustrated desires of the monks at the time of fabrication.

Although the charters are not authentic, they must have been based if not on genuine instruments—and the usually faulty witness lists makes this for the most part unlikely[2]—

---

[1] For a discussion of these charters, see Canon Greenwell's introduction to *F.P.D.*, and Dom David Knowles, *The Monastic Order*, p. 629, n. 4; cf. Wilhelm Levison, *England and the Continent in the Eighth Century* (1946), appendix I, in which he analyses the sources of a set of charters fabricated at St. Augustine's, Canterbury, *c.* 1070 by the professional forger, Guerno, a monk of St. Medard. The Durham charters are printed in *F.P.D.*, pp. xxxviii–lxxv. The earliest date for the exhibition of Bishop William's pseudo-charter is not known; but in 1165 Pope Alexander III confirmed to Prior German the liberties granted by Bishop William to the priors of Durham, without, however, specifying them (Dr. Walther Holtzmann, *Papsturkunden in England* (Berlin, 1930, 1935), ii, no. 120).

For the forged bull of Pope Gregory VII (printed *Scriptores tres*, p. vii and *Papsturkunden*, ii, no. 2), see Holtzmann's prefatory remarks to docs. nos. 2 and 5. He considers that the genuine *preceptum* of Pope Gregory, to which reference is made in Calixtus II's privilege of 1123, has been lost. The genuine privileges of Calixtus II, 1123 (*Papsturkunden*, ii, no. 5), Honorius II, 1126 (ibid., no. 11), Eugenius III, 1146 (ibid., no. 51), Adrian IV, 1157 (ibid., no. 94), Alexander III, 1162 (ibid., no. 107) and Urban III, 1186 (ibid., no. 238) are free from contamination with the forgery. It is referred to and quoted for the first time in the privilege of Celestine III, 1196 (ibid., no. 278), which is therefore the belated *terminus ad quem* for the making of the forgery. Dr. Holtzmann considers that the fabrication is probably based on the privilege of Honorius II. The privileges granted by Calixtus II and Honorius II are of a general and inoffensive nature. The first detailed list of possessions appears in the privilege of Eugenius III, and becomes a regular feature. Revisions of the schedule appear in the privileges of Adrian IV and Celestine III. The claim to be next in dignity to the bishop, with some of the implications, is seen for the first time in the privilege of Adrian IV.

[2] But cf. p. 3, n. 3.

at least on verbal agreements and traditional practice, for extravagant forgeries would hardly have been worth the trouble of making. A mixture of truth and falsehood is to be expected, or a one-sided selection of contents. As a matter of fact the forgeries are closely related to Symeon's chronicle, and in some cases only present in charter form events which he describes as having happened. Thus in the main it seems that the forgeries were designed to justify arrangements which were made informally, and especially to secure documentary proof for changes introduced during the early experimental days. In this character they are an armoury produced in secret for the defence of monastic privileges granted or tolerated by Bishop William of Saint-Calais, a muniment necessary when later bishops tried to disturb the conditions. But they also incorporate some privileges which it is unlikely that the convent had genuinely been granted; and, when these can be distinguished, we learn what additional rights the monks most ardently desired.

The reform undertaken by William of Saint-Calais at Durham was an act of piety, a restoration. He learned that the bishops of Lindisfarne had been monks, living in the closest intimacy with the monastery. William, too, had been monk and abbot, and he took to Durham, and used as a model, the *Consuetudines* with which Archbishop Lanfranc had regulated his own relations with the monastery of Christ Church, Canterbury.[1] In that rule Lanfranc equated bishop and abbot in all respects.[2] What is more, a number of William's acts reveal the view that just as the bishop was abbot in the convent, so the prior was the vice-gerent of the bishop in the diocese. During the rebuilding of the cathedral, that is to say after 1093, William showed Prior Turgot to the people, and announced that he had made him archdeacon, so that he could exercise pastoral care in the diocese under the bishop. And the priors after Turgot were to be archdeacons also.[3] This, says the Durham chronicler,

[1] C. H. Turner, 'The Earliest List of Durham MSS.', *The Journal of Theological Studies* (1917–18), xix. 122.

[2] Printed Wilkins, *Concilia*, i. 328 seqq.; see J. Armitage Robinson, 'Lanfranc's Monastic Constitutions', *J.T.S.* (1908–9), x. 375–88; Rose Graham, 'The relation of Cluny to some other movements of monastic reform', ibid. (1913–14), xv. 184–5.

[3] 'vices suas etiam super illos [*sc.* populos] ei injunxit, ut scilicet per archidiaconatus

Symeon, restored the conditions which had obtained under St. Cuthbert. Nor is it unlikely that several privileges of the same character which appear in the pseudo-charters of the bishop had also been genuinely granted: the right to preside over synods in the absence of the bishop, to administer the spiritualities during the vacancy of the see, and to have the chief voice in the election of the bishop.

Almost contemporary, however, with the Norman adoption of the principle of the monastic cathedral was the beginning of a disharmony within the system. The application of feudal law to bishoprics caused monastic chapters to desire an even more drastic division of the estates, so that the convents could live unhindered through episcopal vacancies and be quit of the services and incidents which affected the bishop alone.[1] And this divergence of interest was soon widened by the appointment of seculars to the bishoprics, and by the emergence of a new attitude of the bishops towards their duties and functions. Hence, in all cathedral monasteries an ever-increasing rift appeared: the bishop tended to leave the cloister and govern the diocese through his own *familia* and his archdeacons and officials; the prior became the routine head of the monastery and aspired to be abbot in all but name; and the estates of the church were divided more radically between the parties. Such a divorce was usually slow and painful; it was caused by constant collision of interest; and the gradual definition of the two competencies came normally through the piecemeal settlement of quarrels.

The general history of the Durham estates and rights is not pertinent to this inquiry; but the process by which the monks secured a share of them is of fundamental importance. And although the truth is obscured by the bias of the

---

officium, Christianitatis curam per totum ageret episcopatum, ita statuens, ut quicunque illi successores fuerint in prioratu, similiter succedant et in archidiaconatu', *Symeonis H.D.E.* i. 129; cf. William of Malmesbury, *Gesta pontificum Anglorum*, ed. N.E.S.A. Hamilton (Rolls Ser.), p. 273, where Turgot's office is called that of a dean. A charter of King William I, with credible witnesses, which can be dated from the witness-list 1086 × 7, includes a confirmation of the archdeaconry, which Turgot holds, to him and his successors. This is the sort of tampering that is found in otherwise apparently genuine copies of eleventh-century charters.

[1] See Dom David Knowles, *The Monastic Order in England*, pp. 625–6.

chronicler Symeon, reinforced by the whole series of forged charters, it seems possible to clear away the fiction.

Bishop William of Saint-Calais had conducted research into the history of the see of Lindisfarne so that his reforms should be as far as possible a restoration.[1] His genuine findings are unknown; but Symeon held the view, certainly wrong for the early period, though probably true for more recent times, that it was an ancient custom of the church that those who ministered to God before the body of St. Cuthbert should have their own lands distinct from those of the bishop.[2] If Symeon's view represents the popular opinion of the day, then it cannot be doubted that pressure was put on the bishop, especially by the monks, to perpetuate or to restore a separate endowment. It would, indeed, be surprising if some working division of lands and revenues between bishop and canons or monks had not existed at Durham in the eleventh century, for assignments of estates *pro victu et vestitu* were usual in cathedral bodies in the south of England.[3] Moreover, certain estates are known to have been granted for this purpose at Durham: both Billingham by King William I and Aycliffe by Scot, son of Alstan, are said to have been given *ad nutrimentum inibi servientium*.[4] In addition to the portion which had been enjoyed by the canons there were in 1083 the estates which had been assigned to the monks before they migrated to Durham—Monkwearmouth and Jarrow. And this double nucleus, to which the monks might be expected to cling, was increased during the early years of their new abode by donations to the church expressly intended for their maintenance, such as the royal grant of Hemingbrough.[5] Hence the Durham monks

---

[1] *F.P.D.*, p. xxxviii; *Symeonis H.D.E.* i. 120–1.

[2] Op. cit. i. 123.

[3] Cf. the position at Canterbury according to B. W. Kissan, 'Lanfranc's alleged Division of Lands between Archbishop and Community', *E.H.R.* liv (1939), 285–93. Canon Greenwell in his introduction to *F.P.D.* was so concerned with refuting the theory that the estates of Durham had been anciently divided that he went to the other extreme, and produced an account of the separation which appears unnecessarily involved. Other historians, operating in a wider field, have ignored the complications and stated baldly that William of Saint-Calais divided the endowments. Cf. H. Böhmer, *Kirche und Staat*, p. 498, Dom David Knowles, *The Monastic Order*, pp. 625–6.

[4] *Symeonis H.D.E.* i. 108; *F.P.D.*, p. xli.   [5] See below, p. 53.

probably at no time lacked estates under their immediate control; and this created a problem to which all parties must have given some thought. The monks, it is clear, were anxious not only to retain what they had, but also to secure an equitable division of the whole possessions of the church, including the new royal benefactions, and to obtain an independent and legal title to their share. For this aim Bishop William can have had little sympathy. All his actions suggest that he had a conception of organic unity in his church. The bishop was to be abbot, and the prior archdeacon. A radical division of estates could have had little appeal for him. At the same time some sort of segregation was a practical necessity. The monks had to have food and wood and revenue; and it was preferable that they should exploit their own estates rather than have a call on a central fund. Archbishop Lanfranc accepted the customary division of estates at Canterbury;[1] and it is reasonable to suppose that William of Saint-Calais would be prepared to do as much at Durham. But even if the bishop would go so far, two problems remained: the extent of the convent's share, and the degree of independence it should be allowed.

The first problem probably resolved into how much was to be added to the territories already under the monks' control. The narrative of Symeon can be read in this sense. The bishop, he says,[2] after settling the offices in the church next segregated the estates, assigning part for the food and clothing of the monks. The gift of Billingham was then renewed by the king in favour of the monks, and the bishop also made a small grant of land. From this account we may understand that the old working division betwen the estates was accepted by Bishop William, possibly modified by the necessity of providing for the dispossessed canons, and that small additions were made to the traditional portion.

Symeon then seems to deal with the question of the division of the new post-Conquest endowments of the church.

---

[1] B. W. Kissan, 'Lanfranc's alleged Division of Lands between Archbishop and Community', loc. cit.

[2] 'Denique terrarum possessiones illorum ita a suis possessionibus segregavit, ut suas omnino ab episcopi servitio, et ab omni consuetudine liberas et quietas ad suum victum et vestitum terras monachi possiderent. . . . Episcopus quoque aliquantulum quidem terrae monachis largitus est', *Symeonis H.D.E.* i. 123.

Bishop and king, he continues,[1] in order that the monks should be preserved from indigence and penury, had provided sufficient lands for their food and clothing; and these lands were always about to be given; but the grant was impeded first by the death of the king and then by the death of the bishop, and never came into effect. From this it could be inferred that the wider scheme, although projected, had not been carried out even in 1104×9, if we accept that date for the composition of Symeon's contribution to the *Historia Dunelmensis Ecclesiae*.[2]

If Symeon's account is read in this natural sense only one obscurity remains: the real nature of the impediment; for he does not tell us why the deaths of king and bishop should have been so catastrophic. And the situation is made even more puzzling by our knowledge that the impeded scheme was in fact fulfilled either within Bishop William's lifetime, or, at the latest, during the three years' vacancy which followed his death.[3] Plans for the rebuilding of the cathedral in 1093 envisaged the convent's construction of the monastic offices at its own expense.[4] The king protected those estates which the monks possessed on the day of the bishop's death (1096);[5] and Ranulf Flambard found them well endowed at his accession in 1099.[6] Only one solution seems possible: the hindrance to the scheme lay eventually more in defect of title than in want of endowment. The wider scheme of partition was achieved *de facto* but not *de jure*.

In the light of this conclusion it becomes clear why the two deaths were fatal to some of the hopes of the monks. The death of William the Conqueror could have removed the possibility of further royal benefactions; but actually he had been most generous to Durham;[7] and it is probably because of the non-fulfilment of his wishes that the monks

---

[1] 'Verumtamen ut sine indigentia et penuria Christo servirent, sufficientes ad victum illorum et vestitum terras eis una cum rege ipse providerat, et jam jamque daturus erat. Sed ne id ad effectum perveniret, primo regis ac postea episcopi mors impedimento fuerat', ibid. i. 124.

[2] Thos. Arnold, *Symeonis opera*, i, p. xix.

[3] King William II was well disposed towards the monastery; cf. *Symeonis H.D.E.* i. 128; and below, n. 5.

[4] Ibid. i. 129.

[5] *Scriptores tres*, pp. xxvii and xxviii (1099 × 1100).

[6] *Symeonis continuatio prima*, i. 141.   [7] See below, p. 53.

lamented his untimely demise. Rightly or wrongly they seem to have considered that the convent had been defrauded of its share of his gifts; and certainly they attributed conditions to his grant of the Yorkshire estates for which there appears to have existed no documentary evidence.[1] According to the monks, then, King William I had intended them to share in his grants to the church of Durham, but had died before this scheme had been properly realized.

The death of Bishop William of Saint-Calais occurred nine years after that of his patron; and he lay dying at Windsor for no inconsiderable time with monks in attendance.[2] This was no sudden and inopportune misfortune; and to regard it as fatal to the scheme implies that it marked nothing more than the final disappointment of long-cherished hopes. Symeon in his prejudice was almost incapable of understanding the bishop's attitude towards the problem. As we have seen, William started with the idea that bishop and monks should form a single community, and could have had no desire to effect a radical division in the estates of his church. But he was pushed remorselessly away from his original conception. The monks seem to have become united against his views, and his exile under King William Rufus, involving not only separation from the monks but acute administrative problems, may have done much to convince him that a duality might be advisable. Nevertheless, he must have come to this conclusion slowly, reluctantly, and perhaps sorrowfully; and he may have allowed the monks an ever wider control over the estates they claimed without at any time recognizing it as anything more than an administrative convenience. The monks must have pressed for a formal warranty, for charters, for a title valid against his successors. And it seems that, whatever hopes he may have raised, William died without giving way. The monks did not underestimate the seriousness of the check. A few years later their forgeries, with lists of the convent's estates, were ready for future use; but for a time they had to rely largely on customary practices and verbal agreements which left them at the mercy of each new bishop.

[1] See below, p. 73.
[2] *Symeonis H.D.E.* i. 133; 'De injusta vexatione', ibid. i. 195.

William of Saint-Calais's successor, Ranulf Flambard, a benefactor of his church, and the patron of the hermit St. Godric, but a secular clerk with a family, not unnaturally hesitated to accept all the conditions he inherited. He encountered an aggressive monastery, already committed to a campaign of aggrandizement at the expense of the bishop, and took a firm stand. He resumed some of the estates he found under monkish control, got rid of Prior Turgot and his archdeaconry, and no doubt regretted the whole of his predecessor's reform. Yet Ranulf weakened in the end; and he restored on his death-bed, as far as he was able, the position which had obtained on the day of his consecration.[1] Even if the monks were successful in implementing this concession during the five years' vacancy after Ranulf's death, the accession of Geoffrey Rufus in 1133 seems to have reopened the inevitable controversy; and some time elapsed before he, too, could be induced to confirm the 'ancient liberties and customs' of the monks.[2] Greed and private interests played their part in this episcopal opposition. Most twelfth- and early thirteenth-century bishops of Durham despoiled the convent of estates and churches in order to reward their families.[3] But their attitude was not entirely unreasonable: they were faced by an ambitious and tenacious corporation, which, if uncontrolled, would have prevented them from being master in their own house. A just balance of interest was hard to keep; and it was not until 1229, when an attempt was made to clear up all outstanding

---

[1] *Symeonis continuatio prima*, i. 141; *Scriptores tres*, pp. xxix–xxx. The restitution included the church of Kirkby Sigston. It was, apparently, Ranulf's nephew, Richard, who had been enriched at the convent's expense. Ranulf's charter was confirmed by Pope Alexander III in 1162 (W. Holtzmann, *Papsturkunden*, ii, no. 107). Ranulf made other concessions to the monks in his last years. He witnessed Archbishop Thurstan's recognition of the convent's franchise in Yorkshire, 1121 × 8 (see below, pp. 60 and 75); and he granted to the monks *pro redemtione anime mee* the tithes from his demesne of Northallerton, Welton, and Howden, *c.* 1125 × 8 [W. Farrer, *Early Yorkshire Charters* (1915), ii. 306].

[2] *Symeonis continuatio prima*, i. 142.

[3] For Ranulf Flambard and his nephew Richard, see note 1; for Hugh of le Puiset and his son or nephew Bouchard, and Philip of Poitou and his nephew Aimery, see below, pp. 33 seqq. Philip's nephew Peter held the convent's church of Howden (*Durham Annals and Documents*, p. 159). For episcopal clerks, cf. Richard of Coldingham, below, p. 25. These are random examples of what must have been a fairly general practice.

differences between bishop and convent, that the history of the partition of the estates can be considered as almost finally closed.

The lack of genuine titles to the conventual estates and the irregularity of the proceedings obscure the conditions under which they were transferred, and may indeed have prejudiced rights which would normally have pertained to the convent's territory. The monks naturally had two main wishes with regard to the churches on their estates: to have the absolute disposal of them, and to divide the episcopal rights in respect of them.

The first claim, besides being dependent on the success achieved in segregating the estates, was intimately connected with the relations of bishop and convent in the church. As long as the bishop was abbot he had complete control over the actions of the monks; even when he withdrew from the cloister his tutelary position was hard to deny and never was entirely destroyed. Whenever the bishop was strong and the prior or the corporate spirit weak, the bishop exercised an influence over the disposal of the convent's churches despite charters in which the right was renounced. This can be seen as late as the thirteenth century. The bishop could always put pressure on the convent to obey his wishes if he so chose, and it was rarely that the monks were moved to rebellion. The convent's legalistic annals report several debates in the thirteenth century in which the weary caution of the seniors is opposed to the ardour of those with less responsibility. Nevertheless, free disposal of the churches was an integral part of the priory's claim to a separate endowment, and the right is included in the forgeries of the early twelfth century, where the canonical distinction, new for England, between the *beneficium* and the *cura animarum* is used.[1] The convent is to have the free disposal of all its churches, and the clerks to whom it grants them are to answer to the prior and brethren for the benefice and all other revenues and to the

---

[1] The distinction became usual in the later twelfth century. Cf. a privilege of Pope Alexander III to Durham, 1160 × 76, 'In parochialibus autem ecclesiis quas tenetis liceat uobis clericos absque impedimento aliquo eligere et diocesanis episcopis presentare, quibus, si idonei fuerint, episcopi curam animarum committant, ut illis de spiritualibus, uobis autem de temporalibus respondeant', W. Holtzmann, *Papsturkunden in England,* ii, no. 149.

bishop of the diocese for the cure of souls.[1] This is a translation of the conception of *Eigenkirchentum* into the language
of the twelfth century.[2] The monks naturally desired to have
the full rights of a proprietor, the power to do what they
willed with their churches, provided that divine services were
maintained.

The second claim, the desire to share the *episcopalia*, was
equitable, and in harmony with the normal procedure when
the joint endowments were divided between the two con-
stituent parts of a monastic cathedral.[3] The convent was
part of the governing body of the church, and naturally
considered that it should hold its private possessions under
conditions as similar as possible to those under which the
bishop would hold his. Moreover, just as the estates were
to be divided, so should the *episcopalia*: according to the
ideas of the time one and all were but particular aspects of
the cathedral church which could be separated and exploited.
Bishop William of Saint-Calais appears to have acted on
this principle when the intitial segregation of lands was made
shortly after 1083. According to Symeon, the monastic
estates were to be entirely free and quit of all service to the
bishop and all custom.[4] The circumstances under which the

---

[1] Pope Gregory VII's wishes are represented by Bishop William as, 'Ecclesias
autem quascumque, me in subsequentibus donante vel adquirente, seu ceteris
fidelibus largientibus, adquisierint, in sua manu et donatione liberas habeant, et
honestis clericis deserviendas committant, qui episcopis de cura animarum tantum,
in quacumque diocesi fuerint, intendant; priori autem et fratribus de beneficiis et
redditibus omnibus ceteris semper attendentes existant . . . Priores vero et fratres
liberam dispositionem in omnibus, tam ecclesiis quam ceteris possessionibus . . .
semper obtineant', *F.P.D.*, xxxix–xl. In one of the false charters of Bishop William
the incumbents are referred to as vicars, and the free disposal is granted thus,
'Omnes vero suas ecclesias in sua manu et libera dispositione habeant, ut semper
de eis quantum potuerint, redditus suos accrescant, ita ut nullus se de ipsis aliquid
intromittat, nisi per consensum ipsorum [priorum] et monachorum licenciam',
ibid., p. xlviii; cf. p. l, and false charters of King William I, ibid., pp. lxvii–lxviii,
lxx, lxxiii–lxxiv, and false charter of Lanfranc, ibid., p. lxxvi, 'Ecclesias suas . . .
libere pro voluntate sua disponant, vel in manu sua teneant, seu honestis personis
de eis tenendas absque omni episcoporum fatigatione vel inquietatione distribuant'.
Cf. H. Böhmer, *Das Eigenkirchentum*, p. 303, n. 2.

[2] Cf. Paul Thomas, *Le droit de propriété des laïques sur les églises et le patronage
laïque au moyen âge* (Bibl. de l'école des hautes études, sciences religieuses, vol.
19, 1906), p. 94.

[3] Rev. E. W. Watson, D.D., 'The Development of Ecclesiastical Organization
and its Financial Basis', *Cambridge Medieval History*, vi. 548–9.

[4] See above, p. 6, n. 2.

division was made at Durham, however, may well have hindered the convent in maintaining these rights, for Bishop William's concessions may have been restricted to the limited area of his first separation, and only by an unsanctioned enlargement could the monks have extended it to all the territory which they ultimately acquired. Hence it is uncertain whether the desires as expressed in the forgeries corresponded entirely with the actual conditions. The restrictive attitude of Bishops Ranulf Flambard and Geoffrey Rufus probably applied to the jurisdiction and liberties of the convent's churches as well as to the extent of the estates.

The altered circumstances in which the convent found itself in the early twelfth century, the changes in the constitutional arrangements which followed the appointment of secular priests as bishops, and the possibility that the accession of each new bishop would herald a scrutiny of its claims, caused the monks not only to plan the warranty of their private estates and the rights which pertained to them, but also to re-define the respective positions of bishop and convent. This restatement of the constitution is a marked feature of the forged charters, which display many characteristics out of harmony with the earliest phase of the reform of Bishop William of Saint-Calais. Claims are made which both reflect changes genuinely made by Bishops William and Ranulf and also reveal unrealized wishes which the new situation had inspired. Privileges of these types in the forgeries are: the prior to be freely elected; the prior to have all the rights and dignities of an abbot; the prior to have the position in the diocese of a dean—there is usually an equation with the position of the dean of York; the prior and convent to have archidiaconal rights in the churches of the monastery.

It will be noticed that in these forgeries Bishop William's conception of the prior as his deputy in the spiritual government of the diocese has been maintained, although under a slightly different form, but that the obverse position has been rejected: the bishop is no longer considered as abbot, and every device is introduced to make the prior and convent independent of him.

The new role claimed for the prior in the government of the diocese—that of a dean—was the result of changes made by Ranulf Flambard. One spurious charter of King William I confirms to the convent the archdeaconry granted by the bishop to Turgot and his successors;[1] but it stands alone in this: the other forgeries create a new position for the prior. We learn from William of Malmesbury that Ranulf Flambard thought Turgot too forward in the exercise of this privilege, and had him appointed bishop of St. Andrews.[2] We find no prior with an archdeaconry embracing the whole diocese thereafter. Instead appear two secular, territorial archdeacons on the usual pattern.[3] The convent seems to have accepted this reform, and to have remodelled its claims in consequence. By equating in the forgeries the position of the prior to that of the dean of York a satisfactory adjustment was made, which maintained the prior as the deputy of the bishop, and put him above, and with a certain control over the archdeacons.[4]

The claim of the prior to be the dean of a chapter doubtless derived principally from the pre-monastic history of Durham. Alone of the dispossessed clerks of St. Cuthbert the dean became a monk in 1083,[5] and it has been suggested that he continued to exercise his functions until 1093 when Turgot replaced him.[6] Turgot was described as dean as well as archdeacon,[7] just as was Leobwine, the deputy of Bishop Walcher (1071–80).[8] Medieval deans are various, and in 1147 Turgot's successors were described as *decani et archipresbiteri*,[9] normally to be understood as a rural dean or dean

[1] *F.P.D.*, p. lxxiv.

[2] Op. cit., pp. 273–4. Cf. Bartholomew of Cotton, *Historia Anglicana*, ed. H. R. Luard (Rolls Ser.), p. 415: 'Hic [*sc.* episcopus Willelmus] hoc privilegium priori Dunhelmensi concessit, ut in toto episcopatu decanus et vicedominus haberetur; quod postea successoribus poenituit.'   [3] See Appendix, below, p. 153.

[4] 'Et quascumque dignitates seu honores decani Eboracenses sub archiepiscopis Eboracensibus et super archidiaconos illius ecclesiae possederint, priores Dunelmenses sub episcopo et super archidiaconos ipsius ecclesiae libere et quiete in perpetuum habeant', pseudo-charter of King William I, *F.P.D.*, p. lxvii; cf. false charters of Bishop William, ibid., pp. xxxix and xlvii.   [5] *Symeonis H.D.E.* i. 122.

[6] Dom David Knowles, *The Monastic Order*, p. 629, n. 4.

[7] See above, p. 3, n. 3 and p. 13, n. 2.

[8] In the *Historia Dunelmensis ecclesiae* (i. 114, 115) he is referred to as archdeacon; in the *Historia Regum* (ibid. ii. 210) he is called a dean, following Florence of Worcester, *Chronicon ex chronicis*, ed. B. Thorpe (Eng. Hist. Soc., 1848), ii. 16.

[9] *F.P.D.*, pp. lx–lxiii. Cf. spurious charter of King William I, 'et jure Decani vel Archipresbiteri ad synoda celebranda et cetera Christianitatis officia persolvenda, ipsius ecclesiae archidiaconis praesideant', ibid., p. lxix.

of Christianity. Clearly there was much confusion at the time; but in later years an equation with the dean of the cathedral chapter of York was understood in this context,[1] and it was probably in that sense that the forgery was originally made.

The creation of the territorial archdeaconries by Bishop Ranulf modified the convent's claim in another way, too; for the monks naturally became interested in the privileges of their proprietary churches in relation to these new diocesan officials. Hence, in the forgeries a claim is made to a personal and flexible archdeaconry in respect of those churches. The prior and convent were to have 'omnes potestates atque omnia jura et vices archidiaconi in omnibus ecclesiis propriis'.[2] In one charter freedom from hospitality and aids of archdeacons and bishops and other vexations and burdens— that is to say, from the episcopal customs—is also included;[3] but this is explanatory. By a reversal of the usual process, archidiaconal jurisdiction is not claimed by assimilating possession of the customs to an archdeaconry, but contrariwise. This boldness in claiming unequivocally archidiaconal jurisdiction is doubtless due to Turgot's archdeaconry and the convent's special position in the constitution. The claim does not appear in the forgeries concerning the franchises in the dioceses of York and St. Andrews.

It will be seen that the monks claim a franchise in two ways: the first is based on the rights of proprietors of churches and the equitable division of the estates and jurisdictions between bishop and convent; the second is an outright claim to an archdeaconry deriving from a modification of Turgot's official position in the diocese. The forgers were making doubly sure. If the convent could not have the complete control of its churches as a proprietor, it would have it as a diocesan official. One characteristic is common to both attitudes: the franchise claimed is personal and flexible;

---

[1] Robert de Graystanes in *Scriptores tres,* p. 69; *Durham Annals and Documents of the Thirteenth Century,* ed. Frank Barlow (Surtees Soc., vol. 155), p. 64.

[2] Pseudo-charters of Bishop William, *F.P.D.,* pp. xlvii, xl, and liv.

[3] 'Sed quietus sit, tam ipse [prior] quam clerici ejus, de hospitiis et auxiliis episcoporum et archidiaconorum, et ceteris gravaminibus et vexationibus', *F.P.D.,* p. liv. For freedom from episcopal aids, see also false charter of Lanfranc, ibid., p. lxxvi.

the privileges are demanded for an indefinite area, churches possessed or to be acquired by the monks.

It cannot be stated with certainty in every case how far the constitutional clauses in the forged charters corresponded with the actual conditions at any particular time. The fabrications reveal the convent's objectives; but its success in attaining them must have fluctuated with the attitude of its bishop. Ranulf Flambard, as we know, atoned for his steady hostility to the convent by a death-bed repentance. Geoffrey Rufus, we are told by Symeon's continuator,[1] after a period of opposition to the rights of the convent, later imitated the example of his predecessors, and bestowed certain liberties and customs on both the church and the monks. He confirmed to the prior all those privileges for which the Fathers of the Church were authority and those which could be justified by undoubted antiquity and ancient custom. It would seem that Bede and the Northumbrian annals—and perhaps Symeon's compilation—had been studied once more, and that after Ranulf's death the cause of the monks began to prosper.

Certain of the claims can be checked individually. We have already seen that the division of the estates was accepted in principle by the bishops, although details of the partition caused friction. There is also evidence that the prior acted as the deputy of the bishop and as the dean. Prior Turgot ruled the diocese in spiritualities during Bishop William's exile (1088–91). Then, too, a dispute between Prior Roger and Archdeacon Wazo in 1147 about their respective positions was settled by judges in favour of the prior after an inquest had been held.[2] Witnesses maintained that the priors had been the vice-gerents of the bishops under William and Ranulf, had been the superiors of the archdeacons *sicut decani et archipresbiteri*, and had enjoyed all the privileges which proclaimed them next in dignity to the bishop. There is no appeal to the yet unpublished spurious charters; but it is clear that in this respect the forgeries corresponded to the

---

[1] 'libertates et consuetudines tam ecclesiae quam monachis more praedecessorum suorum indulsit, et priori ecclesiae, quaecumque vel patrum ecclesiae auctoritas, vel comprobata servaverat antiquitas et prisca consuetudo, benigne concessit', *Symeonis continuatio prima*, i. 142.   [2] *F.P.D.*, pp. lx–lxiii.

facts. On the other hand, it is unlikely that the monks possessed the right freely to elect their priors. In certain cases we know that priors were appointed by the bishops; and the privilege of free election was not firmly obtained before the thirteenth century, and even then was often illusory.

Finally, we come to the convent's claim to have archidiaconal powers within its parishes; and no shred of evidence can be found in support of it. The balance of probability is in favour of the claim being not entirely without foundation; but further than this it would be dangerous to go. It is, indeed, unfortunate that there should be darkness here, for this is the main franchise which the convent was in the end to establish in the diocese of Durham. Thus we start with the scent but not with the sight of our chief quarry.

§ 2. *The Development of the Franchise, 1140–1229*

The monastery of Durham would appear in the first half of the twelfth century to have been well placed for developing a substantial franchise in respect of its parish churches. The project, however, did not prosper in the next century. In the centre of the period between the death of Ranulf Flambard in 1128 and the translation of Richard Poore in 1228 lies the long episcopate of Hugh of le Puiset (1153–95), detached, hard to interpret, unusual in its normality. Before Hugh was the violence and misery of King Stephen's reign with the intrusion of William Cumin into the bishopric. After Hugh occurred the bitterest struggles between bishop and convent in the whole stormy history of the church of Durham. For one-fifth of this century the bishopric was vacant; none of the bishops was a monk; and none, with the exception of Hugh, was acceptable to the chapter. During the vacancies the prior and the archdeacons exercised the spiritual authority; but the archdeacons, although in theory subordinate to the prior, seem in fact to have been dominant.

The episcopate of Hugh of le Puiset is important more for its under-currents than for dramatic or even perceptible developments in the organization of the diocese of Durham itself. In the history of the Yorkshire franchise it is the decisive period; but that very strength which Hugh could use against York subdued the priory at home. Hugh, one of

the greater bishops of Durham and one of the most important men of his period,[1] seems to have treated the monks
firmly although kindly; and, as he restored on his death-bed
lands and liberties of which he had deprived them,[2] it is
clear that he had withstood some of their claims. Hence, in
the convent admiration for the bishop was mixed with a
feeling that its privileges were frustrated, and those who
guided its policy were aware that the forgeries had matured
in its secret archives and that time was running out.

The first years of the episcopate must have been used by
both bishop and convent for stock-taking and reorganization, and, during the reparation of the damaged see, there
may have been a genuine co-operation. But it was probably
at that time that the monks decided on the policy of appropriating their churches, a plan which took them more than
half a century to accomplish, and which was to play its
part in the quarrels with their bishops.

Appropriation proved so difficult because the parish
churches were feudalized. It is not known to what extent
the monks were in direct control of their estates at this time,
whether the ownership of a vill implied manorial exploitation or merely a superiority with fiscal rights; but it is clear
that the convent had not acquired the immediate disposal of
the revenues of its churches. Even at the end of the twelfth
century hereditary parsons possessed several of the convent's
churches,[3] and fifty years earlier this must have been a
general condition.[4] The parsons were doubtless burdened

[1] See Bishop Stubbs's brilliant sketch of Hugh's career in the preface to vol. iii
of his edition of *Chronica magistri Rogeri de Houedene* (Rolls Ser.), pp. xxxiii–
xxxvii: 'Without being a great man, he was always in a great position, and seldom
unequal to the occasion.' For the family of Le Puiset, see also J. L. LaMonte, 'The
Lords of Le Puiset on the Crusades', *Speculum*, xvii (1942), genealogical table, p. 100.

[2] 'Monachis autem terras et libertates, quas eis abstulerat, restituit', *Scriptores
tres*, p. 15.   [3] See below, pp. 33–5.

[4] In 1174, for instance, when the abbey of St. Albans granted to the priory the
churches of Bywell St. Peter and Edlingham in recompense for Durham's surrender
of its claims to the church of Tynemouth, it was agreed that the parson of Bywell
should hold for life and that in the case of Edlingham the clerk of the church should
succeed at the death of the present parson (*Scriptores tres*, pp. liii–lvi). About the
year 1164 both the advowson and the parsonage of Bishop Middleham were granted
to the priory by the owners; but the parsonage was only surrendered for the sake
of the title, and the church was not impropriated [Documents printed by Robert
Surtees, *The History and Antiquities of the County Palatine of Durham* (1816–40),
ii. 384].

with pensions as recognition of their subjection to Durham; but these may not have been substantial in amount.[1] So, in order to increase the revenues which could be derived from the churches, the first task of the monks was to break the grip of these clerical families. When this had been accomplished, they could appropriate at once, or at least keep the gift of the church and the disposal of its revenues in their own hands. Their usual practice seems to have been the appointment of a chaplain who farmed the revenues.[2] This arrangement, although similar in appearance to that of a rectory subject to a pension, was fundamentally different in principle. To help them in the struggle against the parsons, and to provide for any success, the prior and convent secured a number of charters from Bishop Hugh, reinforced by papal confirmations and indults, in which their ownership

[1] For pensions from Ellingham and Castle Eden in the twelfth century, see next note and p. 21, n. 2. The pensions from the Yorkshire churches were almost completely stereotyped by the first quarter of the twelfth century. They were in 1225: St. Peter the Little at York, Skipwith—1 m.; All Saints Pavement at York, Holtby—25s.; West Rounton, Welton—3 m.; Hemingbrough, Howden—5 m.; Walkington—£5; Brantingham, Kirkby Sigston—10 m.; and in 1291 Northallerton was burdened with £20. See *The Register of Walter Gray, Lord Archbishop of York*, ed. Jas. Raine (Surtees Soc., vol. 56), p. 154; *Durham Annals and Documents*, nos. 75, 121, 139–41, 143; *Taxatio ecclesiastica papae Nicholai* (Rec. Com.), p. 302; *Valor ecclesiasticus Hen. VIII* (Rec. Com.), v. 301–2. The percentage of the total value of the church as assessed in 1291 represented by the pension differs widely from case to case. It is noticeable, however, that the Howdenshire churches (except Holtby) were far more lightly burdened than the Allertonshire. Hemingbrough's pension of 5 m., for instance, came only to 2·8 per cent. of its total value in 1291, whereas Kirkby Sigston's pension of 10 m. was a quarter of the whole value of the church.

[2] The history of the church of Ellingham will illustrate this policy (see *A History of Northumberland*, ii. 226, 268–77; *F.P.D.*, pp. 99–102). The church was granted to the convent in the first half of the twelfth century by the proprietor. In 1154 × 6 Bishop Hugh of le Puiset regulated the future disposition of the church. It was ordained that after the death of the rector who then held, the most suitable son of the baron in whose fief Ellingham lay was to succeed; and that on his death the convent was to have the parsonage, but the baron and his heirs were to have the advowson 'sicut alii barones solent habere aliarum ecclesiarum quae in territoriis suis fundatae sunt'. This latter provision was inoperative; the former, however, was fulfilled, and about 1209, after the death of the baron's son—who paid the convent an annual pension of 5s., presumably as a memorial of the agreement, the prior granted Ellingham to a clerk at farm for £10 p.a. The farm was all the more similar to a pension because the clerk was to bear all burdens falling on the church. It is uncertain how long this state of affairs lasted; but the vicarage was not taxed by the bishop until 1273. There could be confusion between rectors paying pensions and chaplains farming the revenues even in 1221 (cf. the cases of Cornhill and Ancroft, below, p. 35).

and free disposal of the parsonage of their churches were recognized, and permission to appropriate was given.[1] The general charters were supplemented by others referring to churches by name.[2] Although Hugh of le Puiset sanctioned the convent's plan of appropriation, it is unlikely that he was entirely sincere, or that he gave active help. When the hold of the hereditary parson was broken, the bishop found a useful gift for his clerks;[3] and certainly by 1195 few churches had been appropriated by the convent apart from Jarrow, Monkwearmouth, and Holy Island, which, as cells, had always been in the hands of the monks.

This failure of the convent to get a secure grip on the temporalities of the churches it had acquired must have severely affected its pretensions. With many parsonages feudalized, vacancies would be few, induction a formality, and the right of gift illusory. In the diocese of York an archidiaconal franchise was created by the monks although they appropriated but one of their churches. Hence appropriation was not essential; but it is certain that it facilitated the process. If the churches were served by monks or stipendiary chaplains there was less likelihood of the bishop

---

[1] Charters of Hugh, 1153 × c. 60 [William Hutchinson, *The History and Antiquities of the County Palatine of Durham* (1785–94), ii. 72 n.] and 1188 × 95 (*Durham Annals and Documents*, pp. 146–7). The confirmation of a charter of Hugh, possibly of one similar to that of 1153 × c. 60, is included in a privilege of Pope Adrian IV, 1157 (W. Holtzmann, *Papsturkunden*, ii, no. 94). In 1164 Pope Alexander III granted Prior German and his successors the free disposal of the convent's churches on the death of the parsons (ibid., no. 119), and Urban III repeated the grant in 1186 × 7 (ibid., no. 245). Cf. also privilege of Alexander III, 1171 × 81 (ibid., no. 208).

[2] In 1175 × 95 Hugh confirmed to the convent the parsonage of Elvet (*Durham Annals and Documents*, p. 146), and in 1154 × 6 and 1163 × 86 the parsonage of Ellingham (ibid.; *A History of Northumberland*, ii. 268 n.). In 1160 × 76 Pope Alexander III confirmed the convent's disposal of the revenues of Northallerton and Norham (Holtzmann, op. cit. ii, no. 148), and between the same dates conceded that the churches of Norham, Northallerton, Howden, Monk Hesleden, Elvet, Bishop Middleham, Aycliffe, and Pittington could be devoted to the cost of alms and hospitality, provided that the consent of the diocesan bishop was acquired (ibid., no. 149). Finally, the same pope in 1171 × 81 confirmed the churches of Norham, Monk Hesleden, St. John's Merrington, and Northallerton to the use of the convent's refectory (ibid., no. 212). The pensions paid by the rectors of those churches were probably already devoted to those purposes.

[3] Elvet and Bishop Middleham, for instance, were granted to Mr. Richard of Coldingham, a clerk of Bishop Hugh. See Holtzmann, op. cit. ii, no. 164, and below, p. 25.

claiming the episcopal customs, and episcopal claims to the custody of vacant churches and to the induction of presentees would have been frustrated. An immunity was protected by the dead hand.

No explicit reference to the convent's archdeaconry can be found during Hugh's episcopate; and the position as regards the episcopal customs is not entirely clear. In 1168 × 9 Pope Alexander III confirmed to Prior German and the convent the church of Holy Island with all its chapels and the other churches which they peacefully possessed, and decreed that those churches should remain free from all synodals and other episcopal customs, since the monks had peacefully possessed this privilege for forty years in accordance with the canonical grants of the bishops of Durham.[1] This proves that the convent claimed the immunity of its parish churches from the episcopal customs; but we may doubt whether the franchise was always respected. When Hugh's successor, Philip of Poitou, levied an aid on the diocese in 1197–8 to reimburse him for the cost of his appointment, the monks were unable to prevent its collection from their own clerks despite their privileges and their complaints.

The position which was to obtain when the churches were appropriated was laid down by the episcopal charters. In an early grant of Bishop Hugh (1153 × c. 60) it is stated that vicars to be placed in the Yorkshire churches when appropriated were to have sufficient revenues to pay *episcopalia jura*,[2] and in a late charter (1188 × 95), which refers to the convent's churches in general, it is decreed that the chaplains of the appropriated churches were to pay the episcopal customs, but that the convent was to be free from all customs, aids, hospitality, and exaction of bishops, archdeacons, and officials in respect of them.[3] The failure to state the reci-

---

[1] 'et ceteras ecclesias, quas pacifice possidetis . . . uobis . . . confirmamus, et eas ab omnibus synodalibus et aliis episcopalibus consuetudinibus ita liberas et absolutas manere sancimus, quemadmodum ab episcopis Dunelmensibus, qui pro tempore fuerint, uobis canonice indulte fuisse noscuntur et uos a quadraginta annis noscimini pacifice possedisse', Holtzmann, op. cit. ii, no. 124.

[2] 'assignatis eis [*sc.* vicariis] portionibus quibus sustentari valeant, et episcopalia jura persolvere, et honeste ecclesiae deservire', Wm. Hutchinson, op. cit. ii. 72 n.

[3] 'capellanos . . . qui ecclesiis et capellis honeste deserviant et episcopalia persolvant. Concedimus etiam ut in ipsis ecclesiis suis quieti et liberi sint inperpetuum

pient of the customs which the vicars were to pay makes these provisions difficult to interpret, and also raises the question whether the convent collected the customs from its clerks and rectors of entire churches. A charter concerning Edlingham and Bywell St. Peter, however, seems to clarify at least the bishop's intentions. These churches had been granted to the prior and convent of Durham by the abbey of St. Albans in 1174 in compensation for Durham's surrender of its rights in other churches. Bishop Hugh's confirmatory charter falls into two parts: the confirmation of the grant and the arrangements for the later disposition of the churches. After the first section the phrase *salvis per omnia nostris episcopalibus* is interlined in the original, and the same safeguard with the addition of *consuetudinibus* is added in the cartulary into which the document has been copied. After the second section, in which permission to appropriate is given and the division of the revenues is arranged, *salvis episcopalibus consuetudinibus nostris* occurs integrally in the text.[1] From this we may conclude that the bishop certainly intended to collect his customs from those churches after appropriation, and that a disagreement over the interim position was settled in the bishop's favour. More generally it may be inferred that Hugh of le Puiset aimed at dividing the spoils: the convent could appropriate if the bishop got the customs.

All these charters were, of course, plans for the future; and when the convent did eventually become strong enough to appropriate, it was also able to repudiate this condition. From the terms of the charter of 1174 it also seems likely that Hugh of le Puiset was collecting, or trying to collect, the customs from some of the convent's rectors;[2] yet towards the end of the twelfth century the monks were without a

---

ab omnibus consuetudinibus, auxiliis, et hospiciis et exaccionibus omnium successorum nostrorum episcoporum et archidiaconorum et omnium officialium', *Durham Annals and Documents*, pp. 146–7.

[1] Charter printed in *A History of Northumberland*, vi. 104 n.

[2] In 1162 × 86 Prior German granted Castle Eden, a chapel of Monk Hesleden, to a clerk: 'Sciatis nos dedisse in elemosinam et presenti carta confirmasse Willelmo . . . capellam de Edene; salvis episcopalibus consuetudinibus; et reddet nobis in singulis annis unam marcam argenti . . .'; he was instituted by Bishop Hugh, 'Nos eum de ecclesia eadem canonice impersonavimus', Surtees, op. cit. ii. 45. The recipient of the customs is, as usual, uncertain.

shadow of doubt themselves collecting the customs from their Yorkshire rectors,[1] and therefore it is possible that similar conditions had prevailed periodically or locally in the diocese of Durham.

If, indeed, the monks were at times in receipt of the customs, their possession of some administrative functions is almost certain. Immunity from the customs is compatible with the subjection of the churches to the ordinary diocesan administration; receipt of them, unless through the hands of the bishops and archdeacons, meant that such functions as visitation were actually performed. Although the picture of conditions under Bishop Hugh is imprecise, the setting of the scene for the dramatic events which followed his death is yet sufficiently clear. The episcopate of Hugh is seen as a period in which the monks, although outwardly quiescent under the strong but not unfriendly hand of their bishop, never accepted defeat, and laid their plans for the future in the secret knowledge of their unpublished forgeries.

The death of Bishop Hugh in 1195 must have seemed to the convent the end of an era, and the ensuing vacancy its heaven-sent chance. Before long its nuncios were in Rome with a copy of the forged bull of Pope Gregory VII—its first public appearance, as far as is known; and in May 1196 the unsuspecting Pope Celestine III granted a privilege, based in part on the forgery, in which was included the right of the prior to the dignities of an abbot and to the office of archdeacon over all the convent's churches and the clerks in them.[2] What is more, shortly after the pope had in the spring of 1197 consecrated at Rome Philip of Poitou as the next bishop, he warned him and his nephew, the archdeacon of Durham, to preserve intact the liberties and possessions of the church.[3]

We cannot know whether it was with confidence or in fear that the monks opened their new offensive; but they can hardly have expected such strong opponents as Philip of Poitou (1197–1208) and his successor Richard Marsh (1217–26) were to prove. Monkish chroniclers, at Durham and elsewhere, represent them as monsters. The intimacy

---

[1] See below, pp. 76–9. [2] W. Holtzmann, op. cit. ii, no. 278.
[3] Ibid. no. 285.

of both with King John is no testimonial to their manners; but their familiarity with the Angevin system of government meant that they were capable if irresponsible administrators, and royal clerks did not always make the worst bishops. Indeed, both Philip and Richard can be regarded as reformers. They found the convent claiming a medley of rights and privileges, many of which were contrary to the common law of the Church, and they each in turn tested the legality of these practices by rough and peremptory methods.

Among the objectionable claims of the convent were those which originated in proprietary rights, but could no longer be justified as such. Examples of this type are the custody of vacant churches and the induction of presentees into them. Both these functions were now allocated to the bishop by ecclesiastical common law,[1] and their unwarranted alienation was considered a pernicious abuse. It is, therefore, not surprising that these efficient bishops should have attacked the convent's claim to them. And besides the question of legality there was the matter of discipline. The sight of *claustrales* performing administrative duties inimical to conventual life cannot have been edifying. Moreover, the monastic claim to be free from the episcopal customs could not fail to attract unfavourable attention from bishops trained under King John; and the convent's possessions and especially its rights of advowson aroused the bishops' cupidity. Both bishops attempted to control the monastery's ecclesiastical patronage, and when the feudalized condition of the convent's churches is considered, even this action will not appear entirely unreasonable.

The battle between the parties was a complex action. Each side groped towards a legal contest; but each avoided getting seriously committed to it. Both bishops probed the convent's *munimenta*; and both seem to have considered a

---

[1] Cf. the arguments in the suit between Mr. Honorius, archdeacon of Richmond, and Geoffrey, archbishop of York, in 1200–1, concerning the alienation of these rights to the archdeacon, *Chronica Rogeri de Houedene*, iv. 177 seqq.; *Decretal.* III. vii. 6, *Quum venissent*. Pope Innocent III upheld the archiepiscopal contention 'quod institutio personarum et custodia ecclesiarum vacantium ad eum in diocesi sua spectat tam de jure communi quam de consuetudine generali'; but he agreed that they could be lawfully alienated.

direct attack too hazardous. Although neither believed in the authenticity of those splendid and dangerous charters, they felt, it seems, unequal to the task of proving their falsity. Nor were the monks disposed to stake everything on their muniments. The forgeries were too valuable, and too vulnerable, to risk in anything except a desperate action. Their proper place was in reserve. Suspicious charters, however, if unsupported by current practice, were weapons without ammunition; and the bishops developed a plan of countering the charters by rival threats, and, while holding them in check, of destroying their value. Hence the bishops renewed their claim to be abbots of the convent; and under cover of this stroke concentrated on destroying the convent's possession of the privileges it claimed. The struggle for possession of, and prescription for, the disputed rights was protracted and sometimes violent. The advantage lay generally with the bishop; and by the time the convent eventually went to law its position had become precarious. It is not, therefore, surprising that the struggle should have been ended by a treaty, and that the false charters had only an indirect influence on the final settlement.

The events of these years are, then, of great importance in the history of the peculiars, and, as the period is exceptionally well documented, it is possible to describe the contest in unusual detail.

While bishop-elect in 1196 Philip of Poitou, the confidential clerk of King Richard, had appointed his nephew, Aimery, archdeacon of Durham. Aimery is represented by the monks as their chief adversary, and as swaying the will of his less active uncle.[1] It is likely that the archdeacon had clashed with the convent before his patron returned from Rome,[2] and he naturally disliked the prior's claim to an archdeaconry which was in the open at last through the papal confirmation of the forged charter of Gregory VII. He lost no time in suggesting to his uncle that the monks had usurped episcopal privileges, and Philip of Poitou listened to his complaints with sympathy. According to the monks,

---

[1] Geoffrey of Coldingham, in *Scriptores tres*, p. 18.

[2] Besides the problem of the administration of the diocese *episcopo absente*, there was also the matter of the church of Aycliffe (see below, p. 33).

the bishop then proceeded to despoil the convent in three ways: by seizing the custody of its churches when vacant, by exacting aids from its clerks, and by disregarding its rights of patronage.[1] We have many indications of the attitude of each party. What the bishop called the rights of his office the monks called 'wrongful vexations'—a phrase which recalls the false charter of Bishop William, 'Notum sit omnibus', in which epscopal vexations were renounced.

The first months of the episcopacy were thus spent by each side in testing the strength of the other. By 1198 Philip of Poitou was prepared for action. He had obtained a papal inhibition to the prior to assign churches, alienate possessions, or institute priors of cells or other obedientiaries without the consent of the bishop, on the grounds that he had among them the place of abbot.[2] This claim was certainly ingenious, and gave him the initiative; but when the inhibition was read in the synod the prior replied that it was null *ex suggestione falsi*, and an unseemly brawl caused the meeting to break up in disorder. The next day the monks counter-attacked by asking Philip for permission to read to him the privileges of the convent. A start was made; but the bishop lost patience, interrupted the lecture, and refused to give credence to their charters.[3] Philip was clearly less credulous than Pope Celestine III.

The dispute was probably a prelude to the celebrated siege of monks in Elvet church by the servants of the bishop.[4] In the same year, 1198, died Master Richard of Coldingham, who had been an important clerk of the late bishop,[5] and rector simultaneously of two of the convent's churches, Elvet in Durham and Bishop Middleham, the second of

---

[1] 'Suggerentes episcopo . . . monachos quasdam libertates usurpasse, quas temporibus predecessorum suorum nullius eos aetas meminerit percepisse. . . . Horum falsitatis assercionibus episcopus assentiens, cervicem erexit, et a clericis eorum auxilia et vacantium ecclesiarum custodias et donationes exegit, et quas ipsi vexationes illicitas dicebant, ipse libertates suo juri debitas asserebat', Geoffrey of Coldingham, loc. cit.

[2] *Calendar of Papal Letters*, ed. W. H. Bliss (1893), i. 4.

[3] Geoffrey of Coldingham, pp. 20–1; cf. p. 19, 'episcopus . . . nec privilegiis ecclesiae fidem daret'.

[4] For descriptions, see Geoffrey of Coldingham, p. 19; *Chronica Rogeri de Houedene*, iv. 69; 'Attestationes testium', *F.P.D.*, pp. 220 seqq.

[5] Cf. Surtees, op. cit. i. 282, 284, 296, 298, &c.

which he had farmed.[1] Bishop Hugh had given the convent permission to appropriate Elvet on the death of Richard,[2] but while the clerk lay dying Prior Bertram and Bishop Philip quarrelled over the future of his churches. Philip said that he should have the grant as he was bishop and abbot; Bertram maintained that it was his right by ownership (*dominus fundi*), prescription, and by being abbot in all but name.[3] When Richard died monks entered both churches. At Bishop Middleham two monks and two episcopal bailiffs remained in joint custody for seven weeks, and, when the bishop finally arrived, the monks had to change their presentee; at Elvet monks who had entered were starved out by the servants of the bishop led by Archdeacon Aimery.[4] This scandalous violence greatly prejudiced Philip's cause. In other cases the bishop was more accommodating, although the monks represented all his attempts to recover episcopal rights as frenzied persecution. Four days after the capitulation of the monkish custodians of Elvet, Philip confirmed the appropriation of the church,[5] and a lawsuit which had been threatening was avoided by the mediation of friends.[6] The bishop also confirmed the convent's right to the free disposal of its churches, provided that his reasonable assent was obtained,[7] and the rest of the episcopate seems to have been fairly peaceful.

The events of 1198 provide us with yet another clue to the motives behind the bishop's attack on the privileges of the monks. The convent's churches were useful as gifts to episcopal clerks, and there is plenty of evidence that the bishops in this period were controlling the convent's right of patronage. The reply of the monastery was to press on with appropriation. According to the tenor of its charters this could be done without the episcopal assent as a simple

---

[1] 'Attestationes testium', *F.P.D.*, p. 250. [2] See above, p. 19, n. 2.

[3] *Chronica Rogeri de Houedene*, loc. cit.

[4] This was not the only hostile action of Aimery in this year. He also disseised with violence the convent of an estate which Henry of le Puiset, a son of the late bishop, had given for the support of monks at Finchale (*Chronica Rogeri de Houedene*, iv. 39–40).

[5] 'Attestationes testium', *F.P.D.*, pp. 239, 248–9; *Chronica Rogeri de Houedene*, loc. cit.; *Durham Annals and Documents*, p. 147.

[6] Geoffrey of Coldingham in *Scriptores tres*, p. 19.

[7] 'cum illius tamen moderato assensu', *Chronica Rogeri de Houedene*, loc. cit.

administrative act; but such a practice was no longer in harmony with the general custom of the church, and appropriation was always a hazardous operation, often requiring the indemnification of many interests. Custody of the vacant church gave a very useful start to the proceedings; it meant, for instance, that the bishop could not intrude a clerk of his own, and then demand recognition of the accomplished fact. Custody also proclaimed the convent's *dominium*, and gave it possession of the church.

Philip of Poitou suffered defeat in his attempt to control absolutely the convent's parish churches, and conditions probably returned to normal, that is to say, with the patronage nominally in the hands of the prior and convent, but with the bishop able to influence the policy.[1] He seems also to have gained no clear victory in the struggle for the custody of vacant churches of the convent's advowson;[2] but he had at least put the monks on the defensive. With regard to his attempts to destroy the immunity of the churches from the episcopal customs, we know nothing more than that he exacted aids from them.

After the death of Philip in 1208 the monks appear to have made strenuous efforts to recover their rights during the long vacancy; but the archdeacon Aimery was one of the royal guardians of the see, and he hindered the process.[3] In 1217 Richard Marsh was appointed bishop by the efforts of the legate and against the wishes of the monks. He had held many royal offices, having been exchequer clerk, sheriff, justiciar, and chancellor, and was selected as a strong man to maintain the royal power. For a time he had been archdeacon of Northumberland, and so must already have come into contact with the claims of the monks.

It is difficult to discover whether or no his policy was at first conciliatory. In the first two years of his episcopate he gave the convent permission to appropriate several of its

---

[1] This episcopal influence seems to have been unofficially recognized by the convent in 1229. One of the objections against Prior Thomas de Melsonby put forward by the king in 1237 to impede his acceptance as bishop was that he had obtained 'Le convenit' simoniacally from Bishop Poore 'eo pacto quod non possent conferre alicui aliquam ecclesiam, irrequisito assensu et consensu suo', *Scriptores tres*, p. lxxiii.

[2] See below, pp. 33–5.   [3] 'Attestationes testium', *F.P.D.*, pp. 220 seqq.

churches;[1] but in the grant in respect of Dalton-le-Dale occurs the saving-clause 'salvo nobis et successoribus nostris jure pontificali et parochiali'. This cannot have been at all satisfactory to the monks, and the church was still unappropriated in 1229.[2] According to Wendover a quarrel arose between bishop and monks, apparently in 1218 or 1219, over certain ancient liberties and customs which the convent enjoyed. Richard asked the monks to show him all their privileges, so that he could remedy any imperfection in their liberty; but the monks suspected fraud, and refused to exhibit their charters. In return the bishop swore that he would convert all their goods to his own use, and that henceforth they should have no peace.[3] Evidently the scene which opened the episcopate of Philip of Poitou was being re-enacted, this time with Richard anxious to discover the exact import of the jealously guarded charters of the monks. Wendover's story, however, is incomplete, for a charter of Richard dated September 1218 is extant,[4] made up of three extracts from the spurious charters of Bishop William, in which the convent's archdeaconry, its free control of its parish churches, and its right to appropriate at will were recognized. Unless this is a draft or a forgery, the convent must in the end have opened its archives and allowed the bishop to collate its privileges. Nevertheless, it is difficult to reconcile this recognition of the convent's liberties with the saving-clause in the Dalton charter, granted only three weeks earlier, or with Richard's later actions. The charter was possibly granted by the bishop during the negotiations over the church of Dalton, and later repudiated.

The rest of Wendover's description of the origin of the quarrel is certainly true. He relates that shortly after this dissension, which we can now regard as a distorted view of the happenings in September 1218, servants of the bishop violently expelled a monk from a church, and that, when the monk complained to the bishop, he replied that his servants

---

[1] Dalton-le-Dale, Aycliffe, and Pittington, Surtees, op. cit. i. 118 and 277; *Scriptores tres*, p. 36; *Durham Annals and Documents*, p. 148.

[2] Richard Poore confirmed his predecessor's grant in 'Le convenit', *F.P.D.*, p. 216.

[3] *Flores historiarum*, ed. H. G. Hewlett (Rolls Ser.), ii. 256 seqq.

[4] Printed *F.P.D.*, p. lxxxvii.

would have done better had they killed him. Clearly this refers to the disputed custody of a church, but whether Bedlington or Ancroft,[1] or even another, is not certain. Later, the chronicler informs us, the monks appealed to the pope, and sent proctors to the *curia* to accuse the bishop. The convent's charges are listed in the papal rescript they obtained, dated June 1220.[2] They make ugly reading, and include the shedding of blood, simony, adultery, sacrilege, and perjury, but they were intended, in a way familiar to medieval controversialists, to defame the character of an adversary, and to prejudice his case. Such truth as they may have contained was subsidiary to the monks' purpose: the main points at issue were the bishop's treatment of the monk in custody of a church and dilapidation, or unlawful alienations. By the rescript, in which details of the complaints are given, Urban III ordered Richard Poore, bishop of Salisbury, and John of Fountains, bishop of Ely, to make inquisition into the truth of the allegations, and return their findings.

A verdict was never obtained. Richard Marsh appealed against the judges, obtained a suspension of action, and set off for Rome.[3] In February 1221 the pope revoked the order for the inquest in expectation of the bishop's arrival;[4] but Richard, who was sick, had made no appearance by June, and the pope renewed the commission to the judges.[5] The inquisition was duly performed, and the findings transmitted to Rome.[6] By great fortune a copy of these invaluable *attestationes testium* has been preserved.[7] The later history of the case is confused, but unimportant. It was the bishop's

---

[1] See below, p. 35.

[2] *Flores historiarum*, ii. 258; *Calendar of Papal Letters*, i. 72.

[3] Rather confused accounts are given by the 'Annales de Dunstaplia', *Annales monastici*, ed. H. R. Luard (Rolls Ser.), iii. 62, 67–8, and by Wendover, loc. cit.

[4] *Calendar of Papal Letters*, i. 78.   [5] Ibid., p. 82.

[6] *Annales de Dunstaplia*, iii. 67–8.

[7] Printed *F.P.D.*, pp. 220 seqq. They have a fifteenth-century title, giving them the date of 1228. The Rev. Wm. Greenwell rightly rejected the date, and, on internal evidence, concluded that they must derive from the episcopate of Richard Marsh. He seems, however, to have been unaware of other materials for the history of the litigation, and made no attempt to place them in their context. Although it is most likely that these *attestationes* are from the possessory case of 1221, it is not impossible that they come from a later stage. The exact date, however, is of no great importance to us.

policy to hinder the pronouncement of a definitive sentence, and probably additional charges from both sides protracted the hearing. In May 1224 the bishops of Bath, Salisbury, Ely, and Rochester were ordered by the pope to endeavour to bring the case to a close.[1] In March 1225 the bishops were apparently trying to secure peace between the parties;[2] but in December 1225 the case between the convent and the bishop with regard to the custody of void churches of the advowson of the prior and monks, alienations and other matters was still pending, and the four bishops were required to send to the pope lawful proofs of alienations of episcopal goods said to have been made by the bishop without the consent of the prior and chapter.[3] The death of Richard Marsh in May 1226 achieved what the courts had failed to do, and the only tangible results of the struggle were the expenses of the litigation. Two years later the monks secured the translation of one of the judges, Richard Poore, a man whom they had unsuccessfully elected as bishop in 1213, from Salisbury to Durham, and in 1229 he negotiated with the convent a concordat on many of the disputed points, which was known as the 'Littera convencionalis', and later as 'Le convenit'.[4]

The *attestationes* are records of fact, and illustrate the many disputes between the parties, for there seems to have been friction wherever the interests of bishop and convent touched. 'Le convenit' is no code of relations; it is based largely on the *attestationes*, and settles only those points on which there had been irreconcilable division. Where there had been no conflict there is no pronouncement, and even more disconcerting is its silence whenever either side had conclusively proved prescription through the inquest.[5] It was apparently also accompanied by 'gentlemen's agreements', only some of which have been recorded.[6] 'Le convenit' has therefore to be interpreted with caution. Although Robert de Graystanes, the fourteenth-century Durham chronicler, calls it *priori et conventui praejudicialis in multis*,[7]

[1] *Calendar of Papal Letters*, i. 97.   [2] Ibid., p. 101.   [3] Ibid., p. 104.
[4] Printed *F.P.D.*, pp. 212 seqq.   [5] Cf. below, p. 80.
[6] See above, p. 27, n. 1. Richard is also reported as promising to make a grant of forest to the monks (Robert de Graystanes, *Scriptores tres*, p. 45).
[7] Ibid., p. 37.

it is impossible to believe that it could have been grossly unfair. It had been the great desire of the monks to have Richard Poore as bishop, and as one of the judges-delegate in the suit he had had ample opportunity for assessing the rights and wrongs. Perhaps the greatest tribute to the fairness of the concordat is that it was constantly respected in later years. It will be seen that our main sources for the history of this important quarrel are unfortunately of the same nature. Owing to the loss of the *libelli* from the possessory case we have no statement of claim from either side, and, owing to the truncation of the hearing, points of law were never argued. But there is no reason to think the attitude of the parties greatly dissimilar from that displayed in 1198.

The *attestationes* and 'Le convenit' are rather disappointing sources of evidence for the degree of acceptance obtained for the convent's claim to an archdeaconry in its Durham parishes at this time. Although it is evident that the pretensions of the monks were generally questioned in this period, the suit only dealt with matters which directly concerned the bishop and which sprang from the initial quarrel. Hence, although the archidiaconal rights of the monks in the diocese of York came under review, for there the bishop as a partner in the liberties was affected, their claim to a similar franchise in the diocese of Durham was not involved. In the latter diocese the main frictional points in ecclesiastical matters were the bishop's endeavour to control the patronage of the monks, his right to levy the customs on the convent's churches, and the rival claims to have custody of and induction into those churches.

It is possible that in the *libellus*, the convent's initial statement of its case, the monks made use of the forged charters, and relied on the grant of the archdeaconry to justify some of the disputed privileges. But as a compromise was eventually achieved on the basis of the findings of the inquisition of 1221, that issue was never joined. The inquisition was concerned with concrete disputes and practices, not with legal claims. Hence the archdeaconry is hardly mentioned. Another contributory cause to the silence is that the charges of the monks were against the bishop alone, and only touched the archdeacons as episcopal agents. The separation of episcopal and archidiaconal function found in the litigation seems prejudicial to the convent's position. The monks claimed a complex of privileges, all parts of which relied on the same charters, but which were unequally supported by possession. Clearly the best policy of the immunist was to reintegrate the alienated *episcopalia*, and to weld together all the parts, so that the strong should support the weak. This the Durham monks failed to do. On the other hand, the wisest course for the diocesan was to break up the agglomeration, to attack piecemeal, and through local victories to undermine the whole structure. And in this the bishops were successful.

The only episcopal customs in dispute—aids and, most likely, hospitality and synodals—are treated as touching the bishop alone. The custom relating to the fines and amercements of justice plays no part in the case—possibly because the monks had no effective possession of ecclesiastical jurisdiction in the diocese of Durham, but more probably because it was held to affect the archdeacon and not the bishop; and hence would only have been involved if the convent's claim to the archdeaconry had ever been argued. In the concordat of 1229 the bishop speaks only for himself, and the convent made a separate agreement with the archdeacon of Durham. This attitude reflects the growing independence of the archdeacon and his establishment as the local ordinary; it seems moreover to indicate that it was not held at this time that freedon from episcopal burdens automatically entailed immunity from the exactions of subordinate officials. If the monks had been attempting to claim an archdeaconry because they possessed episcopal customs, the proceedings of these years must surely have destroyed their efforts. The episcopal policy is indeed most instructive, for it shows how the typical monastic franchise could be disintegrated and defeated. What monks could construct bishops could take to pieces. Fortunately for the convent of Durham, it could display an independent and explicit grant of archidiaconal rights, which was not without value.

The evidence given in the *attestationes* of 1221 is of great interest. On the question whether the monks or the bishop should have the custody of vacant churches of the convent's advowson, evidence was confined to nine churches, all of them rectories, or claimed to be such by the bishop: Aycliffe, Billingham, Low Dinsdale, Heighington, Bishop Middleham, Bedlington, St. Oswald's Elvet in Durham, Ancroft, and Cornhill. Witnesses related what had happened at these churches during recent vacancies in them. We have already described the disputed custody of Elvet and Bishop Middleham, which took place in 1198.[1]

The church of Aycliffe had been granted with the arch-deaconry to Aimery, his nephew, by Philip of Poitou when bishop-elect (1196).[2] The convent must have defeated this attempt to set its right of patronage aside, for another obtained the church,[3] and it was not until this man died some ten years later (1208 × 17) that Aimery was able to renew his claim, possibly on the strength of an agreement made on the earlier occasion. The archdeacon occupied the church; but the monks had decided to appropriate. They disputed Aimery's custody and bought him off with forty librates of land. Their custody was then undisturbed until the accession of Richard Marsh, who in 1217 confirmed the appropriation[4] for which they had obtained papal sanction during the vacancy.[5]

---

[1] Above, pp. 25–6. Another disputed custody of Bishop Middleham took place in 1225. A monk in custody was ordered to quit by the dean of Christianity of Durham, and, when he refused, was excommunicated despite his appeal to the pope (*Calendar of Papal Letters*, i. 108).

[2] *Chronica Rogeri de Houedene*, iv. 14. Aimery succeeded Bishop Hugh's son or nephew, Bouchard de Puiset, as archdeacon. Bouchard had held many parish churches with his archdeaconry—'cum archidiaconatu Dunelmensi ecclesias plurimas ad usum magis deliciarum quam utilitatem animarum paterna provisione possedit' [William of Newburgh, 'Historia rerum Anglicarum,' in *Chronicles of the Reigns of Stephen, Henry II and Richard I*, ed. Ric. Howlett (Rolls Ser.), ii. 441]—and these included at least Aycliffe and Heighington (see below, p. 35) of the convent's advowson. In 1196 he offered the enormous fine of 200 m. when an aid was taken from the beneficed clergy of the diocese *sede vacante* (*Chancellor's Roll 8 Richard I*, Pipe Roll Soc., new ser., vol. 7, p. 257). Aimery may have expected to inherit all Bouchard's benefices, and regarded them as attached to the archdeaconry.

[3] Thomas must have succeeded Archdeacon Bouchard, for he witnesses a document with Mr. Richard of Coldingham, who died in 1198 (*F.P.D.*, p. 127 n.; cf. ibid., pp. 53 n., 169 n.). A Thomas, clerk of Aycliffe, occurs in 1147 (ibid., p. lxiii; cf. p. 157 n.); but the span seems rather too wide for the conflation of the two.

[4] Peter de Derlington, witness for the convent, *F.P.D.*, p. 248; *Scriptores tres*, p. 36; *Durham Annals and Documents*, p. 148; Pope Honorius confirmed Richard's grant in April 1218 (Surtees, op. cit. i. 118).   [5] *Calendar of Papal Letters*, i. 47.

At Billingham the monks had had the advantage of early intelligence of the fatal illness of the parson, Simon the Chamberlain—one of Bishop Hugh of le Puiset's most intimate clerks—for it had been communicated to them by his son, Henry, to whom the church had been promised. Representatives of Prior Bertram (1188–1212) were thus in at the death, and, despite their fears of opposition, had the peaceful custody of the church until the arrival of Henry, who then held it in peace for all his life.[1] Of his institution and induction we are told nothing; but the presumption is that he was inducted by the guardians, and his significant absence from Billingham after perceiving that his father was dying may be explained by the necessity of seeking episcopal institution. During the tenure of Henry, Bishop Philip (1197–1208) gave the monks permission to appropriate on condition that a vicarage was instituted,[2] and on Henry's death the monks had the custody once more,[3] and successfully appropriated. The vicarage was taxed by Prior William of Durham (1212–14), during the vacancy of the see,[4] and it may be surmised that Henry's death could not have occurred at a happier time.

At Dinsdale the parsonage had descended from Norman to his son William le Breton, and thence to William's clerk, Nicholas le Breton, in whom we may see probably a close relation, if not another son. Two witnesses declared that there had been no vacancies, and so no custody.[5] We know, however, that William was instituted to the church by Bishop Philip.[6]

Heighington had been the scene of disputes. Three vacancies are described by witnesses, and there is little agreement between the testimony of the two parties. The episcopal witnesses maintained that after the death of William Hansard in the time of Bishop Hugh (ante 1195), the bishop had had the peaceful custody of the church.[7] Witnesses for

---

1 F.P.D., p. 249; Wm. de Norham, however, said there was no interval, ibid., p. 250.   2 F.P.D., p. 250; charter printed Surtees, op. cit. iii. 392.
3 F.P.D., pp. 249 and 271.   4 Printed Hutchinson, op. cit. iii. 107 n.
5 John de Middeltone, F.P.D., p. 249; Wm. Baard, ibid., p. 250.
6 Printed Surtees, op. cit. iii. 394. Norman was still parson in 1196 (Pipe Roll 8 Richard I, p. 256).
7 Henry Paulin, F.P.D., p. 246; Peter de Heighington, p. 255.

the convent, however, declared that a monk, John, had been in peaceful custody.[1] Similar contradiction is found in the description of events following the death of Archdeacon Bouchard (1196). Witnesses for the monks held strongly that there had merely been ineffectual opposition from the bishop.[2] But there can be no doubt that after the death of German de Pusat, the next rector, the bishop had had the custody, and that this time it had been the attempted entry of a monk which had been repulsed.[3]

Disputed custody had also taken place at Bedlington after the death of the parson, Ralf Harang, in the time of Bishop Richard Marsh, apparently in 1219. The monk who had been sent to administer the church gave evidence that despite the hindrance of the bishop's servants he had acted as custodian, and that he had inducted William de Roeng' into possession on the mandate of the convent.[4]

Witnesses of both parties were in agreement over events at Cornhill and Ancroft during vacancies, and at other times, but the status of the churches and of their incumbents was in dispute. It is clear that, as 'Le convenit' recognized, Cornhill was a chapel of Norham, and Ancroft a chapel of Holy Island, a church appropriate to the convent. But each was growing into a parish church, having burial and baptismal rights, and the mistaken view of some episcopal witnesses is understandable. It is also certain that the incumbents were chaplains who had farmed the revenues; but their farm was indistinguishable from a pension, and they were thought by many to be parsons. Hence, on the grounds that the two chapels were parish churches and rectories, the

---

[1] Walter Freeman, *F.P.D.*, p. 287; cf. Richard le Brun, p. 264, William de Merintone, p. 277.

[2] Anketil, monk, *F.P.D.*, p. 296; Roger Tredegold, p. 297; Peter de Heighington, p. 255; Ric. le Brun, p. 264; Wm., monk, p. 277; Wm. de Merintone, p. 277; Wm. de Bissoptone, p. 298; cf. the story of Reginald Abelin, episcopal witness, p. 243.

[3] Most of the episcopal custodians gave evidence: Oliver fitz Rolland, *F.P.D.*, p. 246; Elyas de Ketton, p. 253; Roger, p. 261; cf. Ric. de Auclent, p. 238, and other witnesses. Reginald Abelin declared that a monk Ralf, the present prior (1214–33), tried to intrude, pp. 242–3; Oliver fitz Rolland stated that it was the monk William, afterwards prior (1212–14), p. 246. It is possible that German de Pusat was a relative of Bishop Hugh and of Archdeacon Bouchard.

[4] Anketil, *F.P.D.*, pp. 296–7; cf. Wm. Crowe, p. 301. For the date see Jas. Raine, *The History and Antiquities of North Durham* (1852), p. 367.

bishop had claimed and fought for their custody during vacancies.[1]

The *attestationes* show that vacancies at seven parish churches only passed under review, although the convent had the advowson of at least twice as many in the diocese. The significance of this is not apparent. If we confine ourselves to the evidence given, it is clear that the convent was in shaky possession of the right of custody in but one of the seven churches, Billingham. The opposition of the recent bishops had clearly been intensive, and there were no Nestors to cast back their minds to a period when ownership of a church gave undisputed custody. The Dunstable annals represent the inquisition as abundantly in favour of the monks, and declare that the judges uncovered *mirabilia, abominalia, et fabulis annumeranda*.[2] Certainly neither Philip of Poitou nor Richard Marsh had been gentle pastors, and their methods of opposition to the claims of the monks must have alienated the sympathy of many. But the custody of vacant churches pertained now by common law to the bishop, although it was commonly performed by the archdeacon under mandate, and sometimes acquired by him through grant or usurpation. The *attestationes* show that the monks were unsuccessful in establishing a prescriptive title to it, or even general possession of it. All indeed was lost unless they could prove by their charters an episcopal grant. Several witnesses were asked by what right the convent claimed custody. Some did not know. A layman characteristically replied that the church in question was theirs.[3] Monkish witnesses referred to the spurious charters with their grant of archidiaconal jurisdiction and the free disposal and control of their lands and churches.[4] But custody was

---

[1] 'Attestationes testium', *passim*.   [2] *Annales monastici* (Rolls Ser.), iii. 67.

[3] Walter Freeman, 'requisitus quo jure monachus habuit custodiam illam [Heighington], dicit se nescire, nisi quod ecclesia eorum est' (*F.P.D.*, p. 288); cf. Roger Tredegold, layman, who said that a monk was at Heighington 'ad custodiendam ecclesiam illam, tanquam ecclesiam monachorum propriam, donec prior disponeret de ea pro voluntate sua' (p. 297); Ric. le Brun, 'de custodiis ecclesiarum requisitus, dicit quod audivit saepe quod monachi debent habere custodiam ecclesiarum de patronatu suo vacancium, sed quo jure ignorat' (p. 264); Peter, prior of Finchale, agreed with Richard, 'excepto quod non recolit utrum hoc fuerit sede vacante vel non' (p. 267).

[4] The monk Anketil, *F.P.D.*, p. 296. The important evidence of the monks G. and Thomas has been lost owing to the mutilation of the manuscript. We get

not an archidiaconal right, and a thirteenth-century bishop would be unwilling to interpret the other clauses in such a sense. Hence it was not unreasonable of Bishop Richard Poore to decide that the convent had no good claim to either the possession or the ownership of the right, and its claims were duly denied in 'Le convenit', which declared that the monks were to have the custody and sequestration of none of their churches in the diocese of Durham.[1]

Almost inseparable from custody, and similar in its nature, was the right of induction. Witnesses gave examples of the convent's sending to its custodians of a church the mandate for inducting its presentee into corporal possession of it.[2] This claim was not specifically denied by 'Le convenit'; but the rejection of the claim to custody was probably considered as comprehending the other. It is true that by the concordat the monastery was given control of the temporalities of its churches in almost the same words as in the false charters;[3] but this grant applied only to the appropriated churches, to which we must now turn our attention.

a tantalizing glimpse of it from the evidence of Henry, the sub-prior: 'Requisitus de custodiis ecclesiarum, concordat cum G. monacho, eo excepto, quod ubi Thomas monachus dixit quod deberent ponere monachos pro recognitione juris sui, iste dicit quod debent habere custodiam; item ubi Thomas monachus dixit episcopum quaesisse ab officio suo si ecclesia esset de eorum advocatione, iste dicit episcopum quaesisse si ecclesia esset de eorum custodia' (p. 280).

[1] 'Custodiae vero et sequestra omnium ecclesiarum, quae sunt de donacione dictorum monachorum in episcopatu Dunelmensi, cum vacaverint, nobis et successoribus nostris, sine aliqua eorundem monachorum contradictione, in perpetuum remanebunt', *F.P.D.*, p. 216.

[2] At Ancroft (*F.P.D.*, p. 223), Cornhill (p. 225), and Bedlington (p. 297); it is implied at Billingham (p. 249) and at Dinsdale (pp. 249–50). At Bishop Middleham in 1198, after the bailiffs of the bishop and monks had been in joint possession, W. Achelun, a monk, presented Mr. Philip de Baillol as parson to the bishop, who accepted him. The monk then handed the key of the church to the bishop, who transferred it to his chaplain, who was to have the custody of the church in the name of the presentee (pp. 250, 301).

[3] 'Omnes vero terras prioris et monachorum Dunelmensium et omnes ecclesias suas, in usus proprios conversas vel canonice convertendas, concedimus . . . quod in sua manu et libera dispositione habeant et teneant inperpetuum, ut quantum poterint semper de eis redditus suos secundum deum augmentent et extendant, ita quod nullus post canonicum eorum ingressum, quantum ad temporalia, se de illis intromittat, nisi per consensum ipsorum prioris et monachorum vel licenciam, sed vicarios suos ad illas ecclesias . . . praesentabunt episcopo . . .; qui vicarii ab episcopo instituti de beneficiis illarum temporalibus, viz. quae dictis priori et monachis debentur, eisdem respondeant, nobis vero et successoribus nostris, quantum ad ipsos vicarios pertinet, de cura animarum, intendant', *F.P.D.*, p. 213.

No question seems to have been asked in the lawsuit about the liability of the convent's churches to episcopal hospitality and aids. The monks, however, had a clear title to exemption *ex privilegio* and probably also were in disputed possession of the immunity. This was recognized by 'Le convenit'. The prior is declared free from episcopal hospitality and aids and from other burdens and vexations in respect of churches appropriated at the time of the agreement.[1] Clearly it is a concession confined to appropriated churches, otherwise the limitation would be meaningless. Apart from the restriction, the language is the same as that in the forgery 'Notum sit omnibus'[2] and the charter of Richard Marsh,[3] except that there is no mention in 'Le convenit' of the immunity being effective against archdeacons. The failure to define the position of the vicars causes ambiguity; but it must be inferred that they as well as the convent were to be immune, for, as almost all the appropriations were recent, the bishop would have stated the liability of the vicars had there been any. Certainly in later years the freedom was understood as embracing the whole church.

The limitation of the franchise to churches already appropriated by 1229 halved the area which had been privileged by earlier charters. Three churches had anciently been appropriated;[4] no parsonage seems actually to have been acquired during the episcopate of Bishop Hugh;[5] but about six were appropriated between his death and 1229.[6] Of the total, seven were in the archdeaconry of Durham,[7] and

---

[1] 'Prior . . . quietus sit in perpetuum de hospiciis et auxiliis episcoporum et ceteris gravaminibus et vexationibus in ecclesiis in usus proprios conversis tempore confectionis hujus cartae', *F.P.D.*, p. 213.   [2] See above, p. 14, n. 3.

[3] See above, p. 28.   [4] Jarrow, Monkwearmouth, and Holy Island.

[5] The parsonage of Branxton had been granted to the convent's infirmary, and the transaction confirmed by Bishop Hugh (charters printed Jas. Raine, *North Durham*, append., p. 139); but it was not appropriated (cf. induction of a parson in 1234, ibid., p. 140) until granted in 1251 by Bishop Walter to maintain a cell at Warkworth (ibid., p. 140).

[6] It is certain that Ellingham (see above, p. 18, n. 2), Billingham (see above, p. 34), and Elvet (ibid., p. 26, n. 5) were appropriated. The appropriation of Dalton-le-Dale (ibid., p. 28, n. 2), Aycliffe (ibid., p. 33, n. 4), and Pittington (ibid., p. 28, n. 1) is likely. In addition papal permission was obtained in 1217, during the vacancy of the see, to appropriate Norham, Monk Hesleden, and 'Medesham' (? Bishop Middleham) (*Calendar of Papal Letters*, i. 47); but whether this had been done by 1229 is not known.

[7] Monkwearmouth, Jarrow, Billingham, Elvet, Dalton, Aycliffe, and Pittington.

two in the archdeaconry of Northumberland.[1] This settlement could hardly have been based on prevailing conditions, because appropriation was a new policy of the convent; nor was it in harmony with the tenor of the charters, although the *ecclesiae propriae* of the forgeries might have been understood in 1229 as *ecclesiae in proprios usus*, and the concession of privileges, as in the charter of Bishop Hugh of le Puiset, had always been associated with appropriation. Most likely it was but a convenient compromise, with a certain mistaken yet equitable justification. In any case the settlement was designed to effect a change in the nature of the franchise which is common to the history of all such privileged areas: it was intended to restrict a fluid exemption.

In 1229, then, the convent's franchise *vis-à-vis* the bishop was defined. It is noticeable that in this affair the archdeaconry proper as claimed in the false charters was not involved, but only the rights deriving from the convent's position as owner or patron and possessor of the episcopal customs. The right to an archdeaconry is considered a matter to be decided with the archdeacons. This theory that possession of the episcopal customs, or the possession of some of them—for the custom concerning justice has not been involved—affects relations with the bishop alone, is a development of considerable importance. The archdeacon, now an ordinary with his benefice, has become an independent power in the bishopric, and claims to an archdeaconry are held to be primarily of his concern. It will be appreciated that the early twelfth-century forgers did well in their redundancy. Had an archdeaconry not been explicitly claimed, little of the convent's franchise would have remained after 1229: the rights of a proprietor and owner of the customs had been reduced largely to financial rights in the churches and some immunities from episcopal demands. The franchise had now been limited to about nine churches. They were to be free from the financial rights of the bishop; but the convent had no episcopal administrative functions in respect of them, such as custody, sequestration, and induction. On the wider issue—the disposal and advowson of all the convent's churches—victory lay substantially with the

[1] Ellingham and Holy Island.

monastery, and it was left with a control as independent as the balance of power would permit.

§ 3. *The Franchise and the Bishop after* 1229

There is not much evidence to show how faithfully the ecclesiastical privileges confirmed to the convent by Bishop Richard Poore in 'Le convenit' of 1229 were respected by his immediate successors. The very absence of recorded conflict, however, is significant; and as the provisions dealing with the temporalities seem to have been observed, there is a presumption that the whole was accepted. Indeed, the period between the translation of Richard Poore and the accession of Anthony Bek in 1284 was disturbed by relatively few internal disputes, and can be regarded as the golden age of the convent.

It seems clear that the monastery was unable to recover any of the *episcopalia* it had lost in 1229. The earliest episcopal registers extant, unfortunately as late as the early fourteenth century, show sequestration of the convent's churches, inquisition and induction performed by the archdeacons under episcopal mandate.[1] It is also significant that the convent's thirteenth-century formularies contain no models for administrative documents concerning the Durham churches beyond those suitable for the owners of advowsons, although the administration of the Yorkshire franchise is well illustrated.[2] Nor do the monks seem to have aspired to more extensive privileges. There is no trace of a desire—none, indeed, would be expected—to introduce an alien bishop into the franchise, and so detach it from the see. In 1249 Walter Gray, archbishop of York, gave the convent the right to have monks ordained, chrism made, and churches of their advowson dedicated by any English or Irish bishop during a vacancy in the bishopric of Durham,[3] and in 1252 Bishop Walter Kirkham gave a similar privilege, effective during his absence from the bishopric;[4] but there is no evidence that such privileges were ever sought for the franchise *sede plena*.

---

[1] *Registrum palatinum Dunelmense*, ed. Sir T. Duffus Hardy (Rolls Ser.), *passim*.
[2] *Durham Annals and Documents*.
[3] *Scriptores tres*, p. lxxix.   [4] Ibid., p. lxxxi.

The bishops on their side seem equally to have respected the convent's rights. The immunity of the monastery's appropriate churches from episcopal visitation fees seems to have been maintained, for Bishop Richard Kellaw's visits (1311–16) appear to have been unaccompanied by protests. Bishop Lewis de Beaumont (1318–33), however, the unlearned relative of Queen Isabella who had been forced on the monks, showed an aggressive spirit. Each time he visited the chapter and the convent's churches a contention arose over procurations,[1] and in 1328, when he respected the immunity of the chapter but exacted a procuration fee from each church, the trouble came to a head.[2] The monks maintained that their appropriated churches were free from episcopal procurations by special privilege, and that they had been in possession of the franchise longer than the memory of man. So, in return for a gift of a hundred marks, Lewis remitted procurations due from the churches for the term of his life and penalties imposed for delicts up to the time of the agreement. Bishop Richard of Bury (1333–45) inspected the charter of Lewis in 1343, and continued the exemption for the term of his episcopate.[3]

If the concession had to be renewed by each bishop, and if it was usually paid for, the convent was in practice only farming the rights. Nevertheless the position was different from that which had obtained in respect of the convent's churches in the diocese of St. Andrews during the thirteenth century. There the convent's rights depended explicitly on a commercial bargain.[4] In Durham the monks had an independent and perfectly sound title to the liberty, which a well-disposed bishop might recognize freely. Yet it is not unlikely that most bishops required some recompense for the surrender, and it seems that no perfect stability was ever achieved, for a late fifteenth-century memorandum records that Bishop Thomas Langley (1406–37) exacted procurations from the convent's churches.[5]

[1] Charter of Lewis, *Richard of Bury, Fragments of his Register*, ed. Wm. Brown (Surtees Soc., vol. 119), p. 183.   [2] Robert de Graystanes, in *Scriptores tres*, p. 105.

[3] *Richard of Bury*, pp. 183–5.   [4] See below, pp. 137–8.

[5] *Richard of Bury*, p. 264. When Bishop Walter Skirlaw took hospitality at Pittington in 1394 an instrument was drawn up recording that it was *ex gratia et permissione* (*Scriptores tres*, p. clxxiii).

Although in the fourteenth and fifteenth centuries the monks had not the freest possession of this immunity, it appears that they had enlarged the area of the franchise. 'Le convenit' confined the peculiar to churches appropriated by 1229; but all later references to the privileged area speak simply of the appropriate churches. Not one qualification of this phrase is to be found in a series beginning in 1271. In 1320 Bishop Lewis de Beaumont, when visiting the diocese, questioned the monks' right to have appropriated churches. The suit was heard by commissaries of the bishop, who gave a verdict for the convent, and justified their appropriation of Jarrow, Monkwearmouth, Holy Island, Witton Gilbert, Whitworth, Bywell St. Peter, St. Oswald's Elvet, Aycliffe, Heighington, Merrington, Dalton-le-Dale, Monk Hesleden, Billingham, Bishop Middleham, Pittington, Norham, Branxton, Ellingham, Edlingham, and Bedlington, together with their chapels.[1] For a present of forty marks Lewis de Beaumont confirmed the sentence in 1325, and Bishop Richard of Bury likewise confirmed it in 1343.[2] A late fifteenth-century memorandum declares that this sentence and the episcopal confirmation of it should be exhibited as a warning whenever the bishop visited,[3] and it was evidently imagined that the privileges extended to all those churches, and not to that portion alone which had been appropriated by 1229.

At what period this process of enlargement took place is uncertain. The first mention of rights applying to appropriate churches comes from 1271.[4] Most, if not all, of the churches in the list of 1320 had already been incorporated by that year, and no more were appropriated in the history of the convent. It is equally difficult to perceive whether the extension of the franchise was gradual, each new member being assimilated on appropriation, or whether there was a sudden usurpation or licensed enlargement. The former hypothesis seems more likely, and, if the terms of 'Le convenit' (*tempore confectionis hujus cartae*) were intended to bar the future, the episcopal attempt to limit the area of the franchise

---

[1] *Richard of Bury*, pp. 181–2.
[2] Ibid., pp. 182–3; Robert de Graystanes, op. cit., p. 104.
[3] *Richard of Bury*, p. 264.   [4] See below, p. 45.

had clearly been a failure. That the peculiar ultimately became fixed was due only to the absence of further appropriation.

§ 4. *The Franchise and the Archdeacons after 1140*

The question of the convent's archdeaconry proper had been ignored by the lawsuit of 1220-6 and by 'Le convenit' of 1229. It was considered a matter which touched rather the rights of the archdeacons than those of the bishop. The archdeacons had, indeed, become the persons most vitally concerned with the franchise, and we have seen that they usually led the attack upon it.

Some negative evidence for the degree of acceptance that the convent's archdeaconry received at the turn of the twelfth century is provided by the *attestationes* from the great lawsuit already discussed. In the course of the dispute over the status of the incumbents of Ancroft, it was conclusively proved that one of them, Geoffrey, had taken an oath of obedience to the bishop (institution) and also to the archdeacon,[1] had attended synods and chapters,[2] and had received chrism from Henry, rural dean of Newcastle, distributing it by the authority of the bishop.[3] The monks seem only to have challenged the interpretation of these facts. According to them, the four chaplains of Holy Island attended the chapters in turn, representing themselves and the mother church, and not *tanquam personae* as episcopal witnesses alleged.[4] Only for Ancroft have we such details; but they seem to show that the monks were not exercising archidiaconal jurisdiction in Northumberland.

One action at Ancroft of the archdeacon of Northumberland, however, besides his attempts as episcopal agent to dispute the custody of the monks, had caused the convent concern. He had demanded hospitality from the chaplain

---

[1] Wm., rural dean of Northumberland beyond Coquet, *F.P.D.*, p. 220; Andrew, a deacon who had been at Ancroft seven years, p. 222.

[2] 'secutus fuit sinodos et capitula tanquam persona', Andrew, loc. cit.

[3] Andrew, loc. cit.

[4] Richard de Houburne, layman, 'De capellanis iiij. capellarum [Ancroft, Tweedmouth, Kyloe, and Lowick], vicibus suis sequentibus capitula pro se et pro matrice ecclesia de Insula, concordat cum G. monacho [evidence lost]', *F.P.D.*, p. 273.

Geoffrey, and, when it had been refused, complained to the chapter. Geoffrey had given way.[1] A deacon, Andrew, who had been at Ancroft for seven years, and who was an episcopal witness, said that he had never seen or heard of an archdeacon seeking or obtaining hospitality there before.[2] Another witness for the bishop had not seen the like in five years.[3] After Geoffrey died a disputed custody took place. The convent appointed a clerk named Hugh;[4] the bishop appointed one Oger, to whom collation was made in the chapter by the archdeacon.[5] The agents of the archdeacon had failed to put him into corporal possession of the church owing to the monks being within, and so presumably a substitute ceremony took place. Oger, however, did gain possession in the end, and the archdeacon took hospitality from him immediately.[6]

This evidence was adduced to prove that the chaplains of Ancroft were parsons. Thus, according to the bishop, parsons, or some parsons, of the convent's churches were liable to give hospitality to the archdeacon. It would also seem that the position in appropriated churches was little different, for the convent appears to have made no attempt to justify Geoffrey's immunity on the grounds that Holy Island was appropriate. Here was an opportunity for proclaiming the rights of the convent, and that it was not taken, and that the monks relied on the argument that Geoffrey was exempt as the chaplain of a chapel, seems to show that the convent had no franchise in the archdeaconry of Northumberland, and did not even claim one. It would be dangerous, however, to draw further inferences applying to the whole diocese. In 1229 the convent was so devoid of archidiaconal rights in Northumberland that it negotiated no concordat

---

[1] Andrew, *F.P.D.*, p. 222; Adam de Ildertone, p. 221; Roger de Witingham, p. 223; Ralf, p. 267.

[2] Ibid., p. 222; Walter, deacon of Norham, a conventual witness, concurred, p. 284.

[3] Roger de Witingham, ibid., p. 223. [4] Andrew, ibid., pp. 222–3.

[5] Adam de Ildertone, ibid., p. 222; Andrew, 'De collacione ecclesiae de Anecroft, facta ab episcopo post mortem G., et de presentacione clerici, cui facta est collatio in capitulo per archidiaconum loci, concordat cum Ricardo, capellano de Siplibotle [evidence defective]', p. 223; cf. Robert, chaplain of Alnham, p. 221, and Roger le Clerk, layman, p. 227.

[6] Roger de Witingham, ibid., p. 223.

with its archdeacon, and so tacitly surrendered its claims. Conditions must have been more favourable to the monks in the archdeaconry of Durham; but the *attestationes* throw no light on them.

When 'Le convenit' was made with the bishop in 1229 a complementary concordat seems to have been arranged with the archdeacon of Durham. In 1271 the holder of this office, Master Robert of St. Agatha, acknowledged before the bishop that the prior of Durham was archdeacon in the churches appropriated to the convent between the rivers Tyne and Tees, and that archdeacons of Durham had exercised jurisdiction in those churches in the name of the prior and not in their own, in consequence whereof they had paid an annual pension to the prior. Thereupon Bishop Robert Stichill gave a verdict for the prior, and it was confirmed by Bishop Robert de Insula in 1276.[1] This probably reveals the terms of the earlier settlement. It will be noticed that in this agreement the franchise is once again confined to the appropriate churches. Clearly the convent's archidiaconal franchise, like the area exempted from episcopal procurations and aids, had been limited to churches appropriated by 1229, and was showing a similar development. Otherwise the agreement is fair enough. The claims of the convent to archidiaconal jurisdiction *ex privilegio* were irresistible in 1229; but the charters may have been almost entirely inefficacious owing to non-user. This position was accurately reflected in the concordat. The convent's claims were fully recognized; but the monks were deprived of the actual exercise of the jurisdiction. The pension may have been but a reminder to the archdeacon that part of his jurisdiction was wielded in a delegate capacity; but, as archdeacons seem to have been anxious to renounce the burden, it was probably substantial, and hence designed to indemnify the convent for the loss of revenue. If the pension did approximate to the farm of the rights delegated to the archdeacon, the convent had not done too badly; but even so later priors struggled to wield the jurisdiction in person.

The refusal of Thomas de Goldburgh, archdeacon of Durham 1308–30 (?), to pay the pension and recognize his

---

[1] Robert de Graystanes, in *Scriptores tres,* p. 46.

vicarial position[1] finally provoked the convent to direct action. In 1319 the prior seized the disputed jurisdiction by visiting all the convent's appropriate churches in the archdeaconry, by appointing officials and servants, and by performing all the archidiaconal functions. In 1321 the archdeacon tried to disturb the convent's possession by visiting in person; but the prior appealed against the project, and the clergy and parishioners successfully resisted it. Bishop Lewis de Beaumont, however, intervened on his archdeacon's behalf. He threatened to depose the prior; he challenged the convent's right to have appropriated churches, sequestrated them, and threatened to give them to his clerks; he compiled a list of the appropriate churches, doubled the assessments, and sent the schedule to the pope with the comment that the monks had become senseless through their wealth. The monks lost heart; and on 5 March 1324, against the advice of their counsel, agreed to compromise. It was settled with the archdeacon that the prior should have full archidiaconal jurisdiction in the churches of Jarrow and Monkwearmouth, both cells of the convent, and in their chapels; the archdeacon in all the rest for life.

When Archdeacon Thomas died on 22 December 1330,[2] the prior immediately resumed the disputed jurisdiction; visited St. Oswald's Elvet on the next day, and on Christmas eve all the remaining churches, personally or through commissaries. He appointed officials, celebrated chapters, and, being thus in possession, appealed lest his possession be disturbed. The bishop was no less active. He granted the archdeaconry to his nephew, Aimery de Beaumont, a deformed creature according to the monastic chronicler, and the convent's peaceful possession was disturbed in July, when the prior was summoned to appear before the bishop

---

[1] For accounts of the disputes and the litigation, see *Registrum palatinum Dunelmense*, i. 203, 266–7, 471, 692, and Robert de Graystanes, op. cit., pp. 103–4, 108–10. In 1312 the case was described as 'super jurisdictione archidiaconali et ejusdem jurisdictionis exercitio in ecclesiis, quas iidem prior et conventus infra archidiaconatum nostrum Dunelmensem obtinent, et super omnibus ea quomodolibet contingentibus, secundum vim, formam, et effectum compositionis et condicti coram nobis inter ipsos dudum habiti', *Registrum palatinum Dunelmense*, i. 203–4.

[2] Graystanes gives 1333; but follows with the information that 23 Dec. was a Sunday. Moreover if 1330 is correct, the terms of the following composition can be made intelligible.

and answer the complaints of the archdeacon. The convent
made little attempt to state a case, employed the best counsel
to put forward a series of technical objections so as to post-
pone a verdict and lengthen its period of possession, and was
finally excommunicated. This time the bishop used the
threat of visiting the chapter as a weapon, and the monks
submitted to a composition similar to that of 1324, except
that it was agreed that when the bishop died conditions were
to revert to those obtaining on 1 January 1331(?). Hence
when Lewis de Beaumont died on 24 September 1333, the
prior once more resumed the jurisdiction, and was so intent
on this that he allowed the archbishop of York to take over
the administration of the spiritualities of the diocese without hindrance.[1]

The tenacity of purpose shown by the convent in the
early fourteenth century had its reward, and by 1377 the
prior's archidiaconal jurisdiction had been extended within
the southern part of the diocese to cover all the monastery's
appropriate churches.[2] The prior styled himself 'archdeacon
in all our churches in the diocese of Durham united and
annexed to us and our convent and monastery'.[3] Chapters
were held fortnightly or three-weekly, except during the
harvest period, usually in the church of St. Oswald's Elvet,
but occasionally in the nave of the cathedral.[4] The president

[1] *Scriptores tres*, p. 119.

[2] Some documents touching the official of the prior's archidiaconal jurisdiction
in the diocese of Durham, deriving apparently from 1377–80, appear among pieces
concerning the official of the bishop and miscellaneous items in a Durham formulary
'Chapter Misc. 421', a paper book of 15 ff., marginally defective, written in several
hands of the late fourteenth century. A register of the chapter's proceedings,
1435–56, is extant ('Capitula generalia prioris Dunelm' 1435–1456'), a paper
volume of 155 ff.

[3] 'Nos Robertus prior ecclesie Dunelm' archidiaconus in omnibus ecclesiis nostris
in diocesi [or infra diocesim] Dunelm' nobis et conventui nostro ac monasterio
unitis etiam et annexis', Misc. 421, ff. 12, 13ᵛ. The bishop addressed him as
'dilecto filio priori ecclesie nostre Dunelm' archidiacono in omnibus ecclesiis suis
nostre diocesis vel eius officiali', ibid., fo. 4ᵛ. Cf. prior's mandate of 1343 announcing
his visitation of Jarrow and Monkwearmouth, 'Johannes prior ecclesie Dunelmensis, archidiaconus in ecclesiis ecclesie Dunelmensi appropriatis' [*Inventories
and Account Rolls of Jarrow and Monk Wearmouth*, ed. Jas. Raine (Surtees Soc.,
vol. 29), p. 235], and style in 1498, 'Thomas, permissione divina prior ecclesiae
cathedralis Dunelmensis, archidiaconus in omnibus ecclesiis sibi et capitulo Dunelmensi appropriatis, unitis, et annexis' (*Scriptores tres*, p. ccclxxxix).

[4] For the nave of the cathedral, cf. *Capitula generalia*, fo. 112 (1453).

of the chapter was the prior's official,[1] or his commissary, who used the services of an apparitor. All churches appropriate to the convent within the archdeaconry of Durham were under the jurisdiction of the court, and a record of the attendance of the nine vicars[2] and the ten parochial chaplains[3] was kept in the fifteenth-century register. The parish of Bedlington (later a detached portion of the county of Durham) and the chapel of Wallsend (within the parish of Jarrow), although both north of the Tyne, also were at times subject to the chapter.[4] The competence of the court extended to matrimonial suits.[5] Appeals from the chapter went to the bishop's audience.[6]

The position in the archdeaconry of Northumberland was rather different. Probably no more than two of the convent's churches there had been appropriated by 1229, and the monks may have thought at first that the maintenance of claims to jurisdiction in respect of them was hardly worth while, for it appears that in 1328 the convent had neither possession of archidiaconal jurisdiction in Northumberland, nor an agreement with the archdeacons like that with the archdeacons of Durham.[7] The growth in the number of the churches appropriated to the convent within the archdeaconry however, must have created an inducement to the recovery of the privileges, and in the fourteenth century the monks planned, and successfully carried out, a brilliant campaign for the recognition of their long-dormant rights.[8]

---

[1] The following styles appear in Misc. 421: 'officialis iurisdictionis archidiaconalis prioris Dunelm' archidiaconi in omnibus ecclesiis sibi et conventui suo Dunelm' in diocesi Dunelm' unitis et annexis' (fo. 5ᵛ); 'nos domini prioris Dunelm', iurisdictionem archidiaconalem in ecclesiis eiusdem prioris et conventus sui clero et populo eorundem habentis, officialis' (ibid.); 'officialis iurisdictionis archidiaconalis prioris Dunelm' in diocesi [episcopatu, fo. 4ᵛ] Dunelm'' (fo. 2ᵛ). Other minor variations occur.

[2] St. Oswald's Elvet, Pittington, Dalton-le-Dale, Monk Hesleden, Billingham, Bishop Middleham, Aycliffe, Heighington, Merrington. Cf. Misc. 421, fo. 5ᵛ and *Capitula generalia, passim.*

[3] Jarrow, Shields, Monkwearmouth, Hilton, Croxdale, Witton Gilbert, Whitworth, St. Margaret's Durham, Wolviston, Castle Eden. Cf. *Capitula generalia, passim.*

[4] The vicar of Bedlington is listed 4 Oct. 1436–16 Apr. 1439 and 9 Oct. 1455; the parochial chaplain of Wallsend 3 Oct. 1437–7 Apr. 1456.

[5] Cf. Misc. 421, ff. 2ᵛ, 4, 5ᵛ.   [6] Cf. ibid., fo. 4.

[7] See p. 49, n. 1. In 1317, for instance, the official of the archdeacon of Northumberland made the inquisition on presentation to the convent's church of Meldon [John Hodgson, *A History of Northumberland* (1820–40), II. ii. 7].

[8] Robert de Graystanes, op. cit., p. 107.

In 1328 the prior and chapter appealed against the archdeacon of Northumberland, who was about to visit the
appropriated churches of the convent within his archdeaconry. At the hearing of the case the prior maintained
that by the convent's charters he was archdeacon in all
churches appropriate to the convent within the bishopric of
Durham, and consequently in Northumberland. The archdeacon replied that from the beginning archdeacons had
exercised their jurisdiction in those churches as in others.
The position is clear: the prior relied on privileges, the
archdeacon on the common law and prescription. The appeal
was merely a manœuvre, and was abandoned. Its purpose
was to disturb the archdeacon's possession, for the possessor
enjoyed so many advantages at law. In 1331 the prior himself visited the churches. The archdeacon appealed, and the
convent came to terms. It was agreed that the archdeacon
was to have full jurisdiction for his life over the convent's
appropriated churches, but that visitation fees were to be
received alternatively by archdeacon and prior. The composition, although marking an advance, was valued not so
much for its terms as for the advantageous position that had
been secured for a renewal of the campaign. The agreement
was made with the prior's visitation unrevoked. Before, the
convent's charters had been void through non-user; now its
counsel maintained that, since the grant in the charters was
of the jurisdiction of an archdeacon, by taking possession of
one part, visitation, possession of the whole had been recovered.[1] The struggle was still in progress at the end of
the century, when John de Wessington, the antiquary who
became prior in 1416, was conducting the case of the convent, on which he composed a memorial.[2] The hamper of

[1] 'Causa inducens priorem ad componendum erat, quod contra visitacionem
prioris archidiaconus appellaverat, et tuitorie ad curiam Eboracensem; quia ergo
prior solas cartas habuit, ante visitacionem illam a possessione vacuas, nec ulla
compositione archidiaconi roboratas, ne tuitorie visitacio facta jam per priorem
adnullaretur, et pro nullo pronunciaretur, sic composuit. Dixerunt tamen aliqui,
quod ex quo privilegium fuit unum de jurisdictione archidiaconatus concessum
priori, per apprehensionem possessionis unius partis erat totius possessio perquisita',
ibid., p. 107.

[2] 'In primis idem Johannes, antequam erat in priorem creatus [ante 1416],
collegit per modum articulorum jura et privilegia archidiaconatus prioris in ecclesiis
suis adversus magistrum Johannem Rekenall, archidiaconum Northumbriae; et

proofs produced in 1312 was still in the muniment room.[1]
In 1396 the prior authorized proctors to make a final concord with Master John de Refham, archdeacon of Northumberland, on archidiaconal jurisdiction,[2] and, as has been
noticed,[3] Bedlington and Wallsend were sometimes subject
to the prior's chapter in the fifteenth century.

By the fifteenth century, therefore, the monks had not only
maintained their theoretical claims, but had recovered possession of the greater part of them. In the period after 'Le
convenit' the convent never forgot that the prior was archdeacon by right, and never hesitated to take up the struggle
with an archdeacon who tried to ignore his vicarial position.
Thus the possibility of exercising the jurisdiction in person
was always present, and was eventually for the most part
realized. Moreover, the privileged area had been restored
almost to its widest extent by the appropriation of some eleven
more churches between 1229 and 1271 and by the recovery
of rights in the archdeaconry of Northumberland. Hence the
programme of the pseudo-charters had, after a long struggle,
been substantially realized.

§ 5. Retrospect

It was by no means unusual, indeed almost normal, for
the chapter of a cathedral to have special rights in its own
parish churches. The chapter formed the council of the
bishop, without the consent of which he should take no
important action, and it was equitable that its ecclesiastical
possessions should be in a privileged position. The claims
of the monks to a franchise within the bishopric of Durham
were, then, neither extraordinary nor unreasonable. It is
their chequered history which requires explanation.

It may be surmised that the original pretensions of the
monks were too immoderate in sum, and that the inevitable
hostility which they aroused from each bishop endangered
even legitimate parts. Perhaps the least acceptable claim of

---

idem articuli valent ad defensionem contra archidiaconum Dunelmensem', *Registrum
palatinum Dunelmense*, iv. 484 n.   [1] See ibid., i. 473.

[2] 'de et super jurisdiccionibus archidiaconalibus certarum ecclesiarum, cleri,
populi, et personarum earundem, ad dictos priorem, conventum, et capitulum, ut
asseritur, pertinentium', *Scriptores tres*, p. clxxviii.

[3] See above, p. 48.

the convent was that the prior should be abbot in all but name. This was designed to cause recurrent and bitter quarrels which continued even through the thirteenth century. Such chronic hostility was bound to react unfavourably on every aspect of the convent's privileges. Monks, much more so than a secular chapter, were disadvantageously placed in any such conflict. The supineness of a prior might cause the loss of many hard-won privileges, and the monks were obliged to suffer in silence.[1] The position of the prior, too, was hard. The convent was under the jurisdiction of the bishop, and his special claims of tutelage were difficult to deny. His visitational rights could be used to put great pressure on the convent, and he could force the resignation of a government distasteful to him. His superior wealth and power made him almost irresistible. As a palatine earl, the shield of the kingdom against the fury of the Scots, he was usually a trusted friend of the king. Not here, as perhaps elsewhere, could the king be tempted to favour the monks so as to weaken the bishop or feudatory. Nor could the convent look to the archbishop of York for help, since its claims were almost equally distasteful to him. The convent's pretensions to govern the see during a vacancy were hotly contested by the archbishops, and there was little reason for the metropolitan to support the monks against their bishop.

The claims of the monks were wide, and the monks were defenceless. Almost any privilege they obtained in the diocese of Durham, especially during the more turbulent centuries, depended on the goodwill of the bishop. If they could have obtained free election, and secured bishops from their own ranks, everything might have been well. But only one Durham monk was raised to the see in the whole of the twelfth and thirteenth centuries. Under these conditions it was almost impossible to gain disputed rights by prescription. Hence, when relatively orderly government came to the diocese, and settlements of the disputes were attempted, the monks could show magnificent privileges albeit little possession of them. The importance of possession was considerable, and Richard Poore no doubt thought himself

---

[1] Cf. Geoffrey of Coldingham on Prior German (1162–86), *Scriptores tres*, p. 8.

generous in conceding some portion of rights ineffectually claimed. When all these factors are considered it must be acknowledged that the monks had not fared too ill. They had forged their titles, and had in the beginning lacked the strength to acquire a firm hold on the rights. But they had been imbued with the tenacity and resilience of a corporation, and those qualities did in time prevail.

II

THE YORKSHIRE FRANCHISE
(HOWDENSHIRE AND ALLERTONSHIRE)

§ 1. *The Origin of the Franchise*

THE ecclesiastical franchise of the convent of Durham
in the diocese of York was an enclave within a larger
immunity—the liberties of St. Cuthbert. These liberties in
the later Middle Ages were composed of two groups of
parishes: Birkby, Cowesby, Leake, Osmotherley, North
Otterington, Thornton-le-Street, Northallerton, Kirkby Sigston, and West Rounton, near the Durham–York boundary,
with Crayke more than half-way to York; and Howden, Brantingham, Hemingbrough, Skipwith, Walkington,
and Welton, to the north of the Humber, with Holtby,
east of York, as a detached member. The northern portion
was known as Allertonshire, the southern as Howdenshire.

The church of Durham possessed estates in Yorkshire
before the Norman Conquest;[1] but the greater part of the
episcopal and monastic fief was acquired afterwards. King
William I, between 1080 and 1086, granted to Bishop
William of Saint-Calais the manors of Welton and Howden,
and to the convent the manor of Hemingbrough with sac
and soc,[2] thus creating a block of Durham estates north of
the Humber, and in 1091 King William II granted the
same bishop the manor and socage of Northallerton with
similar extensive privileges.[3] These estates and their
churches were divided between bishop and convent during
the general partition already described,[4] thus giving the
monks a claim to share the ecclesiastical rights pertaining to
them. But in the twelfth century the franchise obtained
was normally regarded as belonging to the whole church

---

[1] *Victoria County History, Yorks.*, ii. 152.
[2] W. Dugdale, *Monasticon*, ed. Caley, i. 238; Wm. Farrer, *Early Yorkshire Charters*, ii. 302, 315; *V.C.H., Yorks.*, ii. 153.
[3] *Scriptores tres*, p. ccccxxv; Farrer, op. cit. ii. 266; *Symeonis H.D.E.* i. 127.
[4] Above, pp. 4 seqq.

of Durham and the claims of the convent as a matter for internal arrangement.

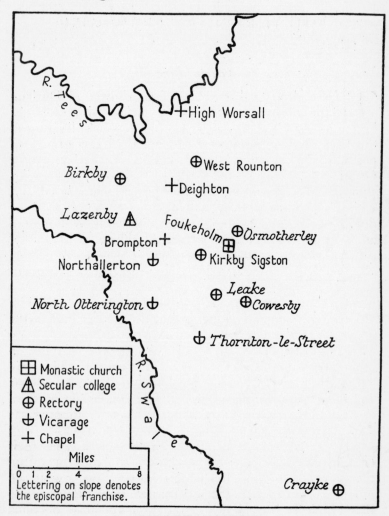

ALLERTONSHIRE

The churches on the estates of the bishopric of Durham in Yorkshire were naturally privileged. The conditions obtaining before the Norman Conquest, when lands had been given in the city of York to provide convenient lodgings for the bishop and Crayke served as a hostel on the journey,[1] are only known from relatively late tradition; but it can safely be assumed that churches when built on those estates[2] would have had all the privileges of a bishop's *ecclesiae propriae* and have looked to the archbishop for chrism alone. The new acquisitions were certainly in this

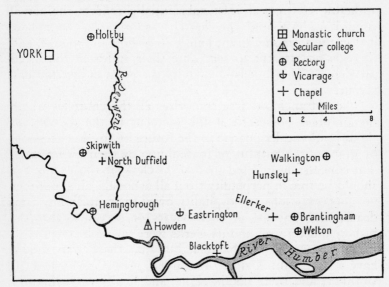

HOWDENSHIRE

position. In 1140 Hugh Sottavagina, precentor and archdeacon of York, the historian of its archbishops, declared that by ancient custom no parochial church of Durham had rendered any financial custom to the metropolitan of York except for 6*d.*, which was paid for chrism. Archbishop Thomas I (1070–1100), he says, ordered them to pay synodal dues, especially as the mother church was in need of restoration (it had been burned in 1069 and sacked in 1075); but Bishop William of Saint-Calais, after consultation with his clerks, forbade them to pay anything except the ancient custom, and in that position matters remained until Arch-

---

1 'Historia de S. Cuthberto', *Symeonis opera*, i. 199.
2 There was a church at Crayke at the time of the Domesday survey (*V.C.H. Yorks.*, ii. 217), and All Saints, Pavement, was in existence (ibid., ii. 191).

bishop Thurstan (1119–40) remitted the fee of 6*d*., because it looked like the purchase of chrism.[1]

A charter of Archbishop Thomas I granting these privileges has been preserved.[2] It is a forgery;[3] but there is no reason to doubt that the portion referring to the position of the Durham churches in Yorkshire, if not based on an authentic charter, at least substantially reflects the actual conditions. Although the charter was forged by the monks, it is in the form of a grant jointly to bishop and monks, and there is no attempt to segregate their rights in the listed privileges. This monastic modesty is a point in the charter's favour.

The enfranchised area comprises all the churches which the grantees possessed at the moment in the diocese, or should canonically possess in the future by royal concession, by grant of the faithful, or by building on their own estates. The concessions granted are that the clerks in those churches should be free in perpetuity from all synodals, aids, burdens or rents, exactions or hospitality owed to archbishops, rural deans, archdeacons, or their vicars or servants; that the bishop and convent and its clerks were not to be compelled to attend synods or chapters, but that those who should have a complaint against them must go to the court of St. Cuthbert and there obtain right; and finally that whatever liberties and dignities Thomas or his successors should pos-

---

[1] *Historians of the Church of York*, ed. Jas. Raine (Rolls Ser.), iii. 68. The document is difficult to date precisely. Raine gives *c.* 1140 × 5. H. Böhmer (*Das Eigenkirchentum*, p. 303, n. 2) suggests 1125 × 40—between the prohibition of the fee for chrism (Westminster Council of Sept. 1125) and the resignation of Archbishop Thurstan (5 Feb. 1140). The *terminus a quo* is 1137, the accession of Prior Roger, to whom the letter is addressed; the *terminus ad quem* is less firm, possibly 1140 or 1144 when successors to Hugh are listed as archdeacon and precentor of York respectively (Le Neve and T. D. Hardy, *Fasti ecclesiae Anglicanae*, 1854). That Hugh should have been consulted by the prior of Durham suggests that both sees were vacant, as, indeed, they were in 1140–3. The date *c.* 1140 seems, therefore, the most reasonable. For Hugh de Soteueim, Sotewame, Sotevagina, or Sottavagina, the author of 'The Lives of Four Archbishops of York', see Raine, ibid. ii, pp. xii–xv, and Raymonde Foreville, *L'Église et la royauté en Angleterre sous Henri II Plantagenet* (Paris, 1943), p. xxxiii. Hugh's evidence should be unimpeachable on this matter.

[2] *F.P.D.*, p. lxxvi.

[3] See above, p. 2. A strange feature is that Hugh de Soteueim (Sottavagina), the historian who had been consulted by the convent about the franchise *c.* 1140, is included among the witnesses.

sess in their own churches and lands these also were to be enjoyed by the bishop and prior in theirs.[1]

The franchise, then, embraced the proprietary churches of Durham, or, eponymously of St. Cuthbert.[2] It did not correspond exactly with the area of the Durham fiefs, for some parts with their churches were in the hands of mesne tenants,[3] and some churches were held by Durham without the corresponding manor.[4] The immunity was personal and flexible, not territorial. All the episcopal customs were alienated except the *cura animarum*.[5] The churches remained within the diocese of the archbishop.

[1] It has been thought advisable to print side by side the words of the charter and its paraphrase in 1281 (see below, p. 84), so that the later interpretation can be fully appreciated:

Charter	1281 *paraphrase*
'Concedo, insuper, confirmo, et praecipio, ut tam ipsi quam ipsorum vicarii liberi et quieti inperpetuum sint ab omni redditu sinodali, et ab omnibus auxiliis, gravaminibus, vel redditibus, exaccionibus, vel hospiciis, tam a me quam ab decanis, archidiaconis, vel omnium nostrorum vicariis et ministris. Sub anathemate eciam prohibeo ne aliquis ulterius ipsos, vel eorum clericos, aliqua sub occasione fatiget, vel ad sinoda vel capitula ire, nisi velint sponte, conpellat. Sed si quis erga eos vel suos aliquam querelam habuerit, ad curiam Sancti Cuthberti Dunelmum veniat, ut ibi qualem debuerit rectitudinem percipiat. Omnes enim libertates et dignitates, quas ego et mei sequaces in ecclesiis propriis vel in terris nostris possederimus, ipsis et Sancto Cuthberto in omnibus ecclesiis et terris suis libere in perpetuum concedimus. . . .'	'qui omnes ecclesias quascumque tenemus in dicta diocesi, vel in posterum adquirere poterimus, liberas et quietas omnino inperpetuum a se et omnibus successoribus suis ab omnibus, que ad ipsum vel ad ipsos successores suos pertinent, seu pertinere poterunt, nobis concessit et liberaliter constituit, et ab omni redditu sinodali, auxiliis, gravaminibus, redditibus, exaccionibus, vocacionibns synodorum et capitulorum quietos fecit et immunes, iurisdiccionem nobis in predictis concedendo, et nos ordinarios constituendo. Insuper omnes libertates, dignitates ac consuetudines, quas ipse et sui sequaces in propriis ecclesiis possederunt, seu possident, nobis et S. Cuthberto in omnibus ecclesiis nostris libere inperpetuum concessit, et a se suisque successoribus liberas et quietas confirmavit.'

[2] Charter of Thomas (*F.P.D.*, p. lxxvii): 'ut omnes ecclesias, quascumque in presenti in diocesiana parrochia mea possident, vel in posterum canonice adquirere poterint, concessione regum, largitione fidelium, vel aedificaverunt in proprio fundo terrarum . . .'; cf. charter of Thurstan (Farrer, op. cit. ii. 274); 'Has libertates eis in perpetuam elemosinam . . . donamus, et easdem tam in omnibus ecclesiis quam in capellis quas amodo in archiepiscopatu nostro canonice adquirere poterint . . . eis . . . confirmamus.'   [3] e.g. West Rounton and Sockburn on the Conyers' fief.

[4] e.g. Holtby, where the convent had but three carucates of land.

[5] 'Quare volo et praecipio ut omnes ecclesias suas in manu sua teneant, et quiete eas possideant, et vicarios suos in eis libere ponant; qui michi et meis successoribus de cura tantum intendant animarum; ipsis vero de omnibus ceteris beneficiis elemosinarum', *F.P.D.*, p. lxxvii.

The statement of Durham rights in the fabrication is reasonable and agrees with the tradition of 1140. The sharp distinction between *beneficium* and *cura animarum*, already noticed in other Durham forgeries,[1] is perhaps a little too precise; but, as Böhmer has remarked, it appears in the proceedings of the London council of 1075.[2] The elaborate rehearsal of archiepiscopal officers who were to be excluded from the franchise—archdeacons, rural deans, and their subordinates—appears slightly anachronistic, but hardly affects the nature of the franchise claimed. It is quite possible that the monks may have amended a genuine charter of Archbishop Thomas I, not to justify this franchise, but to strengthen their title to other and more disputed claims, such as the prior's claim to have all the rights of an abbot, which appear later in the instrument.[3]

The origin, therefore, of the liberties of St. Cuthbert in Yorkshire is quite clear. The traditional position of a bishop's proprietary churches in the diocese of another, as ascertained, for example, by Lanfranc and Anselm in the case of Canterbury,[4] is maintained in respect of the post-Conquest acquisitions of the church of Durham probably by tacit assimilation with the status of churches anciently possessed in Yorkshire, reinforced possibly by a formal surrender of certain episcopal customs by Archbishop Thomas I. The rights left to the archbishop are small; but sufficient to maintain his diocese intact. He reserves his ancient right to provide chrism and charge a fee for it, and he reserves control over the *cura animarum*. By the forgery synods, chapters and courts are denied to the archbishop as instruments of discipline, so that *cura animarum* can mean little more than the institution of priests presented to him by Durham. Hugh Sottavagina's letter of 1140 suggests that Durham clerks had for a time, at least, attended the archiepiscopal synods, and that friction arose over financial demands and not over attendance. It is possible that William of Saint-Calais here as elsewhere modelled his actions on those of Archbishop Lanfranc: originally allowing his clerks

---

[1] Cf. above, p. 11, n. 1.   [2] *Das Eigenkirchentum in England*, p. 303, n. 2.
[3] H. Böhmer considered the whole document reasonable and authentic, ibid.
[4] See above, pp. x and xiv.

to attend the synods of the diocese for pastoral ends, and then withdrawing them after the privilege had been abused.[1]

The later history of the franchise is complicated by the claims of the convent to a share in it. In the Norman period, however, the aim was not necessarily to create an independent position, for in that lay danger to the franchise: the proprietary churches of the convent were less likely than those of the bishop of Durham to attract and retain episcopal privileges. Hence the monks, although anxious to establish their right to the independent ownership of the manor of Hemingbrough and the free disposal of the many churches they claimed on the episcopal estates, were probably equally prepared to shelter from York behind their bishop, and secure from him by domestic arrangement a share of privileges held simply in the name of the church of Durham. Later, however, and especially when the *episcopalia* had firmly adhered to the churches, the convent may at times have been tempted to play a more independent part, and seek from York recognition of its position within the franchise. As the bishop of Durham alone was competent to subtract the churches from the diocese of York, it would have been politic for the archbishops to favour the less dangerous immunist, and there is slight evidence that this course was followed. At the same time it was equally wise for the bishops of Durham to insist on their paramount position in the franchise, and to treat the priory as but a subordinate element in the government of liberties belonging to their bishopric.

The episcopal attitude towards the franchise normally had the conceptual ambiguity to be expected in the possessor of rights which, though sanctioned by tradition, were in some ways at variance with the more progressive ideas of the time, and, moreover, could hardly be expressed in a

---

[1] See above, p. x. A Norman example of a qualified duty of attendance at synods in the twelfth century can also be given. The bishops of Lisieux and Bayeux each held half of the village of Epreville, and the ecclesiastical jurisdiction was minutely divided between the two. Of interest to us is that the priest, who was collated by the bishop of Bayeux and owed no obedience to the bishop of Lisieux, nevertheless obtained chrism, but without charge, from Lisieux and attended the Lisieux synods —'ad sinodum suam ibit, precepta tantum auditurus, non aliquid redditurus vel de aliquo placito responsurus'. See M. M. Bigelow, *History of Procedure in England* (1880), pp. 398–9.

positive terminology. The Yorkshire estates were part of
the bishopric of Durham; but the parishes were not within
the Durham diocese, although some of the *episcopalia* had
been alienated by York. William of Saint-Calais, when he
forfeited his estates in 1088, complained to King William
II that the royal writ had dispossessed him of that part of
his bishopric which was situated in the county of York;[1]
Bishop Hugh of le Puiset (1153–95) regulated the internal
ecclesiastical arrangements almost as an ordinary;[2] and even
in the thirteenth century Durham statutes for the franchise
contained references to 'our diocese'.[3] Although the liberties
were not to be radically attached to the bishopric of Durham,
it seems that this possibility was not destroyed before the
middle of the twelfth century.

Apart from the internal struggle for power between
bishop and convent, the nature of the franchise seems to
have changed little before the accession of Roger of Pont
l'Évêque to the see of York in 1154. Archbishop Thurstan
(1119–40) granted the monks a charter (1121 × 8) in which
the convent's right to certain churches within the franchise
was recognized and the franchise itself was redefined.[4] To
its present possessions and to others which it might canonically possess, Thurstan granted freedom from aids, hospitality and other vexations or burdens of archbishops,
archdeacons, and rural deans. If a common aid were taken
from all the churches in Yorkshire, the archbishop would
notify the prior and convent, and, if they cared to make
a contribution, it would not prejudice their liberty. Certain
rights of justice are also specifically granted. The archbishop states that if he or his successors should have a complaint against any of the convent's clerks, they would accept
the right which the priors would do them for the crime of
those clerks.[5] Hugh Sottavagina attested the financial im-

---

[1] 'me dissaisivit de toto episcopatu meo quem habeo in Eboracensi comitatu',
'De injusta vexatione', *Symeonis opera*, i. 179.

[2] See below, pp. 61 seqq.   [3] Ibid., p. 96.

[4] Farrer, op. cit. ii. 274. Bishop Ranulf Flambard witnesses the charter; it is
possibly part of his 'repentance' in his later years (cf. above, p. 9).

[5] 'Qui [vicarii] prorsus ab omnibus auxiliis, hospiciis, et a cunctis vexationibus
seu gravaminibus ceteris tam archiepiscoporum quam archidiaconorum et decanorum quieti nostro tempore ac omnium successorum nostrorum permaneant. Si
vero nos vel successores nostri quicquam querele adversus aliquem clericorum ipso-

munity in his letter of 1140 already mentioned. Durham churches, he said, paid no money custom to the church of York, not even the ancient fee for chrism which Thurstan had remitted.

At the time when Thurstan dispensed with the fee for chrism the franchisal churches must have been obtaining their holy oils from York, and were, therefore, technically at least, within the diocese of York. But there is no evidence to show who exercised episcopal orders in the liberties, whether it was the bishop of Durham or the archbishop of York who dedicated churches, confirmed boys and girls, and conferred holy orders; nor can it be established who in fact admitted and instituted clerks to benefices, although this right was safeguarded to the local diocesan by the pseudo-charter of Archbishop Thomas I. All these matters were, no doubt, subject to convenient arrangement, and the system in force may have changed from time to time. We must beware of discerning rights where the careless or preoccupied diocesans may have seen nothing but burdens. Neither bishop nor archbishop may always have been anxious to undertake these duties, especially the latter who got no reward for his services. This indifference allowed views basically incompatible to exist without collision. Expediency and custom rather than general principles of law governed the relations between the two powers.

Nevertheless the attitudes of bishop and archbishop were fundamentally irreconcilable, as can be seen from a charter, 'Cum singularum personarum' (1153 × 60), which Bishop Hugh of le Puiset granted to the convent, and in which he expressed his claim to possess episcopal powers within the liberties.[1] He confirmed to the convent the parsonage of its Yorkshire churches, gave it permission to appropriate, and regulated the position of the vicars. The convent's churches listed in the charter are those which occur in Archbishop Thurstan's grant to the monastery; but here they are described as being either on the episcopal demesnes or on other lands which pertained to the bishopric or church of

---

rum habuerimus, rectitudinem quam priores de clericis suis nobis fecerint pro aliquo illorum excessu suscipiemus . . .', Farrer, op. cit. ii. 274.

[1] Hutchinson, *History of Durham*, ii. 72 n. See Farrer, op. cit. ii. 276, for the date.

Durham. Hugh says that he regulates their management
because on him falls the responsibility for the care and
supervision of all churches in his diocese. Hugh is represented by the chronicler Geoffrey of Coldingham as a stal-
wart champion of the rights of Durham;[1] and by this charter
he came as close as possible to usurping the position of the
ordinarius loci.

By 1154 the end of the first phase in the development of
the franchise had been reached. The Norman reform of the
English church had produced an unresolved contradiction:
a reinforcement of *Eigenkirchentum* together with a new conception of the bishop as a territorial diocesan authority.
For a time the older views were dominant; and during that
period franchises, such as Howdenshire and Allertonshire,
were perpetuated or came into being, although the newer
ideas offered enough resistance to prevent the situation from
getting completely out of hand. By the middle of the
twelfth century, however, that isolation of the English church
which the Norman kings had so jealously contrived was once
more passing away; and each new penetration by the ideas
current in western Christendom strengthened the diocesan
against the private proprietor. When Archbishop Thomas
Becket exclaimed that Christ had not said that he was the
custom but that he was the law, he was expressing the new
attitude. Bishops began to look questioningly at the customary liberties, and realized that they were contrary to that
growing body of common law of which they had hitherto
been only half aware. And the new spirit, even though it
did not always generate active hostility to franchisal jurisdiction, at least inspired the ordinaries to scrutinize and
define.

In 1154 Roger of Pont l'Évêque became archbishop of
York. He had been archdeacon of Canterbury and one of
that distinguished group of legists and theologians which
Archbishop Theobald had gathered round him. He was,
therefore, deeply implicated in that momentous influx of
canon law into England during the freedom of King
Stephen's reign for which Theobald of Bec was primarily
responsible. Just as Hugh of le Puiset had acquired a see

[1] *Scriptores tres*, p. 9.

rent by the intrusion of William Cumin, so Roger succeeded to an archbishopric lately distracted by the rival claims and parties of William fitz Herbert and Henry Murdac. Each of the new prelates was equally capable of restoring order; but Roger was probably the better versed in the new jurisprudence. It is significant that among the witnesses to Roger's concordat with Durham is found another who had been a member of Theobald's household, the Lombard lawyer, Master Vacarius, the author of the *Liber pauperum*, England's introduction to the Digest and the Code.[1]

Roger granted a charter to the prior and convent of Durham in the early years of his pontificate (1154×66), which repeats for the most part the privileges confirmed by Thurstan.[2] The convent was to have its ancient liberties and dignities in the archdiocese as approved by Roger's predecessors.[3] It was to have the free disposal of its churches; and the vicars to be placed in them were not to be summoned to synods or chapters, nor were archdeacons or rural deans to vex or require aids or hospitality from them.[4] The specific mention of the burdens of the archbishop's subordinates is probably due to their growing importance in diocesan administration. An even more important change in emphasis is seen in the clause dealing with jurisdiction. Roger states that if any of the convent's chaplains should be guilty of an offence, the complaint was to go to the prior and brethren, who should summon the delinquent to the

---

[1] For Vacarius' connexion with York, see F. Liebermann, 'Master Vacarius', *E.H.R.* xi. 305–14.

[2] Durham Dean and Chapter archives, 1ma 1me Archiep., 4. The date is limited by the presence of Robert de Chesney and Ailred of Rievaux among the witnesses. The Rev. Canon S. L. Greenslade very kindly provided me with a transcript of this charter.

[3] 'Rogerus . . . do et concedo deo et sancto Cuthberto et priori et monachis ei in Dunelmo servientibus omnes libertates antiquas et dignitates quascumque aliquo tempore predecessorum meorum in archiepiscopatu Eboracensi meliores habuerunt, tam in omnibus ecclesiis suis quam capellis et terris et ceteris cunctis suis pertinentibus liberas et quietas a me et meis omnibus successoribus', loc. cit.

[4] 'Preterea constituo et archiepiscopali auctoritate decerno quatinus priori et monachis sancti Cuthberti liceat omnes ecclesias suas et capellas secundum morem antiquum in manu sua habere et ad profectum ecclesie sue secundum quod utilius viderint esse disponere. Vicarios etiam suos, quos in ipsis ecclesiis posuerint, nemo ad synodum vel capitulum venire compellat, neque archidiaconus sive decanus aliquid eis gravamen inferat vel auxilium sive hospicium ab eis exigere presumat, nisi forte hoc ipsi gratis facere voluerint', loc. cit.

court of St. Cuthbert and there make correction. If, however, the chaplains were accused of matters which could not be corrected without the archbishop's help, the prior or brethren were to cause them to be brought into the archbishop's presence, where the case was to be determined.[1]

The exact procedure to be used in hearing these serious cases is difficult to envisage from the words of the charter. It does not appear, however, that the monks were to lose seizin of the case; it seems merely that they were to hear and determine in the archbishop's presence and with his help. All the same this is the first mention of archiepiscopal interference in the judicial immunity of the franchise. There must always have been cases outside the competence of the convent's court; but it is possible that for these the prior had often invoked the aid of the bishop of Durham. It may be, therefore, that in this charter Roger is laying down a procedure of great importance to the bishop but of little moment to the convent. Although Roger detested monks, the tone of the charter is conciliatory: there is no overt encroachment, merely the offer of a helping hand. Even so, it is the cloud on the horizon. The diocesan ordinary is drawing attention to his powers. It is a warning to the prior to remember the limitations of his court; and for the bishop of Durham there is a threat, if not a declaration of war.

We know little about the actual quarrels between Hugh and Roger over the liberties except what can be inferred from the agreement whereby they were composed. Between 1162 and 1167 bishop and archbishop made a 'peace and final concord' by which the position of both Durham's Yorkshire franchise and York's Durham franchise—Hexham—was regulated.[2] Although the prior of Durham was not a party to the agreement, and is ignored by the terms, despite his presence at the negotiations, the concordat is concerned

---

[1] 'Si autem ipsi eorum capellani in aliquo reprehensibiles reperiantur, delata prius priori et fratribus querela ad curiam sancti Cuthberti summoneantur et excessus eorum ibi canonice emendentur. Sin autem talia fuerint de quibus accusantur ut nisi nostro auxilio corrigi non potuerint, prior vel fratres illos in nostra presentia adductos statuent ut litis accusationem equo iudicio terminando decidant', loc. cit.

[2] *Historians of the Church of York*, iii. 79; *Chronica Rogeri de Houedene*, ii. 70; Farrer, op. cit. ii. 275, for the date.

with the whole of Allertonshire and Howdenshire. This raises the question whether the bishop was representing and negotiating on behalf of the whole church of Durham, or was merely dealing with matters which touched him alone —his episcopal powers within the franchise; and the terms of the concordat do not provide a ready answer.

By the agreement each party made concessions to the other. Roger abated some of the rights claimed for York in Hexham;[1] Hugh surrendered certain if not all of his episcopal rights in Yorkshire. But it is less easy to determine whether he also relinquished the totality of Durham's claims to franchisal jurisdiction, including those of the prior. In the section of the concordat which refers to the Yorkshire liberties the churches of St. Cuthbert are listed. As the first complete statement of the area, the list is of some interest. The churches are scheduled under archdeaconries, and there is no respect for the territorial divisions of Howdenshire and Allertonshire. There is also no recognition of an internal division of the liberty between bishop and prior. The churches listed are those of which the advowson was in the hands of the bishop and convent,[2] and not those on the Durham fief.[3] It is clear that the liberties of St. Cuthbert still maintained their personal and flexible character. Churches of which the advowson had been surrendered or sub-infeudated were no longer considered part of them, although they may still have enjoyed some of the privileges, and all the Yorkshire churches of St. Cuthbert were on the same footing. But in the concordat, just as in Roger's charter to the convent, there is no statement that fresh acquisitions of Durham would participate in the rights. The

---

[1] The church of Hexham was to receive chrism and oil from the church of Durham 'as is the custom'. The prior of Hexham was to attend the Durham synods, and the clerks and canons were to receive orders from the bishops of Durham. The parishioners were to visit Durham at Pentecost if they desired without interference from either of the contracting parties.

[2] The churches are listed as follows: archdeaconry of John fitz Letoldus (Cleveland), Hemingbrough, Skipwith, Northallerton, Birkby, Osmotherley, Kirkby Sigston, Leake, North Otterington, Crayke, and Holtby; archdeaconry of Geoffrey (York), All Saints in Ousegate, St. Peter-the-little, and a mediety of St. Trinity in Goodramgate; archdeaconry of the treasurer (E. Riding), Howden, Welton, Brantingham, and Walkington.

[3] West Rounton, for instance, is omitted, because it was on the mesne fief of the Conyers.

F

schedule itself suggests an attempt at definition. This particular delimitation, however, was not to be permanent.

The privilege granted by Roger to the clerks in these churches is that they should be immune from synodals. No mention is made of the other episcopal customs; but that is probably because they had not been involved in the quarrel, for, with reference to two chapels which were in dispute, the archbishop says that, if they are adjudged to the bishop, no more will be exacted from them than from the other churches of St. Cuthbert. This interpretation is reinforced by the terms of a bull of Pope Alexander III, 1171×80, which the bishop and monks must have secured in confirmation of this settlement. In it immunity from synodals is expressly recognized, and the residuary rights are lumped together as freedom from other exactions.[1] It may be concluded, therefore, that the position as described by Hugh Sottavagina in 1140 was unaffected by the concordat: the churches remained free from all financial customs due to York.

Although the negative side of the franchise was thus salvaged, the positive character was gravely impaired, if not completely destroyed. It was agreed that if clerks of the scheduled churches or laymen from the demesne manors of St. Cuthbert in Yorkshire should do anything deserving ecclesiastical punishment, they should be corrected by the archbishop after a warning had been sent to the bishop so as to allow him or his representative to be present.[2] If this clause be taken at its face value it would seem entirely to abolish Durham's ecclesiastical jurisdiction in Yorkshire; yet it is difficult to reconcile with this interpretation the omission of reference to the court of the prior and the failure to secure entry for the archdeacons of York into the franchise. Although the liberties belonged to the whole church of Durham it is hard to believe that jurisdictional rights confirmed by the archbishop to the prior only a few years earlier could be abrogated in this way, with no more formality than the

---

[1] Farrer, op. cit. ii. 280; W. Holtzmann, *Papsturkunden*, ii, no. 193.

[2] 'Si vero clerici earundem ecclesiarum vel laici de dominicis B. Cuthberti in Eboraciscira, aliquid dignum ecclesiastica castigatione [correctione, *Hoveden*] perpetraverint, per archiepiscopum emendabitur, tali prius facta submonitione quod episcopus interesse poterit vel minister ejus', loc. cit.

attachment of the prior's seal to the agreement. It is possible, of course, that the prior made a parallel renunciation which is no longer extant.[1] The second difficulty is that the immunists could not have been deprived of the whole of their jurisdiction without the transference of some of it to the archdeacons of York,[2] for the archbishop can hardly have intended any but the graver cases to go before his own tribunal. But the interference of archdeacons in the franchise would have been such an innovation that provision would surely have been made for it had it been envisaged. It is worthy of notice, however, that when the archbishop instituted Roger as parson of Howden in 1173 × 6, he inserted *salvo jure episcopali et officialium nostrorum* in the certificate.[3] This would suggest that the archbishop held that his subordinates had rights in the franchise; but Roger's preferment had been opposed by the convent, and it seems dangerous to draw wide inferences from this text.

Even if the concordat did not entirely destroy Durham's franchisal jurisdiction in Yorkshire, and was in fact but a development of the terms of Roger's charter to the convent, securing that serious cases from the whole franchise should go to the archbishop, and not to the bishop of Durham, it was a serious set-back for Hugh of le Puiset. Roger had vindicated the integrity of his see, and implicitly denied that Durham had episcopal rights within his diocese. Although both parties made concessions in the concordat, the bishop of Durham made the greater. The circumstances in which the treaty was negotiated are unknown, for the document appears in Roger of Howden's chronicle

[1] Roger's charter to the monks can be dated 1154 × 66, the concordat 1162 × 7. The two documents do not seem to be exactly contemporary, for the lists of witnesses are different. Although the chronological sequence cannot be proved, it seems reasonable to suppose that the charter is the earlier, for it shows no sign of arising out of a dispute, and may therefore have been secured from the archbishop shortly after his accession.

[2] The archdeacons seem to have established their position in the judicial hierarchy quite firmly by this time; cf. the Constitutions of Clarendon, 1164, cap. viii (*Select Charters*, arranged and edited by Wm. Stubbs, revised by H. W. C. Davis, 9th ed., p. 165).

[3] Farrer, op. cit. ii. 307. For associated documents see W. Holtzmann, op. cit. ii, no. 148; 'Attestationes testium', *F.P.D.*, p. 279. This is Roger of Howden, the chronicler, who succeeded to the parsonage on the resignation of his father, Robert.

as an isolated piece. Hugh's political career seems to have been outstandingly tranquil during this period: he was in steady favour with the king, moderate and discreet during the Becket trouble, and his only vagary seems to have been a partiality for the Anti-pope Victor IV in 1159–60. Geoffrey of Coldingham calls him *in omnibus fortunatissimus*;[1] but his star must have been in eclipse at this time.

Negotiated partitions of franchisal jurisdictions were quite common in north-west France, but rather earlier than this English example. It has been held that such agreements reveal the growing power of the ordinary rather than the application of a new principle.[2] It is true that franchises were seldom unlawful *in se*, and that their fate depended much on the relations between the interested parties; so that had we more information, vicissitudes in their fortunes could no doubt be attributed to causes even more immediate than the increasing authority of the diocesan bishops. The validity of the concordat between Hugh of le Puiset and Roger of Pont l'Évêque was to be without prejudice to the rights of either church after the deaths of the parties; and this limitation was later invoked by Bishop Hugh, who survived his metropolitan. Yet behind the trivial occasion, and behind the resurgence of episcopal power, was the establishment and application of a principle: the principle that there was a normal system of government for western Christendom, as defined and ruled by the common law of the Church. And where this principle was observed the immunist faced constant danger, for the burden of proof had fallen on him.

The see of York was vacant for ten years after the death of Archbishop Roger (1181), and Hugh of le Puiset probably lost no time in renouncing the terms of the concordat, for he had been treasurer of York before his election to Durham, and might therefore be expected to work harmoniously with the capitular administration *sede vacante*. In 1182 × 3 the convent secured from Pope Lucius III confirmation of the liberties granted it by the charters of

---

[1] *Scriptores tres*, p. 9.
[2] Lemarignier, *Étude sur les privilèges d'exemption*, pp. 216 seqq.

Archbishops Thomas and Thurstan[1]—the omission of reference to Roger's charter is significant, and in 1185 × 7 Bishop Hugh and the prior and convent sent attested copies of these charters for the pope's inspection.[2] In this way earlier conditions were restored. There seems, indeed, to have been no limit to Hugh's ambition in his old age. He aspired to make himself supreme in the north during King Richard's absence on the third Crusade, and so, in order to remain without an immediate ecclesiastical superior, was from the beginning one of the bitterest opponents of the promotion to York of that unfortunate and difficult bastard of King Henry II, Geoffrey Fitzroy.[3] Although Geoffrey had no vocation for the Church, and his temper kept him few friends, it must not be forgotten that many of the difficulties he encountered in obtaining and holding York were due to the long vacancy in the archbishopric, which had encouraged the independence of a rebellious suffragan and of an anarchic chapter.

Geoffrey faced the situation with determination and fearlessness. In the period before his consecration he was sometimes willing to bribe Hugh of le Puiset, although it went against the grain. In December 1189 he offered to confirm the appointment of Hugh's son or nephew, Bouchard, as treasurer of York—part of King Richard's attempted settlement of the quarrels; and he also promised to confirm the bishop's privileges and the conventions made between Hugh and Archbishop Roger of Pont l'Évêque.[4] It would be interesting to know which conventions were in mind. If our interpretation of the agreement of 1162 × 7 is correct, it would seem unlikely that Hugh should have desired its confirmation. Nor does that treaty appear to have been revised through later negotiations, for after Roger's death

---

[1] W. Holtzmann, *Papsturkunden*, ii, no. 223; 'Libertates insuper ecclesiarum ad monasterium ipsum spectantium, sicut in autenticis scriptis bone memorie Thome et Turstini archiepiscoporum Eboracensium continentur et nunc sine controuersia obseruantur . . . confirmamus.'

[2] Farrer, op. cit. ii. 265.

[3] The main authorities for Geoffrey's quarrels with Hugh are *Gesta regis Henrici secundi Benedicti abbatis*, ed. Wm. Stubbs (Rolls Ser.), vol. ii; *Chronica R. de Houedene*, vol. iii; Gerald of Wales, 'De vita Galfridi archiepiscopi Eboracensis', *Giraldi Cambrensis opera*, ed. J. S. Brewer (Rolls Ser.), vol. iv.

[4] *Gesta regis Henrici*, ii. 100–1.

Durham appealed to the charters of his predecessors. Perhaps Geoffrey was making a derisory offer. In any case the charters were not to be issued until after his consecration. He was certainly not prepared to pay Hugh of le Puiset's price.

In March 1190 Richard imposed a three years' exile from England on Geoffrey and on his full brother, Count John; and the ecclesiastical struggle shifted to Rome. Geoffrey sought his confirmation and consecration as archbishop; Hugh supported the party of opposition, and, on his own behalf, endeavoured to secure confirmation of Bouchard's appointment and the permanent abrogation of York's authority over the bishopric of Durham. Early in 1191 Bouchard carried the day at Rome; but the death of Pope Clement and the accession of Celestine III in April caused a complete change of policy at the *curia*. Geoffrey's election was confirmed and his consecration ordered; the grant of freedom to Durham was rescinded, and Hugh was ordered to make his profession of obedience to Geoffrey. In August Geoffrey was consecrated at Tours, and on the strength of permission to return to England which Richard had given him in July 1190, possibly in bad faith, the new archbishop decided to go back immediately and revenge himself on his enemies. A summons to the bishop of Durham to make obedience and answer for his injuries to the archbishopric was dispatched in advance; but Geoffrey's capture by Richard's viceroy, William Longchamp, and the stirring events which succeeded it, postponed the hearing of the case. On 1 November 1191 Geoffrey was enthroned at York, and the battle with Durham could be resumed.

Some of Geoffrey's complaints concerned Hugh's behaviour in the Yorkshire franchises. According to the *Gesta Regis Henrici*[1] Hugh was accused by Geoffrey of usurping the rights of the church of York by taking Peter's Pence and the Whitsuntide processions and offerings from the churches of Howden, Hemingbrough, Skipwith, Brantingham, Kirkby Sigston, 'Homdeleie', Northallerton, and Wal-

---

[1] 'tum quia idem episcopus Dunelmensis jura ecclesiae Eboraci, scilicet le Rom-peni, et processiones hebdomadae Pentecosten de ecclesiis . . . detinuit occupatas', loc. cit. ii. 226.

kington ('Waldington'). Roger of Howden gives Geoffrey's summons in which the charge is that Hugh, not fearing to put his sickle into another man's harvest, had usurped the spiritual administration of Geoffrey's clerks and parishioners, and had for two years despoiled the church of York of the processions and Pentecostal oblations anciently due to it from Howdenshire and Allertonshire.[1] This financial dispute is difficult to interpret in detail. Although Geoffrey is complaining about the treatment of his diocese in the period between his election and consecration, as the reference to 'two years' proves, the actions of the bishop of Durham which caused offence were no doubt but a continuation of his earlier behaviour. The diocese of Durham did not contribute to Peter's Pence. The annual contribution of the diocese of York to the English total was £11. 10s.; but ten times that amount was actually collected in the twelfth century;[2] and during the vacancy of the see the profit should have gone to the crown. The churches involved by name in the quarrel are those of the convent, of which an almost complete list is given, the omissions being the churches in the city of York, and Welton and Holtby, although the last may be disguised in 'Homdeleie'. It looks, therefore, very much as though Hugh of le Puiset had been collecting and pocketing this tax from the whole of the franchise, thereby reducing the surplus which the archbishop hoped to enjoy, and that Geoffrey was trying to stop this practice in the parishes of the convent at least. In this matter Hugh's behaviour reveals his greed and ambition rather than his juristic attitude towards the liberties.

[1] 'responsurus praeterea quod jam per biennium ecclesiam nostram Eboracensem debitis ei processionibus ab antiquo, et oblationibus in diebus Pentecosten, scilicet, Hovedensire et Alvertonsire, contra juris ordinem spoliare praesumpsisti, et falcem in alienam messem mittere non formidans, clericis et parochianis nostris spiritualia ministrare usurpasti', loc. cit. iii. 169. In the early fourteenth century the archiepiscopal peculiar of Churchdown (Glos.) was to be attacked in a similar way. Bishop Giffard of Worcester demanded Pentecostal fees and Peter's pence from the franchise, and the attempt was resumed by Bishop Maidstone (A. Hamilton Thompson, 'The Jurisdiction of the Archbishops of York in Gloucestershire', *Trans. of the Bristol and Glos. Arch. Soc.*, vol. xliii, pp. 153 seqq.).

[2] See *Pipe Rolls 28 Henry II–34 Henry II*. The amount collected varied between £103 and £118. Cf. also O. Jensen, 'The "denarius Sancti Petri" in England', *Trans. R. Hist. Soc.* (new ser.), vols. xv and xix, and Rose Graham, *English Ecclesiastical Studies* (S.P.C.K., 1929), p. 311.

The Whitsuntide processions and offerings, which Hugh was accused of diverting from York to Durham, were, of course, due to the mother church of the diocese, and certainly here Hugh's actions represent an attempt to attach Howdenshire and Allertonshire to the diocese of Durham. Again there is uncertainty about the position of the bishop's share of the franchise; but once more it is possible to infer that the archbishop was trying to reduce Durham's episcopal rights in Yorkshire by objecting to Hugh's treatment of the convent's possessions, if not of the whole franchise, as part of his bishopric. If this inference is correct we have an example of how the growing independence of the priory within the franchise had become an Achilles' heel and could affect the over-all claims of the church of Durham. We are not informed how these aspects of Hugh's dispute with Geoffrey were settled. The quarrel was basically over obedience, and the later stages of the case seem to have been unconcerned with the franchise. Nor is much known about the later history of Peter's Pence and the Pentecostal offerings from the two shires; but it appears that the former was collected by the archbishop at least from the convent's share of the liberties in the second half of the thirteenth century.[1]

The episcopate of Hugh of le Puiset was a decisive period in the history of the Yorkshire franchise, although not in the way which occasionally seemed possible. It is clear that the ambiguous status of the liberties offended both Hugh and Roger of Pont l'Évêque, and that each, if unimpeded, would have solved the problem in the same way—by abolishing the franchise. Yet although each champion seemed in turn to have decisive victory in his grasp, for each it proved illusory. As so often in medieval war the strategic possibilities could not be exploited to the full. Roger's success was undone by the long vacancy after his death. Hugh's counter-offensive was checked by the accession of Geoffrey Fitzroy. The schemes of neither side, however, should be seen as an operational plan. Bishop and archbishop were men of affairs; they took their chances as they came. We may often discern purpose in what was only an opportunist move, perspicuous intention in a groping towards an end of which they were hardly aware. What cannot be denied is the instinctive dislike of the abnormal shown by both sides once the Church had a standard pattern to which they were accustomed. In this drive to normality Durham had the harder task, for it had to overcome the inert resistance of the common law of the Church; and anything short of total victory at this point meant eventual failure for Durham's wider claims. But if the franchise could neither be absorbed in the bishopric of Durham nor brought within the ordinary administration of the diocese of York, there was by 1195 another shape to which it could be moulded, and through transformation into a sort of archdeaconry it could assume again an appearance at once familiar and acceptable to the ideas of the time.

§ 2. The Convent and the Franchise, 1083–1229

The history of the partition of the property of the church of Durham between the bishop and the convent has already been described.[1] In Yorkshire the monks put forward the rather unusual claim to the possession of all the churches on the episcopal manors. The monkish recorder of the royal grant of Welton and Howden says that the king enjoined the condition that all churches on the estates were to be transferred to the monks, and that this was done, the convent receiving the churches of Howden, Brantingham, Welton, Walkington, and Skipwith.[2] The monks also held that the grant of Allertonshire was made under similar conditions, and a spurious charter of Bishop William, ostensibly of the same date as the royal benefaction, purports to concede to the monks the churches of Northallerton, with its chapel of Brompton, and Kirkby Sigston at the order of the king.[3] This scheme of King William I may possibly

---

[1] Above, pp. 4 seqq.

[2] See above, p. 53, n. 2. In the false charters 'Ego Willelmus sedem episcopatus' and 'Notum sit omnibus' (F.P.D., pp. xxxviii-liii) the bishop is only represented as granting Howden, Brantingham, Welton, and Walkington, and in the equally spurious charter 'Quia rerum status' (ibid.) Walkington also is omitted.

[3] 'Omnesque libertates, quas ipsis in ceteris ecclesiis suis prius cartis nostris concessi, in istis plenissime possideant. Hec omnia precipiente domino meo Willelmo rege . . . feci, qui Alvertone scire S. Cuthberto et episcopo ejus in perpetuum dedit. Has vero ecclesias monachis S. Cuthberto servituris pro salute anime sue

represent that part of the convent's endowment which was in some way frustrated. However that may be, the convent obtained in the twelfth century all the churches on the episcopal manors in the south of Yorkshire and on the lands of the bishop in the city of York, and, with considerably more difficulty, two of the parish churches on the manor of Northallerton.

The pecuniary and judicial rights pertaining to these churches were probably divided at the time of the allocation, thus putting the convent of Durham in the complicated position of being subject to two diocesan bishops. The bishop of Durham, as head of the church and the capital owner of the alienated *episcopalia*, naturally exercised a tutelary control over the monastery's parochial affairs. At the same time the archbishop of York, as the *ordinarius loci*, had rights, which, although more restricted in practice, were capable of the greater development. It must not be imagined, however, that this position, although difficult clearly to reconstruct, was not perfectly well defined at the time. The fragmentation of benefices and offices, which can appear obscure to us, consisted in nothing more than the dispersal of concrete rights, usually expressed as financial customs. It is probable that the convent, like the bishop of Durham, looked to the archbishop of York only for the provision of chrism and possibly for the institution of priests, and that

dedit et mihi donare precipit.' Farrer, op. cit. ii. 266. Farrer's opinion that this charter is genuine cannot be maintained. In the first place it should be noticed that the bishop refers to his earlier charters by which he granted liberties to the convent's other churches, and it is hard not to believe that these are the spurious charters 'Ego Willelmus' and 'Quia rerum status', which do not refer to the Allertonshire churches. A third pseudo-charter of the bishop 'Notum sit omnibus' lists two Allertonshire churches, Northallerton and Brompton, and omits Kirkby Sigston. According to Canon Greenwell, the forgeries were perpetrated in the first quarter of the twelfth century, and it is, therefore, inconceivable that they should omit all or one of the churches if William's grant of the three had been genuine. Farrer's charter must be considered the last of these fabrications. It is significant that the convent's title to Kirkby Sigston, which is supported by this charter alone, was frequently attacked by the bishops in the twelfth century, and was not established beyond dispute until 'Le convenit' of 1229. The charter under discussion has, however, one apparent sign of validity—a superb list of important witnesses, in which there is no discord, and which enables Farrer to consider it simultaneous with William II's grant of Allertonshire to the bishop, December 1091. Obviously the monks transferred this attestation from the royal grant, which has disappeared, to their fabrication.

it approached the bishop of Durham for such other episcopal services as were required. As we have seen, the
pseudo-charter of Archbishop Thomas I did not envisage an
independent position for the convent; and normally the
archbishops of York were content to ignore the priory as
an immunist in its own right.

Nevertheless the convent in its quarrels with the bishops
of Durham must have been tempted to secure the support
of the archbishops of York, and to get the sanction of the
latter for rights which may often have been in dispute. It
was in a position to play the one against the other, and this
policy, although but dimly apparent, must have had some
effect on the development of the nature of the franchise.
The charters obtained by the monks from Archbishops
Thurstan and Roger, already discussed from the point of
view of the privileges granted in them,[1] are good examples of
how the monks could use the services of the diocesan bishop.
The former is also interesting as providing the first list of
the convent's proprietary churches in Yorkshire. These are
Howden, Welton, Walkington, and Brantingham; in York,
St. Trinity in Goodramgate, St. Peter-the-little, and All
Saints Pavement in Ousegate; and Holtby, Hemingbrough,
Skipwith, Brompton, Northallerton, and Kirkby Sigston.
The same churches are listed in Bishop Hugh of le Puiset's
charter 'Cum singularum ecclesiarum' (1153 × 60).

The attempts of the convent to throw off the special
tutelage of the bishop and to acquire not only its full share
of the church endowments but also its unhampered disposition of them came to a head during the episcopates of Philip
of Poitou (1197–1208) and Richard Marsh (1217–26); and
their course together with the settlement in 1229 under
Bishop Richard Poore have already been described in so
far as they affected the convent's franchise in the diocese
of Durham.[2] The *attestationes* of the great lawsuit also
describe friction within the Yorkshire liberties, and give us
much information about them at a most interesting transi-
tional period. The main ecclesiastical dispute seems to
have been over the rights of advowson, with the division of
the franchisal jurisdiction as a subsidiary ingredient. The

---

[1] See above, pp. 60–1, 63–4.   [2] See above, pp. 22 seqq.

three principal questions concerning the ecclesiastical peculiar on which witnesses were examined were: the advowson of churches in Allertonshire; the advowson of churches in Howdenshire and Weltonshire (or Weltonsoke); and the withdrawal of suit from the chapters of the bishop in Allertonshire.[1] It seems that the archbishop of York was not directly involved in the litigation. The internal arrangement of the franchise was still considered a domestic affair.

The position of the bishop in Allertonshire was described by Master Reginald, the warden of the hospital of St. James, near Northallerton, an establishment founded by Bishop Philip of Poitou and under the control of the bishops. Reginald said that the bishop of Durham had archidiaconal rights in Allertonshire. Bishops Hugh of le Puiset and Philip of Poitou, he declared, had enjoyed the right, and had appointed their deans, and Philip de Ulecote (one of the royal guardians of the see after the death of Philip)[2] had appointed his.[3] It was the task of the convent to prove that this statement was biased and incomplete. The monks had no difficulty in showing that they were in receipt of the episcopal customs from their own churches. Master Reginald himself acknowleged that in Allertonshire the churches of the monks neither gave hospitality nor paid synodals to the bishop or his dean.[4] For the monks it was affirmed that they took hospitality from all their churches except Kirkby Sigston.[5] To justify such rights the convent could have

---

[1] 'De advocationibus ecclesiarum de Alvertonsire; de advocationibus ecclesiarum de Hovedensire et Welletonsire [or Welletonesoke]; super subtractione sequelae capitulorum episcopi in Alvertonsire', F.P.D., pp. 251-4 seqq.

[2] Philip of Poitou died in April 1208, and Philip de Ulecote and Aimery, nephew of the late bishop and archdeacon of Durham, are noticed in 1209 as guardians of the see [Rot. litt. pat. (Record Com.), p. 91]. In 1212 Earl Warenne was an additional custodian (ibid., p. 94). The see was vacant until the appointment of Richard Marsh as bishop in 1217.

[3] 'Requisitus super subtractione sequelae capitulorum episcopi in Auuertonsire ... dicit eciam quod episcopus Hugo et episcopus Philippus fuerunt in possessione juris archidiaconalis, et posuerunt decanos suos, et Philippus de Vlecotes posuit decanum suum, et temporibus praedictis vidit iste capellanos pro ecclesia illa sequi capitulum episcoporum, et in tali possessione obierunt', F.P.D., p. 251.

[4] 'ecclesiae monachorum non faciunt hospicia neque dant sinodalia episcopo vel decano suo', ibid.

[5] Evidence of Robert of Howden, Durham monk, 'Item dicit quod interfuit aliquando hospiciis captis in omnibus ecclesiis supradictis, praeterquam de Kirkeby

appealed to the charters of Archbishops Thurstan and Roger, and also, possibly, but with less confidence, to the grant of Bishop Hugh, 'Cum singularum ecclesiarum'.[1]

The receipt of fines and amercements could be divorced from the wielding of jurisdiction. But with the two archiepiscopal charters in their archives, in which their jurisdiction had been recognized, the monks could not be expected to tolerate a limitation of that kind within the franchise. Certainly by the time of the lawsuit the convent could show the maintenance or the establishment of possession of coercive jurisdiction. It is interesting to find among the objections put forward by the king in 1237 to Thomas of Melsonby, prior of Durham, to secure the quashing of his election to the bishopric, some which concern this matter. The king alleged that Thomas had been the instigator of the litigation, and that he had despoiled the bishopric of its rights and liberties by usurping jurisdiction over its churches in Allertonshire, which liberties the bishops of Durham had possessed and used up to the time of Bishop Richard Poore.[2] The king was using any stick with which to beat the unfortunate Thomas who did not become prior until four years after 'Le convenit'; but this objection shows nevertheless that the monks had both claimed and secured jurisdiction in Allertonshire. The *attestationes* illustrate the convent's possession. The warden of the hospital of St. James, Master Reginald, when asked about the withdrawal of suit from the chapters of the bishop in Allertonshire, replied that until two years ago the chaplains and parishioners of Kirkby Sigston had attended the chapter, and had answered in all things before the dean of the bishop, just as other chaplains and parishioners of that same deanery.

Sigestone' (*F.P.D.*, p. 299); of Mr. A. de Melsembi, 'Dicit etiam quod saepe interfuit hospiciis captis cum priore et monachis in singulis ecclesiis, praeterquam in Kirkebi Siggestone, quod non debet fieri hospicium sicut intelligit (p. 281); cf. evidence of Richard le Brun (p. 264), Wm. de Acle (p. 268), Reniger (p. 274), Henry, the sub-prior (p. 280), Helye de Rana, sub-prior of Coldingham (p. 282), and of Wm. de Bissoptone (p. 298).

[1] See above, pp. 20 and 61.

[2] 'Item . . . quia ipse usurpavit libertates ecclesiae Dunelmensis, utpote jurisdictionem ecclesiarum suarum de Alvertonsir, quas libertates episcopi Dunelmenses habebant, et eis utebantur, usque ad tempora episcopi Ricardi qui ultimo decessit', *Scriptores tres*, p. lxxiii.

When asked if the chaplains of Kirkby Sigston or of other churches belonging to the monks took an oath of obedience to the bishop or his dean in Allertonshire, he said he did not remember, but he had heard it said for certain that some of them took the oath of obedience and fidelity.[1] Another witness produced for the bishop also maintained that the chaplains and parishioners of this church used to do suit at the chapter of the bishop's dean, but acknowledged that he had never been present when any of the monks' chaplains had taken the oath of obedience and fidelity to the bishop and his dean.[2]

The rights and wrongs of that particular case are unimportant. The title to Kirkby Sigston had been in frequent dispute between the bishop and the monks, and was expressly confirmed to the convent in 'Le convenit'. But the silence of the episcopal witnesses on certain matters and evidence produced by the convent make it clear that the monastery had fully implemented the terms of the two archiepiscopal charters, and had become an equal, if not preponderant partner in the liberties of St. Cuthbert. Although there is no explicit mention of a chapter held by the prior, or of his dean, or even of his archidiaconal rights, it is unlikely that Kirkby Sigston would have been withdrawn as an isolated unit from the bishop's jurisdiction. It must have joined the other churches, of which the patronage indubitably belonged to the monks. The convent's title to Northallerton was based on the earliest forged charters, and had never been challenged since the period of segregation.[3] No questions were asked during this litigation about its jurisdictional attachment, and it may be presumed that it was not subject to the bishop's court. West Rounton, also, had been granted between 1174 and 1190 by the Surtees and Conyers for the maintenance of lights round the body of St. Cuthbert, and the purpose of the gift, if not the terms of the charters, ensured that it was to be in the hands of the

---

[1] F.P.D., p. 251.   [2] Geppe Werri, a layman, F.P.D., p. 251.

[3] Mr. Reginald, warden of the hospital of St. James, and an episcopal witness, when asked about the advowson of the churches of Allertonshire, said that Northallerton and Brompton were on the demesne of the bishop, that the convent had had them *in proprios usus* from ancient time, and that he was unaware that the bishop had ever presented (F.P.D., p. 251). Also see above, p. 73.

monks.[1] This church is not even mentioned in the suit. It is also noticeable that both the *attestationes* and the royal objections of 1237 make no mention of Howdenshire. In that division of the liberties the monks had the manor of Hemingbrough and an almost unchallenged title to the advowson of all the churches. As jurisdictional rights in Allertonshire alone were in dispute, it is almost certain that the bishop did not claim such rights in Howdenshire.

On the positive side witnesses for the monks affirmed that monks took hospitality from all their churches except Kirkby Sigston,[2] and we learn incidentally of the convent having the custody of Howden when vacant,[3] and inducting its presentee into the corporal possession of Brantingham.[4]

From a consideration of this evidence it can be inferred that Kirkby Sigston alone had been withdrawn from the episcopal to the conventual court in recent years. There were witnesses in the suit who could recall events which occurred under Bishop Hugh, but probably no one whose memory extended even to the time of the concordat with Archbishop Roger. For our knowledge of conditions in the period behind the recollection of these witnesses we are dependent on the archiepiscopal charters, and these may give a distorted picture. It is clear that the episcopal witnesses in 1221 were of the opinion that the bishop should have jurisdiction in Allertonshire, and that there the monks were interlopers. This may disclose the traditional division of the liberties between bishop and convent. A partition based on the two distinct territorial units into which the Durham estates fell had administrative advantages, and, up to the late twelfth century, did not greatly clash with a

---

[1] Charters printed Surtees, *History of Durham*, iii. 393–4; Farrer, op. cit. ii. 285–6.

[2] See above, p. 76, n. 5.

[3] Thos. de Askelbi, layman, witness for the bishop, saw monks in custody of the church of Howden for almost three weeks after the death of the parson Roger (the historian), 1202 (*F.P.D.*, p. 257); cf. papal mandate, December 1202, to the bishops of Ely and Norwich, on the showing of the prior and monks of Durham, to institute to a void vicarage a fit person, presented to the archbishop of York by the convent, but whom the archbishop has delayed to admit, and meanwhile to cause the monks to enjoy the fruits of the benefice (*Calendar of Papal Letters*, i. 12); cf. also evidence of Richard le Brun for the monks (*F.P.D.*, p. 264). The king, too, seems to have had a finger in the pie; see the strange entries *Pipe Roll 4 John* (Pipe Roll Soc., new ser., vol. 15), pp. 65, 67.

[4] Evidence of Jordan de Brantingham, *F.P.D.*, p. 295.

scheme of division according to ownership, for the title to Kirkby Sigston had been in dispute, and the advowson of West Rounton was a late acquisition of the convent. The case of Northallerton alone was intractable; and, as it seems to have been appropriated in the time of Bishop Hugh— the only incorporation in this period of a church of the convent in Yorkshire—it may have been given its special position on that occasion.

The background to the quarrel over the jurisdiction of the bishop's chapter in Northallertonshire seems to have been the convent's attempt to disrupt a geographical division of the franchise and substitute to its advantage a partition based on advowson. The claims of the monks were natural and equitable, for these franchisal rights were bound up with the ownership of churches; the archiepiscopal charters had recognized the convent's rights; and a prescriptive title against the bishop was being created.[1] The conditions which prevailed at the turn of the twelfth century are by no means clear; but it is evident that by 1221 the convent had almost achieved its ambition, for it could show possession of and prescription for jurisdiction over all churches of its advowson, except Kirkby Sigston, where the process was not yet complete. This position was accepted by Bishop Richard Poore. 'Le convenit' ignores the subject, and so did not disturb prevailing conditions. The convent had become a partner in the liberties in its own right.

§ 3. *The Nature of the Franchise, 1195–1229*

From the evidence given in the lawsuit it is clear that great changes had taken place and probably were still taking place in the nature of the franchise. The most striking innovations are that a witness speaks of the bishop's archidiaconal jurisdiction, and that the franchise was regarded not as a complex of rights but as a privileged geographical area.

The position of Bishop Hugh of le Puiset was not that of an archdeacon in Yorkshire. His authority was normally

---

[1] Cf. answer of Richard le Brun, witness for the convent, to the question by what right the monks took hospitality, 'dicit quod aliam racionem nescit, nisi quod ita usi sunt ab antiquo', *F.P.D.*, p. 264.

episcopal, if not ordinary. Clearly, however, that had changed. The warden of the hospital of St. James in 1221 may have been inaccurate and untechnical in his description of the bishop's powers; but to him the bishop appeared as an archdeacon. Thus the freedom from attendance at archiepiscopal synods had changed into a right to hold synods which took the form of archidiaconal chapters; the freedom from archiepiscopal visitation fees had changed into a right to visit and collect fees which approximated to an archdeacon's procurations; and the jurisdiction wielded in the chapters was approaching the limited competence of an archdeacon's. The bishop's executive representative in Allertonshire is called by witnesses a dean. 'Dean' is one of the commonest medieval administrative terms; but this dean must have been similar to a rural dean or dean of Christianity, normally a subordinate of the archdeacon; and, although the title in no way restricted the authority exercised,[1] it may have contributed to the formation of popular opinion.

Behind this reduction of scope lay undoubtedly the archbishop's development of his inherent authority as the local ordinary. Even in its weakest moments York had clung to some rights, and that tenacity had been momentous. As canon law became more widely studied and the common law of the Church prevailed over the custom of England, the local ordinary regained his strength. Just as in the Anglo-Saxon period general conditions in Church and State favoured the disruption of the powers of the ordinary, so in the twelfth century they strengthened him against the despoiler. The reopening of free intercourse with Rome and the integration of the English ecclesiastical courts within the universal judicial system meant a tide of definition in which many irregularities must perforce be washed away. Hence the bishops of Durham tended to lose their episcopal powers in Yorkshire, and their franchise consequently appeared as an archdeaconry, for, as has already been remarked,[2] the *episcopalia* then left in the hands of the immunist were those

---

[1] Cf. the Evesham dean in the Vale, below, pp. 90 and 107.

[2] See above, p. xvi. For a further discussion of this phenomenon, see below, pp. 111–12 and 147.

normally exercised by the archdeacons. The alienated
episcopalia had in fact been reintegrated on a lower level.
Yet it cannot be assumed that this was necessarily the view
of the bishops of Durham; and it is noticeable that even as
late as the fourteenth century they avoided limiting their
competence by describing their jurisdiction. The convent,
however, may have been quite satisfied with the way in
which the franchise had developed. The prior of Durham
could be an archdeacon, if hardly a bishop; and the exercise
of an ordinary jurisdiction in the liberties was probably
more satisfactory than a disputed claim to a share in the
wider episcopal pretensions.

It will have been noticed that in both the diocese of Durham and the diocese of York the possession of written titles
played little part during the formative period of the franchises. In both cases effective possession of the privileges
claimed and the attitude of the local diocesan were the
determining factors. In Durham the monks could obtain in
the twelfth century no documentary confirmation from their
bishops of immunities that were in constant dispute; in
York, where the franchise was supported by long and peaceful possession, archiepiscopal charters were freely granted.
Wise immunists strengthened their muniments in time of
peace, and the future usually justified their foresight; but
until *quo warranto* proceedings became usual, charters,
whether authentic or fraudulent, were a luxury. The charter
of Archbishop Thomas I, which the monks had forged, had
an influence on events in Yorkshire no greater than the
other forged instruments had on the history of the Durham
franchise. It was, of course, concealed during most of the
twelfth century. In 1171 × 80 Pope Alexander III recognized that the churches of the bishop and convent in the
province of York had enjoyed freedom from synodals and
other exactions for forty years[1]—the convent's favourite
term for the possession of its immunities in this period,
although greater than the minimum period for prescription,[2]

[1] Farrer, op. cit. ii. 280.
[2] According to Gratian, privileges could be taken from bishoprics by thirty
years' prescription, from monasteries by forty, *Decretum*, pars II, caus. xvi, qu.
3 and 4. Cf. an incident in the Evesham case before Pope Innocent III (see below,
p. 84, n. 3), Marleberg reporting: 'Et proferens rotulum nostrum incepi legere

and less than the term which could be calculated if the forgeries were used. The genuine charters of Thurstan and Roger, while keeping closely to the sense of the forgery, manage to avoid repetition. Indeed, the first mention of the forgery is found in 1182 × 3.[1]

By the second half of the thirteenth century, however, the fabrication had become hallowed by age, and was considered by the monks their principal title deed. In April 1281, during the great quarrel with Archbishop William Wickwane, Prior Richard of Claxton wrote a letter to Master William de la Corner, a proctor of the convent, who was then archdeacon of Northumberland, asking him to come and give the convent advice.[2] In the course of the prior's exposition of the case, he glances at the general position of the convent's churches in Yorkshire, mentions the privileges of Archbishops T[homas], T[hurstan], R[oger of Pont l'Évêque], and W. (? Walter Gray), and dwells particularly on the spurious charter of Thomas, from which he gives long extracts. He claims that the concessions of Thomas had been confirmed by many popes, who had examined the original documents, and that the immunities had been held from the foundation of the church of Durham by that title.

We have seen that the charter surrendered various pecuniary customs and consequently the duties which produced the revenues, and was designed to recognize the normal rights enjoyed by a bishop over his proprietary churches in the

attestationes quae ad hoc faciebant. Et dominus papa, taedio affectus, conversus ad adversarium nostrum dixit, "Num opus est lectione attestationum? num praescripserunt?". Et dixit magister Robertus [counsel for the bishop of Worcester], "Revera praescripserunt". Et dominus papa, "Ut quid ergo laboramus?". Et adversarius, "Pater sancte, nos didicimus in scolis, et haec est opinio magistrorum nostrorum, quod non currit praescriptio contra jura episcopalia". Et dominus papa, "Certe et tu et magistri tui multum bibistis de cervisia Anglicana quando haec didicistis" ', *Chronicon abbatiae de Evesham*, ed. Wm. Dunn Macray (Rolls Ser.), p. 189. The possession, however, must be *bona fide* and *justo titulo* to qualify for prescription; cf. ibid., p. 190.

[1] See above, p. 69, n. 1. Cf. also papal confirmation, dated March 1227, to the prior and convent of Durham of the liberties granted to their churches in the province of York by Thomas, sometime archbishop of York, and approved by Thurstan and Roger, his successors (*Calendar of Papal Letters*, i. 116).

[2] Letter in *Placitum inter W. archiepiscopum Ebor. et capitulum Dunelm.*, British Museum Cotton MS., Julius D. iv, fo. 127ᵛ.

diocese of another. It was differently interpreted in Richard
of Claxton's letter to Master William de la Corner, where it
is summarized as 'He freed us from all synodal dues,
aids, burdens, rents, exactions, and summonses to synods
and chapters, by granting us jurisdiction in those churches
and appointing us ordinaries',[1] and the ordinary jurisdiction
was considered that of an archdeacon.[2] This summary
would also apply to Thurstan's charter, and can be regarded
as the normal thirteenth-century Durham view of the concessions. The principle of exegesis is significant. The priory
extracts a general principle from the terms, and then relies
on the common law of the Church applicable to that principle, rather than on the precise terms of the grants, to
justify the details. If Thurstan's concessions were equivalent to the grant of archidiaconal jurisdiction, then the prior
had all the powers of an archdeacon regardless of any failure
to list each and every right in the charter. This was a policy
which the monks had been unable to maintain in the diocese
of Durham.

The archbishops, on the other hand, even in the thirteenth
century, tended to regard the franchise as a bundle of individual exemptions, and to resist the attempt to consolidate
them into an ordinary jurisdiction. According to their
attitude each separate right must have a title, and the concordat of 1162 × 7 treated the franchise as a complex of
rights which could be freely divided and truncated. These
conflicting attitudes were no doubt purely opportunist, and
hardly represent a fundamental cleavage of opinion between
the parties on the nature of a benefice.

The history of suits concerned with such franchises makes
it clear that in the absence of sound principles of historical
criticism and of a science of diplomatic the verdicts bear
little relation to absolute right and wrong.[3] Thus there is

---

[1] See above, p. 57, n. 1, for text.   [2] See below, p. 94.

[3] Compare, for example, the case between the abbey of Evesham and the bishop
of Worcester over the exemption of the abbey and the monastery's franchisal jurisdiction in the Vale. Evesham's charters, on which its title ultimately depended,
were flagrant forgeries, and were stigmatized as such by the opposing side. But
Innocent III tugged at the cords, cardinals peered at their seals, and no one, except
the counsel of both parties, could see anything wrong with them (*Chronicon abbatiae
de Evesham*, pp. 160–1).

little profit in attempting an objective examination of the titles to these franchises. And in this case there is not even an original creation to scrutinize and expound. Thurstan merely confirmed a franchise already in existence, and Archbishop Thomas I probably did no more than extend an immemorial practice. Nevertheless, the alienation of certain episcopal customs was an accepted fact, and the privation of the archdeacons and rural deans of fiscal rights within the liberties clearly envisaged their exclusion. In process of time all institutions and administrations tend to approach the normal, and it was becoming usual in the twelfth century to understand a surrender of the episcopal customs as a tacit grant of archidiaconal rights.[1] We can say, then, that it was inevitable that the monks should interpret the early charters as granting archidiaconal powers, and, by a natural development, have laid emphasis on the convenient assimilation rather than on the letter of the charters. But it is equally clear that the archbishop had no intention of encouraging that interpretation and tendency. Hence there were probably divergent views of the nature of the franchise from the very beginning.

By aiming at the creation of an ordinary jurisdiction in Yorkshire the monks did not necessarily prejudice the wider claims of the bishops of Durham. The liberty of the convent was originally a franchise within a franchise. Yet the development of one part on those lines, and clearly within the framework of the diocese of York, may well have reacted on the bishops' position. The decisive period seems to have been the episcopate of Hugh of le Puiset. After his narrow failure to subjugate the convent's Yorkshire jurisdiction to his episcopal power and radically to attract the whole franchise to his diocese, the monastery seems to have played for its own hand. In acquiring archidiaconal powers it satisfied its own ambition and endangered the claim of the bishops, for the paramountcy which the bishops of Durham enjoyed over the whole franchise could no longer be interpreted as an episcopal, still less as an ordinary, authority. Howdenshire and Allertonshire were not to be the diocese of Durham in microcosm. Crayke alone was detached from the diocese

---

[1] Lemarignier, op. cit., pp. 174–6.

of York.[1] The remainder felt the influence of the more limited aims of the convent.

The franchise had also by 1229 changed in its spatial conception. In the lawsuit a witness for the bishop speaks of his having archidiaconal rights in Allertonshire, and several refer to his chapter for Allertonshire. The king in 1237 uses a similar phrase. We have suggested that a convenient territorial division of the liberties had, under monkish pressure, given place to a new partition based on patronage; and, as Northallerton and Kirkby Sigston of the convent's advowson were certainly within Allertonshire in 1221, it was anachronistic, although prudent, to apply such a geographical description to the competence of the bishop's court.

The shires were not ecclesiastical in origin. They were survivals from the pre-Norman social and economic organization of Northumbria, and represented groups of dependent vills.[2] The Durham possessions in Yorkshire included at least three shires: Allertonshire, Howdenshire, and Weltonshire;[3] but by the twelfth century their original features were being effaced by a feudal nomenclature. The ecclesiastical franchise was by its nature seldom exactly coterminous with the Durham baronies in Yorkshire or with the submerged shires. Up to the thirteenth century it was flexible, and embraced the proprietary churches and demesne manors of the church of Durham, and them alone. Consequently the three York churches and Holtby, which had not been members of the shires, were within the franchise, while West Rounton and Thornton-le-Street, parts of Allertonshire, were without. So it was not until the area of the franchise had by a process of consolidation been for the most part realigned with the main territorial estates of the church of Durham in Yorkshire that it could be described with much accuracy as Howdenshire and Allertonshire, and by

[1] John Ecton, *Thesaurus rerum ecclesiasticarum* (1742), p. 673 (3rd ed., 1763, p. 542). There are no references to it in the archiepiscopal registers. It remained a detached part of the county of Durham until modern times.

[2] J. E. A. Jolliffe, 'Northumbrian institutions', *E.H.R.* xli (1926), pp. 1–31.

[3] Weltonshire and Weltonsoke were used indifferently in 1221 (*F.P.D.*, pp. 251–4). In Bishop Hugh's charters the latter term seems always to have been used. Cf. 'Hugo ... omnibus hominibus suis de Hovedenesire et Welleton soka salutem' (Farrer, op. cit. ii. 302 *bis*, 324).

that time the shires had almost entirely lost their original significance, as the disappearance of Weltonshire as a separate entity shows. But once it became possible to refer to the liberties of St. Cuthbert as the shires, it became their usual designation. Thus the shires acquired a predominantly ecclesiastical significance, and, in this way transmuted, took on a new lease of life.[1]

The first clear example of describing the ecclesiastical franchise as a shire comes from the lawsuit.[2] It is symptomatic of a change in conception. A process of definition is seen in most monastic liberties.[3] An unsuccessful attempt to stabilize the convent's franchise in the diocese of Durham was made in 1229.[4] In north-west France the process occurred rather earlier; but English conditions were generally backward. The development is natural and understandable. Both administrative routine and the need for administrative efficiency must have worked for stability and concentration; and in this process the influence of secular geography is likely to have been dominant.

By the second half of the thirteenth century, when classified episcopal registers become available, the change has taken place. The exempted churches are not all of the patronage of bishop and convent, nor are all their churches privileged. In the south of Yorkshire there is no change. Holtby, although geographically detached, remains in the franchise. But in the north the York churches of the convent, St. Peter-the-little and All Saints Pavement, are excluded.[5] In compensation all the churches on the episcopal manors of Northallerton, with its berewicks and socage, and Osmotherley are now included, although the advowsons of Thornton-le-Street and North Otterington had been granted to the hospital of St. James near Northallerton. Crayke, although still within the liberties, is now part of the diocese

---

[1] As the result of another mutation Howdenshire is now perpetuated as a parliamentary constituency.

[2] Cf. use by the early-twelfth-century forgers, above, p. 73, n. 3, and by Archbishop Geoffrey of York, above, p. 71.

[3] Lemarignier, op. cit., pp. 118 seqq.   [4] See above, pp. 38–9.

[5] The mediety of St. Trinity in Goodramgate had been surrendered by the convent to the archbishop shortly after 1235, so as to consolidate the church [*Register of Archbishop Walter Gray*, ed. Jas. Raine (Surtees Soc., vol. 56), pp. 69 and 174]. For a detailed analysis of the franchise, and authorities, see below, p. 92.

of Durham. It is likely that a treaty had been made between Durham and York, and that the guiding principle had been administrative convenience. The liberties had been consolidated. They had also been stabilized. There is no change in the composition of the peculiar between the thirteenth and nineteenth centuries.

It is impossible to say with certainty whether the change had occurred by the time of the litigation of 1220–6. It is true that Allertonshire is used to describe the province of the bishop's dean, although this can only have been a loose application, for Northallerton itself was outside the jurisdiction of that officer. Nor can the omission of reference in the conflict to the York city churches be taken to mean that they were outside the franchise, for the bishop had no claims on them. Archbishop Walter Gray's register, which covers this period, also provides no conclusive evidence. The register is not classified, and there are no references to the liberties as such. Hence it cannot be settled conclusively whether the liberties had been consolidated at this time, and, as fifty years later, were composed of two territorial blocks called Allertonshire and Howdenshire. But, if not completed, the change was certainly coming. The statements that the bishop had archidiaconal rights in Allertonshire and the phrase 'the bishop's archidiaconal chapter for Allertonshire' are symptomatic of a new conception of the franchise, territorial rather than personal. Rights which were once detached fragments of the archbishop's *beneficium*, to be applied by Durham to its mutable total of proprietary churches, have been anchored to a tangible geographical area.

It will be noticed that appropriation played little part in the development of the franchise. The appropriation of Northallerton must have been of considerable importance in the internal relations between bishop and convent; but the proprietor's hold on the temporalities of the churches seems to have been of no significance in determining the respective positions of York and Durham. The convent's churches in the franchise appear, indeed, to have been as uncontrollable in the twelfth century as were its Durham churches.

Howden provides a good example of the difficulties which

faced the monks. Probably in the hands of hereditary parsons in the twelfth century,[1] its great value made it the prey of external powers once the feudal hold had been broken.[2] The first thirteenth-century rector was a nephew of the bishop of Durham, and his successor was the archdeacon of Durham. The nephew of the archbishop of York followed, and then came the provost of Beverley. There is no reason to think that any of these were free appointments of the convent.[3] At this point, about the year 1239, the convent tried to appropriate the church; but King Henry III forced the monks to present his clerk and adviser John Mansel. A papal bull was then obtained giving permission for Howden to be appropriated after Mansel's death. But it was never used: the monks must have realized that the act would arouse too much hostility, and in 1265, after the death of Mansel, the convent converted Howden into a collegiate church of five prebends. Even this change, from which the priory gained no financial advantage, indeed it lost its pension and procuration fees, was opposed by the king, and that notorious pluralist, Bogo de Clare, had to be bought off with a substantial pension. Howden, because of its princely revenues, is probably an extreme example; but the convent's inability to appropriate any of the churches except Northallerton proves that there were everywhere considerable obstacles to this policy. In the Yorkshire liberties the identity of the immunists was probably more important than the actual internal condition of the franchise.

The administration of the liberties by bishop and convent is but scantily illustrated by the proceedings of the lawsuit. The bishop appointed a dean; but the prior's dean is not mentioned. In the later thirteenth century the prior appointed an official,[4] and so did the bishop in the early fourteenth.[5] The *attestationes* provide many instances of monks in custody of vacant churches and inducting the incumbents in the diocese of Durham,[6] and some examples of similar

---

[1] See above, p. 67, n. 3.

[2] For a history of Howden, see *Durham Annals and Documents*, pp. 159–72.

[3] A layman, asked in 1221 about the advowson of Howden, Welton, Brantingham, and Walkington, said, 'credit quod ad praesentationem monacorum, sed saepe vidit clericos episcopi eas habere', *F.P.D.*, p. 257.

[4] See below, p. 102.   [5] See below, p. 104.   [6] See above, pp. 26, 33–5.

practices in Yorkshire.[1] It therefore appears likely that the franchisal jurisdiction was directly administered by the convent. This practice may have been considered obnoxious later, and a reform introduced so as to confine monks more stringently to the cloister. The change in the nature of the bishop's representative can probably be explained by considering the experience of the abbey of Evesham.

Up to the early thirteenth century Evesham appointed a dean in the franchise of the Vale, who was a clerk, and was granted the office for life.[2] This dean is expressly called a dean of Christianity on occasion, and so cannot have been greatly dissimilar from the ordinary rural deans. The exact status and functions of that dignitary, however, have never been satisfactorily defined.[3] Some hold that he had an ordinary jurisdiction, but the competence of the jurisdiction, and the relations between dean and archdeacon are difficult problems. Evesham, by making a life grant to the dean, seems to have recognized him as an ordinary, and this was found to have grave disadvantages. Marleberg complains that these clerical deans, secure by the terms of their charters, neglected their duties to the grave prejudice of the monastic title to the liberties, and also oppressed the incumbents by travelling with a large retinue. The position was so unsatisfactory that in 1202 the abbey managed to expel Roger fitz Maurice, canon of Hereford, and appointed Marleberg himself as dean. Henceforth monks held the office.[4]

It is not unlikely that the bishops of Durham experienced similar disadvantages in the appointment of deans, and substituted officials, who could have no pretensions to an inherent jurisdiction.[5] Unfortunately the *attestationes* give

[1] See above, p. 76, n. 5, p. 79, n. 3.

[2] *Chronicon abbatiae de Evesham*, pp. 187 and 194 seqq.

[3] See Wm. Dansey, *Horae decanicae rurales* (2nd ed., 1844); Pierre Andrieu-Guitrancourt, *Essai sur l'évolution du décanat rural en Angleterre d'après les conciles des xiie, xiiie et xive siècles* (1935); A. Hamilton Thompson, 'Diocesan Organization in the Middle Ages', Raleigh Lecture on History, 1943, *Proc. of the Brit. Acad.*, xxix. 167 seqq.

[4] *Chronicon abbatiae de Evesham*, p. 196. For the stipend of the dean, see ibid., p. 210.

[5] In the Canterbury peculiars, however, the deans of the immediate or peculiar jurisdiction of the archbishop, who were normally granted the equivalent of archidiaconal jurisdiction, seem to have remained vicars. See I. J. Churchill, *Canterbury Administration*, pp. 62 seqq.

us little information about the Durham dean in Allertonshire.
Beyond the facts that such an officer had been appointed
before 1195, and that he celebrated the chapters, little is
certain. The impression is gained, however, that the appointments were infrequent, and so, perhaps, for life, or for the
term of the episcopate, and that the competence of the dean
was quite extensive. The statement of one witness that
Philip de Ulecote, one of the royal guardians of the see
during the nine years' vacancy after the death of Philip of
Poitou, had appointed his dean, is rather surprising. As
the convent would normally have had the administration of
the spiritualities *sede vacante*, it seems that either the deanery
was considered part of the temporalities, possibly through
confusion with the bishop's lay officials in Allertonshire, or
the guardians were usurping control of the spiritualities.
Certainly the archdeacon Aimery, another of the guardians,
and nephew of the late bishop, was an enemy of the monks.[1]
At the end of the next century, however, it was the archbishop of York, who had by then supplanted the chapter as
administrator of the spiritualities *sede vacante*, who had control of the episcopal share of Allertonshire during a vacancy.[2]

Although tantalizing and scanty on some subjects, evidence from the *attestationes* enables us nevertheless to come
to some conclusions about the nature of the franchise at the
turn of the twelfth century. The alienation of *episcopalia* in
favour of the proprietary churches of Durham has produced
a franchise which is consolidating into a fixed territorial
archdeaconry in which the convent has become the senior
partner.

§ 4. *The Franchise after 1229*

When we can resume an examination of the liberties in the
second half of the thirteenth century all signs of immaturity
have disappeared; everything is orderly and stabilized. The
extent of the franchise is easy to define:[3] Allertonshire is

---

[1] See above, pp. 24 and 33.   [2] See below, p. 110, n. 3.

[3] The component churches are listed in the *Taxatio Papae Nicholai* (Rec. Com.),
p. 302. Their membership can be tested by the existence of administrative documents of the convent and of the bishop concerning them, and by the archiepiscopal
treatment of them. An admission to All Saints Pavement, York, in 1281 is entered
under 'Jurisdictio de Hovedene' in Archbishop Wickwane's register [*Reg. Wickwane*, ed. Wm. Brown (Surtees Soc., vol. 114), p. 232]; but another admission in

made up of the bishop's churches of Birkby, Cowesby,
Leake, Osmotherley, and Crayke, the last now exempt also
from the archiepiscopal jurisdiction; the convent's churches
of Northallerton, Kirkby Sigston, and West Rounton; and
those of the hospital of St. James, North Otterington,[1] and
Thornton-le-Street.[2] Howdenshire is composed of Howden,
Eastrington,[3] Brantingham, Hemingbrough, Skipwith,
Walkington, Welton, and Holtby, all belonging to the
monks. The convent had jurisdiction over the churches of
its advowson: the bishop over the rest. The female priory
of St. Stephen, Foukeholm, in the township of Thimbleby
and the parish of Osmotherley, and two religious houses
within the convent's parish of Northallerton, the hospital of
St. James, the wardenship of which was in the bishop's gift,
and the hospital or collegiate chapel of Lazenby, seem also
to have been subject to the bishop's jurisdiction.[4] When
the prior and convent confirmed the establishment of the
college at Lazenby in 1291, they safeguarded the parochial

1283 appears under the archdeaconry of York (ibid., p. 45), and this became usual.
All Saints was no longer within the franchise, and the first entry was a mistake.
The church of Normanton-upon-Soar, in the diocese of York, but in the county
of Nottingham, the advowson of which with five carucates of land, two mills, and
some other pertinencies had been acquired by the convent before 1158 (charter
of King Henry II, *F.P.D.*, p. lxxxiii), appears never to have been within the franchise. It is not always clear in the archiepiscopal charters whether the privileges
were accorded to the possessions of St. Cuthbert within the shire or the diocese of
York; but the predominant factor in the exclusion of Normanton was probably
administrative convenience. The convent may never have wished to insist on its
rights.

[1] Granted to the hospital before 1209 by Bishop Philip of Poitou, *Cal. Rot.
Chart.*, 1199–1216 (Rec. Com.), p. 184b.

[2] Geoffrey de Upsall granted the advowson of Thornton to the hospital in 1247
(*V.C.H.*, *Yorks, N. Riding*, i. 458).

[3] Eastrington was still considered a chapel of Howden in 1265, when the mother
church became collegiate (*Durham Annals and Documents*, nos. 130–6a). But the
new arrangement, by the appropriation of the chapel's endowments to the college,
necessitated the creation of a vicarage in Eastrington (ibid., no. 138), and so,
by the end of the century, it was considered a parish church [*Taxatio Papae Nicholai*,
p. 302; *Register of Archbishop John le Romeyn*, ed. Wm. Brown (Surtees Soc., vols.
123, 128), ii. 97].

[4] Cf. below, p. 106. The visitation of 1315 covered six of the seven churches and
the two hospitals. The omission of the priory is natural; the exclusion of Crayke
suggests that it was administered as part of the diocese of Durham. A papal rescript
of 1330 lists the two hospitals, the priory, and all the seven churches, except Leake,
as belonging to the bishop's jurisdiction (*Calendar of Papal Letters*, ii. 320).
The reason for the omission of Leake is uncertain. It remained within the franchise
[John Ecton, *Thesaurus rerum ecclesiasticarum* (1742), p. 676].

rights of the mother church and also their ordinary jurisdiction. This and other documents concerning the foundation were inspected and copied by a notary public in 1343.[1]
The circumstances under which the college was subtracted
from the jurisdiction of the convent are unknown. There
had also been trouble over the position of the hospital at
Northallerton.[2]

The monastery of Durham treated its share of the liberties, although it fell geographically into two parts, as a unity.
One official was appointed;[3] and there was but one seal.[4]
The address in the conventual administrative documents
was 'all rectors of churches, vicars, &c., or their proctors,
within the liberties of St. Cuthbert in Howdenshire and
Allertonshire'[5] with an optional addition of 'and pertaining
to the patronage of the prior and convent'.[6] Although the
bishops of Durham in the early fourteenth century called
their share of the liberties 'the spirituality of Allertonshire',[7]
despite the fact that the episcopal franchise comprised only
part of Allertonshire, it is clear that the territorial shires were

[1] 'indempnitate matricis ecclesiae nostrae de Alvertone in juribus, libertatibus,
decimis, oblationibus, obventionibus, ac jurisdictione nostra ordinaria nobis in
omnibus semper salvis', *Richard of Bury, Fragments of his Register*, p. 177.

[2] Robert, vicar of Northallerton, when 'ill and out of mind', had, under episcopal
pressure and without regard to the rights of the prior and convent and of his
successors, remitted most of his parochial jurisdiction over the hospital. He was
forced by the monks to come to his senses and sue Reginald, warden of the hospital,
for restitution of the rights. The case was heard by the chapter of York, who
decided in the vicar's (styled 'rector') favour. The date of the case may be 1208 × 15
(*Register of Walter Gray*, pp. 177–80).

[3] See below, p. 102. Cf. expression 'officialem liberatis B. Cuthberti de Alvertun
et Hovedenschir', 'Gesta Dunelmensia A.D. 1300', ed. R. K. Richardson, *The Camden
Miscellany, xiii*, pp. 10 and 23.

[4] Mr. Peter Kellaw adhered to Prior Hoton in 1300 and refused to surrender
the seal to Bishop Anthony Bek. The bishop said, 'Stultus est . . . quoniam detinet
sigillum officialitatis de Hoveden' et Alvertonschir'', *Gesta Dunelmensia A.D. 1300*,
p. 44. Cf. also, 'Et ad majorem fidem faciendam sigillum officialitatis libertatis
B. Cudberti in diocesi Ebor. per modum collacionis apponi procuravi', 1303,
Register of Archbishop Thomas of Corbridge, prepared by Wm. Brown, ed. by A.
Hamilton Thompson (Surtees Soc., vols. 138, 141), ii. 134.

[5] 'Hugo, prior Dunelmensis, discretis viris ecclesiarum rectoribus, prebendariis,
vicariis, capellanis, ac aliis clericis infra libertates B. Cuthberti in Hovedenaschyre
et Alvertonaschyre, Ebor. dioc., constitutis, salutem in domino', *Durham Annals
and Documents*, no. 71; cf. nos. 72, 89, 93–4.

[6] Ibid., nos. 86, 94.

[7] 'Jurisdictio spiritualitatis nostrae de Alvertonshyre', *Registrum palatinum
Dunelmense*, i. 56 and 187; *Richard of Bury, Fragments of his Register*, p. 50.

of little importance in the internal administration of this Durham peculiar.

The rights claimed by the prior in the liberties are those of an archdeacon. The prior usually styles himself as exercising, as an ordinary, archidiaconal powers within the liberties of St. Cuthbert in Howdenshire and Allertonshire,[1] and claims to have ordinary and immediate jurisdiction over subordinates and parishioners of all churches of Howdenshire and Allertonshire subject to him.[2] Nevertheless, the franchise was a little greater than a normal archdeaconry.[3]

The bishops of Durham, on the other hand, seem to have avoided limiting their competence by a precise description. An idea of their attitude can be obtained from statutes intended for the franchise, 1240×81.[4] In the preamble to the statutes it is stated that the parochial churches of Durham enjoy the special dignities and liberties accorded to the mother church. In the diocese of York they are immediately

---

[1] Cf. 'Robertus de Insula, sacrista Dunelmensis, gerens vices domini Hugonis, prioris Dunelmensis, fungentis vice ordinaria iure archidiaconali infra libertates S. Cuthberti in Hovedenaschyre et Alvertonaschyre', *Durham Annals and Documents*, no. 134; 'Quia execucioni officii archidiaconalis, quo fungimur in hac parte, personaliter interesse non possumus', ibid., no. 72.

[2] 'habens iurisdiccionem ordinariam et immediatam in subditos et parochianos omnium ecclesiarum de Hovedenaschyre et Alvertonaschyre sibi subiectarum', ibid., no. 86.

[3] See below, p. 103, n. 4.

[4] For these statutes see C. R. Cheney, *English Synodalia of the Thirteenth Century* (1941), pp. 69–73. The manuscript is Brit. Mus. Stowe 930, in which the statutes form the first item. The manuscript is written in a mid-thirteenth-century book hand, and a small part of each page is obliterated by damp stain. Professor Cheney kindly lent me his photostats and transcript. The statutes are largely derived from the version of Bishop Richard Poore's statutes current in the diocese of Durham, but use is also made of those issued by Robert Grosseteste for the diocese of Lincoln. The date of this recension is, therefore, *post* 1240; but it is not later than 1281, for on fo. 6, at the end of the statutes is written in a second hand, 'Anno gracie m^{o}cc^{m}olxxx^{m}oxiij Kal' Martii hospitatus fuit dominus Petrus de Monteforti miles'. The issuing authority is not stated. It is possible that they were intended to be used in both parts of the liberties, and certainly little editing would have been required for their adoption by either partner in the franchise. Such evidence as there is, however, favours the bishop as the issuer of this recension. It is as follows: (*a*) the tone of the preamble; (*b*) the reference to the deans (see below, p. 104); (*c*) the reference to the diocese (see below, p. 96). The general modification of the language is equivocal, for the bishop of Durham had no longer episcopal powers in the liberties. If, however, it is held unlikely that he would modify his style when in an archidiaconal capacity, the present recension may be regarded as an edition of episcopal statutes for the liberties, badly edited for use in the convent's share of the franchise.

subject to Durham, so that the archbishop of York cannot take procuration fees from them or make corrections in them. The liberties have been granted for the honour of God and the glory of St. Cuthbert and for the reformation of morals. Lest, therefore, the privilege and liberty should be accounted a cloak for licence, the statutes are promulgated for the correction of the clergy, who are the vice-gerents of the issuing authority.[1] The sixty-one chapters which follow are mostly concerned with the orders, morals, and conversation of parish priests. When the rights of an ordinary are concerned, the position of the archbishop of York is always safeguarded. Moreover, the language of this recension of the statutes is modified from the mandate of a bishop and diocesan to an exhortation more suitable to an archdeacon. The categorical *praecipimus* is, except in two cases, changed to a softer word—*monemus, amonemus, exhortamur, rogamus, volumus,* or *consulimus,* and *filii karissimi* is usually changed to *filii.*

[1] 'Inter ecclesias siquidem Angli(e . . . Dunelmen)sis dignitatum et libertatum prerogativa (. . .) insignis, etiam ecclesias ipsas parochial(es sibi subie)ctas libertatum et honorum speciali gratia pre(ci)ngere gratulatur. . . . Talium siquidem ingressus in templum domini per dominum pro quanto magis ministerium quoniam autem vices nostras geritis in ecclesiis in quibus ministratis, que quidem nobis capite commisse noscuntur, in extremo examine coram tremendo iudice de nostra pariter et vestra negligentia seu incuria si negligentes fuerimus vel ignavi rationes nos reddere formidantes, nostro pariter et vestro periculo in hac parte nolumus occurrere. . . . Quibus iam statutis tanto maiorem re(verentiam adhibere) debetis ac ardentiori studio amplecti eadem, quia in custodiendis illis retributio mu(lta, quanto ecclesiam) Dunelm', que mater est ecclesiarum sibi subiectarum, ea promulgasse seu publicasse cognoveritis (*2–3v.* . . . chorum fuerimus) qui domino permittente vices agimus ecclesie memorate. Quod autem mater sit eccle(sia predicta) sanctorum patrum archiepiscoporum Ebor' satis declarant ac manifestant statuta et privilegia special(*1–2 v.* eidem) indulta, per que cetere ecclesie sibi subiciuntur immediate, ita quod nulli licet in ecclesiis ip(sius parochial . . . *1 v.* seu) procurationes vel correctiones seu aliqua alia preter ecclesiam Dunelm' nisi per ipsius inc(uriam seu negligen)tiam vel approbationem hec contigerit. Cum igitur hec privilegia premissa eidem sint concessa ad hono(rem et laudem dei et sancti C)uthberti confessoris gloriam specialem et sacrosancte ecclesie, ad plantandum que ad virtutum (spectant decorem, ad ev)ellendum et eradicandum que obvia sunt rationi et profectum salutis animarum impediunt, ne (privilegium vestrum) dici possit iusticie velamentum nec libertas transeat in servitutem peccati et ex gratia surgat sollicitudo, ne sitis quasi acephali et quasi grex ruens per devia sine pastore, nobis pariter et vobis, (qui vices) nostras agitis, omnibus modis procurandum et providendum est ut oves que nostre sunt et ex nostro ovili (pro deo) vocem nostram audiant diligenter et intelligant, ne per eas dici possit quod scriptum est: Equum quippe est ut qui (sacris) minime obedientiam statutis accommodant ab ecclesia habeantur extorres.', ff. 3–3v.

Although the rights of the archbishop of York are pains-takingly recognized, and the phraseology of the document is appropriate, a studious ambiguity of description is most noticeable. The text of the preamble is slightly mutilated in the manuscript, but there seems to be no mention of the elusive archdeaconry. The franchise is described as deriving from the special dignities and liberties of the mother church of Durham. There is, indeed, a certain archaism of thought. Durham is the *mater ecclesia*; the parish churches in York-shire are immediately subject to it and entrusted to the bishop in chief; and the incumbents are the episcopal vice-gerents.[1] In the body of the statutes the franchise is thrice called 'our parish',[2] and twice there is a reference to 'our diocese'.[3] The same cautious attitude seems to prevail in the early fourteenth century, when no description of the franchise appears in the published episcopal administrative documents.

The archiepiscopal administrative documents of the second half of the thirteenth century are closer in style to the episcopal than to the conventual forms, and betray an approach in some ways at variance with that of the priory. There is noticeable throughout a difference of emphasis; for whereas it was advisable for the convent to state boldly its claims in every administrative document, it was equally politic for both bishop and archbishop to maintain a non-committal attitude. The one might hope for more; the other for less. There is also a certain artificiality about the arch-bishops' attitude. They ignored entirely the partition of the franchise between bishop and convent, and, if a division was recognized, it was that between the two shires.

The treatment of the liberties in the archiepiscopal regis-

---

[1] Cf. Bishop Hugh's attempt to attract the Whitsuntide processions and offerings from the liberties to Durham, above, pp. 70–2.

[2] Cap. 1 (fo. 3ᵛ): '*Imprimis in virtute spiritus sancti* consulimus, monemus, atque hortamur in domino, *ut omnes ministri* ecclesiarum parochie nostre *et precipue sacerdotes*'; cap. 5 (fo. 4): 'rogamus, monemus, et exhortamur in domino *ut omnes ministri* ecclesiarum parochie nostre *in sacris ordinibus constituti*'. Words in italic follow the original version of the statutes. See also below, p. 104, n. 6.

[3] Cap. 6 (fo. 4): priests shall expel their concubines '*nisi* officio altaris in nostra diocesi voluerint *privari*'; cap. 59 (fo. 8), re apostate priests: 'monemus sacerdotes nostros, ut cum aliquis talis inventus fuerit in diocesi nostra . . . denuntietur archiepiscopo ut per eum comprehendatur'.

ters from Walter Giffard (1266–79) to Henry Newark (1298–9) is not entirely uniform;[1] but the use of a separate section, divided into years, entitled 'Spiritualitas de Hovedenashire et Alvertonashire' became standard practice.[2] The contents of these sections are almost entirely made up of institutions to churches; and it is clear that in this connexion neither the territorial nor the jurisdictional division was regarded as of any importance. However, when geographical considerations affected the administration, the shires were sometimes employed as units. In 1280 a notification of the appointment of a collector of Peter's Pence applies to Howdenshire alone;[3] in 1288 a special commission for collecting first fruits in Allertonshire was issued;[4] and in 1290 the spiritualities are entered separately in the list of summonses to convocation.[5] In the 'Taxatio ecclesiastica papae Nicholai' of 1291 Howdenshire and Allertonshire have separate treatment, and the latter is further divided between bishop and convent.[6] But when the archbishop of York acted on the assessment, he respected the two geographical units, but ignored the partition between bishop and convent.[7] It may be inferred that when the administrative unit was the archdeaconry, the archbishop often found it convenient to treat Howdenshire and Allertonshire as peculiars in the archdeaconries. But in the arrangement of the registers and in the terms of the general commissions no regard is given to any partition based on the patronage of the churches.

In a similar way the archbishops ignored the administrative

---

[1] Cf. *The Register of Walter Giffard, Lord Archbishop of York*, ed. Wm. Brown (Surtees Soc., vol. 109), p. 289 (and p. 285); *The Register of Wm. Wickwane, Lord Archbishop of York*, ed. Wm. Brown (Surtees Soc., vol. 114), pp. 228–33; *Reg. Romeyn*, ii. 31, 247.

[2] *Reg. Corbridge*, ii. 132–5; *The Register of Wm. Greenfield, Lord Archbishop of York*, prepared by Wm. Brown, ed. A. Hamilton Thompson (Surtees Soc., vols. 145, &c.), v. 145.

[3] *Reg. Wickwane*, p. 229.   [4] *Reg. Romeyn*, ii. 35.   [5] Ibid. i. 33 and 41.

[6] 'Taxatio prebendarum ecclesie Hoveden' necnon ecclesiarum et vicariarum existencium in spiritualitate de Hovedenshire'; 'Taxatio ecclesiarum existentium in spiritualitate episcopi Dunolm' in Alvertonskire'; 'Taxacio ecclesiarum existencium in spiritualitate prioris Dunolm' in Alvertonshire' (*Taxatio ecclesiastica Papae Nicholai*, p. 302).

[7] In 1289 there is a mandate to the keeper of the spirituality of Howdenshire and Allertonshire to cite those within that jurisdiction in arrears with payment of taxation to appear at York (*Reg. Romeyn*, ii. 36); but in 1293 and 1294 the two shires receive individual treatment (ibid. ii. 41).

arrangements actually operative within the liberties, and preferred to consider that there was a 'keeper of the spirituality' in each shire. Mandates were sent to the appropriate keeper according to the situation of the church concerned, and episcopal or conventual deans, officials or special commissaries were as such ignored. The form is usually the same in the case of Allertonshire for the churches of the bishop, convent, and hospital; and for the last two the address is always 'the keeper of the spirituality of Allertonshire'. Sometimes, however, the prior's administrative officer is addressed by name,[1] and occasionally he is styled 'the vice-gerent of the prior of Durham'.[2] Once we find Archbishop Giffard actually taking an interest in the identity of the prior's official. Gilbert, vicar of Northallerton, who had been acting as official, died in September 1267, and when the convent presented his successor to the vicarage, the archbishop wrote to his official, saying that he did not know by whom the inquisition should be made, but that it should be done in the customary manner, 'ut, jurisdictione cujuslibet sive libertate salvata, faciamus exinde quod est nostrum'.[3] Unfortunately such magnanimity was unusual for Archbishop Walter Giffard. We do not know who performed the inquisition; but the archbishop sent the commission to induct to Adam of Darlington, then rector of Dinsdale in the diocese of Durham.[4] Adam frequently acted as a proctor of the convent, and probably had received a special commission from the prior for this performance.[5]

The studied anonymity of the *custos spiritualitatis* usually found in the archiepiscopal registers was certainly to some extent fictitious. A formulary preserved in John le Romeyn's register refers to documents addressed to the keeper as models;[6] yet one cannot but feel that there is a certain artificiality in the terminology of the registers, and suspect that the archbishops aimed at treating the liberties as two

---

[1] See below, p. 102, nn. 4–6.   [2] *Durham Annals and Documents*, nos. 74, 77.
[3] *Reg. Giffard*, p. 43.   [4] Ibid., p. 22.
[5] In 1281 he inducted Adam de Barneby into West Rounton during the great quarrel with the archbishop (*Reg. Wickwane*, p. 232). He was also acting as the prior's representative within the liberties in 1289 (*Reg. Romeyn*, ii. 36). Adam was probably too occupied with the legal activities of the convent ever to have been a resident official.   [6] *Reg. Romeyn*, ii. 187.

exemptions in the archdeaconries, but frequently lapsed into more natural forms. To sum up: in the thirteenth century, certainly in the second half, the liberties were divided between bishop and convent on a principle that disregarded the shires, and did not always respect the parish boundaries. For the archbishop, however, the territorial division was of more moment, because it allowed him, when convenient, and in matters not touching archidiaconal jurisdiction, to associate each part with an archdeaconry, despite the theoretical complication by which Howdenshire was divided between Cleveland and East Riding. And so the archbishop attempted to maintain the misleading distinction in his mandates between the keepers of the spiritualities of Howden and Allerton, and did not normally recognize the actual internal administrative divisions.

The same cleavage between the York and Durham attitudes is seen in the matter of the nature of the franchise. The assimilation of the Durham rights in the liberties to the ordinary jurisdiction of an archdeacon has already been discussed.[1] When Durham conventual administrative documents become available it has become common form. The prior has archidiaconal powers as an ordinary, and usually says so.[2] The archbishops, however, while recognizing the franchise, never mention archidiaconal rights, not even in their occasional attacks on the liberties. They prefer to regard the peculiar as a bundle of separate exemptions. This non-committal attitude is understandable. There was no point in encouraging a franchise, which complicated the diocesan administration, by recognizing a jurisdiction claimed as ordinary, when an alternative and less compromising form was available. The attitude merely expressed caution, and not active hostility. Periodic clashes occurred, naturally, for no jurisdiction is static; but frontal attacks on the liberties were reserved as a weapon to be produced in any serious quarrel with the convent on any subject. The threat of expensive litigation was, indeed, a useful lever.

Despite, then, a difference in attitude, the individual rights of the convent were normally recognized by the archbishop. When Howden was made a collegiate church in

---

[1] See above, pp. 80 seqq.　　　　[2] Ibid., p. 94.

1265, the ordainers, canons of York, reserved all rights, customs, and liberties of the prior and convent in the church, except the exaction of pensions and procurations, which the monks had renounced; and this settlement was confirmed by the archbishop and the papal legate.[1] In 1280 the parsonage of Skipwith was made a prebend of Howden, and the archbishop, after settling the vicarage, safeguarded the annual pension, visitation and procuration, and all other rights and liberties which the convent had in the church.[2] These other rights were the ordinary archidiaconal functions.

A good selection of documents illustrating the administration of the convent's share of the liberties in the second half of the thirteenth century has been preserved in the formularies and letter-books of the monastery, and the archiepiscopal registers are extant for this period. The available evidence for the administration of the bishops' share of the franchise, however, is mostly rather later in date, coming mainly from the episcopates of Richard Kellaw (1311–16) and Richard of Bury (1333–45).

It seems clear that the prior and not the convent was archdeacon in the liberties. In both the spurious and genuine charters privileges are granted to the prior and the monks jointly.[3] This position is maintained intact: the franchise belonged to the whole convent.[4] But the office of archdeacon pertained to the prior alone. This is true also in the diocese of Durham.[5] All administrative documents concerning the franchise go out in the name of the prior, and not, as with all other business correspondence, in the name of the prior and convent.[6] As the convent could sue and be sued, be the patron and the parson of churches, and generally conduct itself as a corporation, there seems no good reason why it should not also have been an archdeacon. The distinction, moreover, between the prior and convent as the joint possessors of archidiaconal jurisdiction and the prior alone as archdeacon is very fine, and its maintenance implies that it must have had significance.

[1] *Durham Annals and Documents*, nos. 130–6a.   [2] *Reg. Wickwane*, p. 231.
[3] Cf. above, pp. 11, n. 1, 20, 56, 60 and 63.
[4] Cf. above, pp. 46, n. 1, 50, n. 1, and below, p. 109.   [5] See above, p. 47.
[6] Cf. above, p. 93, n. 5; *Durham Annals and Documents*, pp. 130 seqq. For the normal form, cf. below, p. 113, n. 1.

It was not unusual in other monasteries having similar franchises for the sacristan to act as archdeacon.[1] There are rudimentary traces of this practice at Durham, but no evidence that the delegation of function to the sacristan was the normal expedient. At Durham it is the prior who appoints the officials,[2] and those administrative writs which are issued at the convent seem to go out exclusively in the prior's name. The prior visits;[3] the prior collects and gives acquittance for the procuration fees,[4] warns rectors to pay their pensions[5] and debts,[6] sequestrates and relaxes sequestration,[7] issues licences to beg within the liberties.[8] The prior excommunicates,[9] and sues out the royal writ of *Significavit*.[10] This may, of course, be a distorted picture, resulting from the type of evidence that has survived; but the active participation of the prior in the administration is at least a limiting factor.

One delegation of the prior's archidiaconal powers to the sacristan of Durham, is, however, extant.[11] Robert de Insula was given a general commission and power of attorney probably in 1265 in connexion with the scheme by which Howden was changed into a collegiate church. The delegation of powers is complete, and there is no time limit in the document as it stands. The commission is far wider in competence than those appointing an official in the liberties. But the prior was by no means *functus officio* as a result of the delegation. Robert de Insula describes himself as the vicegerent of the prior, and was indifferent whether the answers to his mandates were addressed to him or to the prior.[12] The

---

[1] Dom David Knowles, *The Monastic Order*, p. 606. For the sacristan as archdeacon at Bury St. Edmunds see M. D. Lobel, *The Borough of Bury St. Edmund's* (1935), pp. 42–7. Mrs. Lobel considers him to have been the vicar of the abbot and not an ordinary. He employed a dean of Christianity as executive officer.

[2] *Durham Annals and Documents*, nos. 70, 72–3.

[3] Ibid., nos. 89, 90.   [4] Ibid., nos. 78–9.   [5] Ibid., nos. 83, 141–2.

[6] Ibid., nos. 80–2.   [7] Ibid., nos. 78, 81, 83.   [8] Ibid., nos. 93–5.

[9] Cf. Hoton's actions in 1300, 'Quare dictus prior eosdem conspiratores propter suam manifestam offensam nominatim excommunicavit in scriptis, precipiendo . . officiali suo de Alverton' et Hovedenschir' per litteras suas quatinus dictam suam sentenciam in eosdem canonice latam per omnes ecclesias parochiales in dicta libertate, cum maior affuerit populi multitudo solempniter publicaret. . . . Et dictus . . officialis secundum quod sibi iniunctum fuerat absque dissimulacione protinus adimplevit', *Gesta Dunelmensia A.D. 1300*, pp. 10–1, and cf. p. 23.

[10] *Durham Annals and Documents*, nos. 85–7.

[11] Ibid., no. 71.   [12] Ibid., no. 134.

Durham position possibly is, then, that the sacristan was considered the most suitable obedientiary for receiving a delegation of the prior's archidiaconal powers, but that it was not a prescriptive right or duty. It is of interest that the monk associated with Robert in 1265 in connexion with the Howden reform was Henry of Hornecastle, later sacristan of Durham, and recently, if not actually, sacristan of Coldingham.[1]

The routinal administration of the franchise was in the hands of an official, who was normally a clerk with a benefice in the liberties, just like an ordinary rural dean, whom he must greatly have resembled, except that the official's jurisdiction was entirely delegate, whereas a dean's was probably only so in part. Some of the holders of the office during this period are known: Master John of Brompton, rector of Welton, 1258×65;[2] Master Lambert de Gervim, John's successor as rector of Welton, 1265×73;[3] Gilbert, vicar of Northallerton, 1267;[4] Master Michael, rector of Walkington, 1281–2;[5] Master John of Dalton, vicar of Skipwith, 1287;[6] Master Adam of Darlington, rector of Dinsdale and prebendary of Howden, 1289;[7] Peter Kellaw, the brother of the future bishop, probably at this time rector of All Saints in Ousegate but soon to be vicar of Northallerton, 1300.[8] It is possible that the beneficed clergymen of the franchise served according to a rota, a system which was sometimes used with the rural deanery.[9]

The appointments to the officiality throw little light on

---

[1] *Durham Annals and Documents*, no. 127, and see p. 218.   [2] Ibid., no. 70.

[3] Ibid., no. 72. John is found as rector of Dinsdale in 1262 (ibid., no. 116). Lambert occurs in 1244 as rector of Bedlington (*North Durham*, p. 368), and in 1265 he resigned the church of Kimblesworth because he had been appointed to Welton (*Durham Annals and Documents*, nos. 143–4). He cannot have held Welton long, for Mr. Hugh of Evesham resigned it in 1272 (*Reg. Giffard*, p. 57).

[4] *Reg. Giffard*, p. 43; cf. *Durham Annals and Documents*, nos. 74, 78.

[5] *Reg. Wickwane*, pp. 232–3.   [6] *Reg. Romeyn*, ii. 33–4.

[7] Ibid., ii. 36. Adam had been rector of All Saints Pavement, York, while studying at Bologna (*Durham Annals and Documents*, no. 145). He was a typical clerk of the convent.

[8] *Gesta Dunelmensia A.D. 1300*, p. 44. Peter was admitted to All Saints Pavement in 1281 (*Reg. Wickwane*, p. 232). He is listed in *Fasti Dunelmenses* as vicar of Northallerton 1302–11, rector of Sedgefield 1311, and died 1313.

[9] Felix Makower, *The Constitutional History and Constitution of the Church of England* (1895), p. 325.

the powers conferred. Master John of Brompton was appointed 'our official in all our churches within the liberties of St. Cuthbert in Howdenshire and Allertonshire', and given the power to do all things within the competence of a true official;[1] to Master Lambert de Gervim the prior committed his powers (*vices nostrae*),[2] and in a third form the office of the officiality with powers of canonical coercion is granted.[3] The official sequestrated the goods of a church on the death of an incumbent;[4] he received the archiepiscopal letter of inquisition, which he executed;[5] and finally obeyed the mandate to induct the presentee into corporal possession.[6] He must have held the chapters; and he carried out the orders of the prior and the archbishop. It is likely that the limitation on the official's powers was merely practical, secured not by the form of the commission, but by custom and the active intervention of the prior.

For matters outside the normal routine special commissaries seem to have been appointed. Two special commissions from 1265 concerned with Howden church are extant, and have already been discussed in so far as they illustrate the sacristan's position in the franchise. Robert de Insula, the sacristan, was given full powers of visitation, receiving the oath of obedience and reverence from the clerks, inquiring into their legitimacy, conduct, orders, and knowledge, hearing and determining causes and complaints, and punishing contradictors and rebels by suitable ecclesiastical censure.[7] This was a delegation of all the most important archidiaconal functions. For the actual sequestration of the church, a crucial, and in this case difficult operation, the monks Henry of Hornecastle and T. de N. were given a special commission.[8] This expedient was also used in the jurisdictional sphere. About the year 1265 the men of North Duffield, parishioners of Skipwith, complained to the prior in letters patent with six seals attached that the

---

[1] *Durham Annals and Documents*, no. 70. [2] Ibid., no. 72. [3] Ibid., no. 73.
[4] Mandate of Prior Hugh to his vice-gerents, 1265, 'Cum custodia et sequestrum omnium ecclesiarum vacancium in baronia de Hoved' ad nos tam de iure quam de antiqua et approbata consuetudine pertinere noscatur', ibid., no. 127.
[5] Cf. letter of inquisition and reply, 1267, ibid., no. 74, and *Reg. Greenfield*, v. 146.
[6] Archiepiscopal registers, *passim*.
[7] *Durham Annals and Documents*, no. 71. [8] Ibid., nos. 127–8.

rector, Master Emery de Rochechouart, had failed to maintain the due service of a chaplain in their chapel. The rector was warned to amend his ways, should the complaint be true, failing which the prior delegated his powers to two rectors, one of whom was, or both were, to hear the case.[1]

The administration of the bishop's share of the franchise seems to have been similar to that of the conventual. The bishop visited,[2] appointed his subordinates, gave licences to preach within the franchise,[3] and generally supervised affairs. We have seen that the bishops of Durham appointed deans at the turn of the twelfth century as their agents.[4] This practice seems still to have been followed in the middle of the thirteenth century. In what are probably episcopal statutes for the franchise (1240 × 81)[5] there is a reference to 'rectors of the churches of our parish who are our deans'.[6] The representative of Richard Kellaw, however, is usually styled on the archiepiscopal model *custos spiritualitatis*[7] or *custos jurisdictionis*;[8] but in 1314 the bishop appointed Master William de Alverton his official and keeper of the jurisdiction,[9] from which it can be inferred that the keeper was in effect an official. Bishop Richard of Bury in 1338 appointed an official of the exempt jurisdiction of Allertonshire,[10] and in 1339 and 1344 addressed mandates to the official of his jurisdiction.[11] One reference in the register of Richard Kellaw is also found to a dean of the jurisdiction,[12] and this raises the question whether a rural dean was used as well as a keeper or official in the administration. There is no evi-

---

[1] *Durham Annals and Documents*, no. 84.

[2] Statutes for the franchise (see above, p. 94, n. 4), cap. 62, 'Statuimus etiam quod in singulis ecclesiis in Ebor' diocesi ad nostram visitationem spectantibus post susceptionem litterarum nostrarum de visitatione facienda, omnes cause tunc temporis mote et non terminate nostre discussioni, cum ad partes illas venerimus, reserventur' (fo. 8).

[3] Statutes for the franchise (see above, p. 94, n. 4), cap. 48, 'Ne sine archiepiscopi litteris vel nostris predicatores admittantur' (fo. 7).

[4] Above, pp. 89–91.   [5] See above, p. 94, n. 4.

[6] Cap. 7, '*Concubine sacerdotum frequenter moneantur* a rectoribus ecclesiarum nostre parochie qui sunt decani nostri *et precipue a sacerdotibus in quorum parochia commorantur*' (fo. 4). The original version (Poore, cap. 9) runs, 'Concubine sacerdotum frequenter moneantur ab archidiaconis'.

[7] *Registrum palatinum Dunelmense*, i. 187, 305, 353, 390; ii. 729.

[8] Ibid. i. 56.   [9] Ibid. i. 581.   [10] Ibid. iii. 217.

[11] Ibid. iii. 305; *Richard of Bury, Fragments of his Register*, p. 50.

[12] *Reg. pal. Dun.* ii. 724.

dence that the convent made use of rural deans as deputies to its official, and the area subject to the bishop was smaller than the monastery's share. But whereas the prior appointed local clergymen as his official, the bishop seems rather to have employed members of his *familia*, and the additional services of a dean may therefore have been required. The one reference is in a mandate to the dean or his deputy to sequestrate a church. This was work similar to that normally performed by the bishop's keeper, and, in the liberties of the convent, by the prior's official. Hence it is possible that we have here merely an archaic synonym for keeper or official; but the available episcopal documents relating to the administration of the franchise are so few, that no safe conclusion can at present be drawn.[1]

Master Thomas of Levisham, a clerk who had seen long service under the bishops of Durham,[2] was superseded as keeper by Master Henry de Alverton in 1311.[3] In 1313 Sir Robert of Brompton, chancellor and receiver of Durham and master of the hospital of St. James,[4] is found as keeper.[5] In 1314 Master William de Alverton was appointed keeper and official,[6] and in 1338 Bishop Richard of Bury gave a commission as official to his clerk of the same name,[7] who is found in 1340 as vicar of Aycliffe.[8] From these instances

---

[1] In York's peculiar of Churchdown the spiritual officer of the archbishop was called dean, warden (keeper), or official in the second half of the thirteenth century; but towards the end of the fourteenth century the duties of the dean and official were separated (A. Hamilton Thompson, 'The Jurisdiction of the Archbishops of York in Gloucestershire', op. cit., pp. 115–19).

[2] He had been a clerk of Bishop Robert de Insula (*Calendar of Patent Rolls*, *1277*, p. 202; *1283*, p. 185 n.; *Scriptores tres*, p. xcvi) and of Bishop Anthony Bek (*C.P.R.*, *1292*, pp. 504–5; *F.P.D.*, p. 183 n.; *Gesta Dunelmensia A.D. 1300*, p. 45). He is found in 1288 as rector of Stanhope and prebendary of Chester-le-Street; in 1301 he was master of Greatham hospital, and in 1310 prebendary of Osmotherley (*Fasti Dunelmenses*). He did not die in 1311, as stated in *Fasti Dunelmenses*; he was still acting for the bishop in 1315 (see below, p. 107, n. 2).

[3] *Reg. pal. Dun.* i. 56.

[4] Chancellor of Durham, 1313–14 (ibid. i. 454, 589), and receiver, 1313–15 (ibid. i. 468; ii. 762). He occurs as rector of Middleham (Yorks) in 1315, was appointed prebendary of Auckland in 1316, occurs as prebendary of Lanchester in 1315, and as master of the hospital of St. James in 1310, 1322, and 1326 (*Fasti Dunelmenses*).

[5] *Reg. pal. Dun.* i. 305, 353, 390.   [6] Ibid. i. 581.

[7] Ibid. iii. 217; he also received a mandate of the bishop in 1344 (*Richard of Bury*, p. 48). Cf. his employment in 1340 (*Reg. pal. Dun.* iii. 305).

[8] *Reg. pal. Dun.* iii. 289.

it appears that the bishop appointed clerks of his *curia* with local associations rather than incumbents of churches within the jurisdiction as his official. On two occasions special mandates were sent to the vicar of Northallerton,[1] presumably episcopal clerks in a church of the monastery. The bishop's official in the jurisdiction had a seal and rolls,[2] and his competence, despite his title, clearly extended over but a part of Allertonshire.

One commission of the officiality or keepership is extant,[3] and general powers are given, with special notice of competence in jurisdictional matters. The keeper or official sequestrated churches,[4] inducted presentees,[5] and held inquisitions relative to the defects of the edifices and ornaments of churches.[6] In 1339 Richard of Bury ordered the official to do justice to a man who had complained that his wife had been taken from him.[7]

Like the prior the bishop used special commissaries for hearing important suits and for other matters. In 1312 Bishop Richard Kellaw committed his powers to the keeper of the spirituality and the master of the hospital of Lazenby in the case between the prioress and nuns of St. Stephen's Foukeholm and the prebendaries of Osmotherley over the chapel and revenues of St. Stephen.[8] In 1315 Master Richard de Eryum, *jur. civ. prof.*, rector of St. Nicholas, Durham, had a commission for hearing a case touching the prebends in the church of Osmotherley.[9] In 1341 the mandate for inducting the master of Lazenby into corporal possession of the chapel and manor was sent to three persons, the vicar of Northallerton, the receiver of the manor, and a clerk.[10] Visitation, too, seems normally to have been performed by special commissaries. In 1315 the bishop appointed the same Master Richard de Eryum, now styled prebendary of Lanchester, as his deputy to visit his monasteries, hospitals, churches, and chapels, religious and secular persons of his jurisdiction,[11] and the duties of the keeper

---

[1] In 1316, *Reg. pal. Dun.* ii. 808; in 1341, ibid. iii. 409.
[2] Ibid. i. 56.   [3] Ibid. i. 581.
[4] Ibid. i. 305; ii. 724; *Richard of Bury*, p. 48.   [5] *Reg. pal. Dun.* iv. 123.
[6] Ibid. i. 353, 390; *Richard of Bury*, p. 50.   [7] *Reg. pal. Dun.* iii. 281.
[8] Ibid. i. 187.   [9] Ibid. ii. 737.   [10] Ibid. iii. 409.
[11] Ibid. ii. 739; cf. ii. 753.

were to cite attendance on the appointed days, and generally
to prepare for the visit.[1] During the visit Richard excommunicated the rector of Cowesby for contumacy and
sequestrated his benefice.[2] In 1316 the bishop ordered
Master Peter de Fyssheburne, vicar of Northallerton, to
absolve the rector from the sentence and to impose a suitable
penance, but not to relax the sequestration without a special
mandate. To aid Master Peter the bishop enclosed the
comperta of the visitation.[3] Hence it appears that the division
of authority in the liberties of St. Cuthbert had had little
effect on their nature, and that the two parts were similarly
governed.

By claiming archidiaconal powers the priors had consolidated their jurisdiction, but they had also limited it. In
the Evesham franchise of the Vale the abbey enjoyed
episcopal rights. It had its presentees ordained and instituted, its churches dedicated, and its chrism and holy oil
provided by a bishop of its own choice; it collected Peter's
Pence; and it had cognizance of matrimonial suits, a jurisdiction constantly denied to the archdeacon.[4] There is no
evidence that Durham convent ever aspired to such liberties.
Some archbishops were careful to safeguard their right of
institution by reservations and memoranda.[5] The emphasis
was laid on the oath of canonical obedience, and Archbishop
Thomas Corbridge took the precaution of having the proceedings recorded by a public notary.[6] There seem, indeed,
to have been cases of a presentee trying to evade archiepiscopal institution;[7] but these were probably due to the
laziness of the clerks. The priors appear to have been content with an archidiaconal jurisdiction, and to have maintained in this period a purely defensive attitude towards the
archbishops. Nor at this time do the bishops seem to have
aspired to powers much beyond those of an archdeacon.
They were careful, however, to avoid claiming an arch-

---

[1] Ibid. ii. 729.

[2] The custody of the sequestration was granted by the bishop to Mr. Thomas
of Levisham in October 1315 (ibid. ii. 753).   [3] Ibid. ii. 808.

[4] *Chronicon abbatiae de Evesham*, pp. 187, 194.

[5] Memoranda, *Reg. Romeyn*, ii. 41; *Reg. Corbridge*, ii. 132–4; reservation, *Reg.
Romeyn*, ii. 36.

[6] *Reg. Corbridge*, ii. 133.   [7] Cf. below, pp. 113–14.

deaconry, and so were left in a position to encroach should the opportunity arise.[1]

Relations between the archbishops of York and the franchisal authorities were relatively peaceful in the second half of the thirteenth century. None of the disagreements was of great moment; they were either due to the inevitable friction of jurisdictions, or incidental to some other quarrel. They do, however, further illustrate the administration and nature of the franchise.

An interesting conflict between the convent and the archbishop of York took place in 1272, which resulted in a full acknowledgement of the Durham rights of sequestration, inquisition, and induction. Archbishop Walter Giffard had shown himself rather uncertain in 1267 as to the position of the liberties, but his temper had been conciliatory. In 1272 he blundered badly, but not perhaps entirely through ignorance.

After the death of Sir Richard of Middleton, prebendary of Howden and rector of Hemingbrough, the convent presented Master Hugh of Evesham, later the famous cardinal, to the church, and Sir Robert Burnel, the friend of King Edward I, to Welton, which Hugh had resigned. On 18 August the archbishop directed the letter of inquisition to the dean of Christianity of Howden. This variation of terminology may have been innocent, but it caused the prior's official to ignore the mandate, and its execution was entrusted to the official of York, who was to give the presentees custody of the churches should the inquisition result in their favour.[2] To increase the injury, the official of York took advantage of the hold he had obtained on Hemingbrough to sequestrate the goods of the late Sir Richard and levy therefrom a debt owed to the archbishop. This naturally raised

---

[1] In 1840 the three peculiars, the episcopal peculiar of Allerton and Allertonshire, and the dean and chapter peculiars of Allerton and Allertonshire, and of Howden, Howdenshire, and Hemingbrough, which had not changed in area since the later thirteenth century, were apparently all on the same footing. See George Lawton, *Collectio rerum ecclesiasticarum de diæcesi Eboracensi; or collections relative to churches and chapels within the diocese of York* [and] . . . *diocese of Ripon*, pp. 5–6. The franchisal authorities possessed the right of granting probates and administrations of persons dying within the parishes and not having left *bona notabilia*, and the right of contentious jurisdiction.

[2] *Reg. Giffard*, p. 57.

a storm, and in January 1273 the archbishop began to give way, grudgingly and rather dishonestly. He informed his official that as he did not want a suit or contention to arise between him and the convent at that moment, the official was to relax the sequestration of Hemingbrough, and, *quasi sub dissimulationis umbra cautius transeuntes*, to proceed no farther on this occasion, but to request the keeper of the spirituality of Howden to maintain the sequestration under the form sent to the official.[1] The convent, however, appears to have refused the compromise, and in July the archbishop excommunicated certain persons, two of them relatives of the late rector, for violating his sequestration of the church.[2] But by November Walter Giffard had realized that his position was untenable, and he made full amends by revoking the sequestration, returning the money, and annulling all sentences. He acknowledged his error, and recognized the rights of the convent. 'We have learned', he wrote, 'that by the authority of certain authentic documents, which they have shown us, and of long-standing custom the sequestration of Hemingbrough and of all churches of their patronage in Howdenshire and Allertonshire pertains of right to the prior and convent.'[3]

In the sixties or seventies Adam of Darlington as proctor of the convent made appeals against the archbishop of York and his official, perhaps on different occasions. The circumstances of the disputes are unknown, for these are isolated documents; but the complaints are of interest. In each the proctor states the convent's right to jurisdiction in the liberties. He claims that the cognizance of spiritual cases, the visitation of churches, the correction of the crimes of priests, clerks and parishioners and men, and all other things which pertain to the *forum ecclesiasticum* belonged to the prior and convent of Durham by ancient, approved, and hitherto pacifically observed custom.

In the appeal against the archbishop of York, Adam protested against an archiepiscopal visitation of the liberties.[4] Nothing shows more clearly the relative strengths of Durham and York than the latter's restricted power of visitation.

---

[1] *Reg. Giffard*, p. 125.   [2] Ibid., p. 304.
[3] *Durham Annals and Documents*, no. 98.   [4] Ibid., no. 96.

Whereas the archbishops of Canterbury enforced their metropolitical visitations on the whole province in the course of the thirteenth century,[1] York was even opposed by the convent of Durham *sede vacante*, and was never able to secure the right of visitation *sede plena*.[2] The visitation of the Yorkshire franchise should have been less difficult, for there the archbishop's ordinary powers were concerned, and all the weight of the common law of the Church was behind his right to visit during a general visitation of his diocese. Yet there is no evidence that he had ever visited the liberties in the twelfth and thirteenth centuries.[3] In the later period this must have been a legacy from the ambiguous status of the franchise as a bishop's enclave, a status protected by appeals such as this; and the appeals, although doubtless regarded by the archbishop as 'frivolous, frustratory, unjust, null and invalid', seem nevertheless to have had the power to deter. Even so, the Durham position was anomalous, and must, if resolutely and persistently attacked, eventually give way.

The convent came to terms with the archbishop before 1328; but the provisions of the compromise are not available. A quarrel between the bishop and Archbishop William Melton in 1328, however, reveals the rival views.[4] In that year the diocesan decided to visit Allertonshire. Lewis de Beaumont prepared to resist, and naturally desired the convent to support him; but as Lewis had ridden roughshod over their own rights,[5] the monks refused to break their agreement with the archbishop. Thereupon the bishop undertook the defence of the whole of Allertonshire with an army he had raised. The archbishop retreated, waited

---

[1] I. J. Churchill, *Canterbury Administration*.

[2] W. H. Frere, *Visitation Articles and Injunctions of the Period of the Reformation* (Alcuin Club Collections, xiv, 1910), i. 84–6; A. Hamilton Thompson, *The English Clergy and their Organization in the Later Middle Ages* (1947), pp. 1–2.

[3] On 21 March 1311, *sede Dunelmensi vacante*, Archbishop Greenfield appointed a keeper of the spirituality of Allertonshire (*Reg. Greenfield*, v. 148), and on 21 April gave notice of a visitation of the spirituality, which actually took place. There is no evidence, however, that the convent's churches were visited, nor, as the bishopric was vacant, is it clear in what capacity the visitation was made; but, being so closely associated with the appointment of a keeper, it is probably to be regarded as a case of devolved jurisdiction.

[4] Robert de Graystanes, in *Scriptores tres*, p. 106.

[5] See above, pp. 41 and 46–7.

until the army had been disbanded, and renewed his claims.
Once more the army was summoned; once more the archbishop retired. Lewis at length saw that he was being
fooled, and confined his activities to the law courts.[1] He
claimed prescription against the archbishop on the grounds
that bishops of Durham had always visited, and the archbishops never. William Melton replied that the bishop had
no episcopal rights in Allertonshire: he did not institute or
destitute, confirm children or ordain clerks, and therefore
could not visit in connexion with such matters; to claim
prescription for visitation he must first prove prescription
for the *episcopalia*, which he could not. To this theory Lewis
objected that the exercise of episcopal powers and the
inquiry into their operation were two separate things; the
latter, for example, could be delegated to someone who was
not a bishop—and frequently was—while the former could
not. To dedicate a church and to inquire whether it was
properly dedicated were quite distinct operations; hence the
right of visitation could be obtained independently of the
exercise of *episcopalia* by prescription or privilege. Lewis
clearly had some clever advisers; but the armies and the
suit had been expensive, and, to the amusement of the monks,
the bishop finally made a compromise with the archbishop
similar to that secured earlier by the convent.[2]

This Durham dispute over visitation is not only remark-
able for its late enunciation of the more extreme claims of
an immunist against the diocesan, but also provides an
excellent example of that cheapening of alienated *episcopalia*
which occurred generally in the late twelfth and early
thirteenth centuries.[3] By surrendering procurations the
diocesan had virtually alienated to the immunist his right
to visit. But at a later date he reaffirmed his inherent
responsibility for the cure of souls and consequently his

---

[1] A résumé of part of the case is given in a papal brief, May 1330 (*Calendar of Papal Letters*, ii. 320).

[2] In 1331 Archbishop Melton confirmed the semi-episcopal powers of the arch-deacon of Richmond; but he safeguarded his right of visitation. See A. Hamilton Thompson, 'The Registers of the Archdeaconry of Richmond, 1361–1442', *The Yorkshire Archaeological Journal*, vol. xxv (1920), pp. 135–9; *Historians of the Church of York*, iii. 248–50.

[3] Cf. above, pp. 80 seqq. and below, p. 147.

hardly deniable right of visitation. Hence episcopal visitation was laid above the visitational right of the immunist, depressing this to a subordinate level. A similar process had occurred with the rights of the archdeacons proper.[1] *In episcopo ecclesia est.*

The other appeal made by Adam of Darlington, this time against the archbishop's official, probably represents a more legitimate grievance: it was lest he despoil the prior and convent of their rights and jurisdiction by summoning priests, clerks, and parishioners of the convent's vills and churches to plead before him as a result of a simple complaint.[2] The prior, as archdeacon, had a court of first instance in the liberties, from which lay an appeal to the archbishop or his official. It was a natural tendency for important litigants to try to jump the first stage; but the convent could not regard it with complacency. We have, fortunately, a good example of this practice from the archiepiscopal registers, and one which might easily have caused such an appeal. On 28 April 1280 Archbishop William Wickwane wrote to Master Adam de Fyleby, canon of Howden, ordering him either to readmit a woman, who had complained that he had unjustly repelled her from the Lord's table, to the sacraments, or to appear personally before him by such a day to explain the cause of his denial.[3] There might possibly have been a denial of justice in the archidiaconal chapter of the liberties, yet in that case one would have expected the archbishop to say so; more probably the woman had gone direct to the archbishop, and so deprived the prior's court of its jurisdiction. Such a practice was the cause of friction between many levels in the judicial hierarchy. It caused grave trouble between Archbishop John Pecham and his suffragans,[4] and it is not at all surprising to find an example of it here.

It is interesting to notice that this mandate to Master Adam de Fyleby was sent at the very time when the great quarrel between the convent and Archbishop William Wick-

---

[1] W. H. Frere, op. cit. i. 47–59. The similar, although not strictly analogous process, by which in the thirteenth century the archbishops of Canterbury superimposed their metropolitical visitation on the diocesan system, can be compared.

[2] *Durham Annals and Documents*, no. 97.   [3] *Reg. Wickwane*, p. 229.

[4] *Registrum epistolarum fr. J. Peckham*, ed. C. Tryce Martin (Rolls Ser.), i. 329.

wane was breaking out. In that same year the convent presented Master Adam de Barneby to the church of West Rounton, and the letter of presentation was undoubtedly on the usual model.[1] The archbishop, however, objected to the absence of *obedientia* in the greeting, and the monks protested, with justification as it seems, that they did not owe obedience to the archbishop, and had never included the word in their letters of presentation. This dispute was still developing when the bishop of Durham died and the archbishop decided to visit the diocese *sede vacante*. Certain of opposition from the convent, Wickwane gave way on the original dispute, and admitted Adam to West Rounton, lest a quarrel, in which he was clearly in the wrong, should prejudice the later and more important issue. Hence in the tedious lawsuit, which lasted until a compromise in 1286, the position of the Yorkshire churches was left unquestioned, and it was only the monks who sought to introduce the matter in order to prove that the archbishop was prejudiced and hostile.

The most general attack on the liberties in this period was made by Archbishop John le Romeyn; yet it sprang patently out of a much more limited dispute, and was only intended to put pressure on the convent. On 3 August 1289 the mandate to induct Thomas de Goldburgh to the prebend of Skipwith was sent by the archbishop to Master Adam of Darlington, the prior's official.[2] This was a special act of grace, for Thomas had not yet received institution, and the mandate for induction included a proviso that the presentee should go to the archbishop personally for institution within a competent time. Thomas had not attended by February 1290, and the prior's official received a mandate to cite him to appear, in which Romeyn rehearsed his acknowledged

---

[1] *Scriptores tres*, pp. 58 seqq.; 'Placitum' (*ut supra*, p. 83, n. 2). The form of address given in the 'Placitum', fo. 124, agrees with that appearing in a Durham formulary (*Durham Annals and Documents*, p. 234, mem. 3, no. 5), which is, 'Reverendo patri in Christo &c., archiepiscopo Ebor', Anglie primati, devoti sui T. prior et conventus talis ecclesie, salutem et tam devotam quam debitam cum omni honore reverenciam; alii ullo episcopo, sic: promtissimam cum omni devocione reverenciam; vel sic: et tam devotam quam debitam cum omni reverencia obedienciam.' The controversy was revived in 1428 (*Scriptores tres*, p. ccxvi), and John de Wessington wrote a memorial on the subject (ibid., p. cclxix).

[2] *Reg. Romeyn*, ii. 36.

right of institution. In June the official himself was cited to appear and answer for contempt and disobedience,[1] and in August the archbishop decided to put pressure on the monks. He had the prior and convent cited at Howden, Northallerton, and Durham to appear before him and reply to certain articles touching their churches. They were called upon to explain *inter alia* by what right they had appropriated Northallerton and Eastrington, and by what authority they had usurped visitation, correction, and other jurisdictional matters in the other churches, to the peril of their souls, the prejudice of the archbishop of York, and the scandal of many.[2] This must have stirred up the convent to have a few words with Thomas de Goldburgh, and in November 1291 the archbishop issued a commission for the hearing of the reasons alleged by Thomas and his brother Anthony why they should not receive canonical institution to their prebends.[3] This is the last trace of the incident, and it is likely that the whole affair blew over.

§ 5. *Retrospect*

A bishop's possessions in the diocese of another were usually privileged; but the eventual nature of the franchise was not predetermined. In some cases the area might become a detached portion of the owner's diocese, as with the Canterbury estates; but in Yorkshire the bulk of the franchise was assimilated approximately to an archdeaconry. When the relative strengths of the two parties are considered, this stunted development needs explanation. York, with its large but poor and imperfectly organized province, secured few metropolitical powers. Its uneasy supremacy over the Scottish sees provided no precedents for the subjection of the bishop of Durham, whose temporal powers produced exceptional independence; and though it naturally clung to its diocesan authority, it would appear to have been incapable of withstanding Durham encroachment had the

---

[1] *Reg. Romeyn*, ii. 38.

[2] Ibid. ii. 97. The fact that Romeyn questioned the appropriation of Northallerton, effected in the twelfth century (*F.P.D.*, p. 251; Farrer, op. cit. ii. 277, 281, 291; *Calendar of Papal Letters*, i. 47), shows that he had his tongue in his cheek. Cf. similar behaviour of Bishop Lewis de Beaumont (above, p. 42).

[3] *Reg. Romeyn*, ii. 39.

pressure been uniform and sustained. Durham, however, filched Crayke alone from the other diocese.

It is possible that the structure of the diocese of York contributed to this result. Its immense size and the unusual autonomy of some of its archdeacons[1] produced a loose texture in which the immunist may have found little incentive to strive for more radical powers. Within these conditions, if we disregard the concessions made by Bishop Hugh of le Puiset to Archbishop Roger of Pont l'Évêque—probably, indeed, more of a symptom than a cause—the fundamental reason can probably be found in the ever-increasing part played by the convent in the liberties. In proportion as the monks became the owners of the franchise, so did not only the possible claims of the immunists diminish but the episcopal interest in the maintenance of wider pretensions decrease. Howdenshire reacted on Allertonshire, and in Allertonshire itself, an area which geographically was easy to detach, the monks were there to disrupt the unity. Crayke, although deeply embedded in the alien diocese, was a purely episcopal estate; and its fate can be compared instructively with that of the convent's churches in the city of York. Thus the disharmony within the church of Durham seems to explain the history of its Yorkshire franchise. In one case, where the bishop's estates alone were involved, the immunity was developed to its logical conclusion; where bishop and convent were uneasy partners an archidiaconal franchise was secured; and where the convent was sole proprietor not even these lesser rights could always be retained.

1 The position of the archdeacon of Richmond was all but episcopal. He could perform every episcopal function except those inseparable from the bishop's order. See A. Hamilton Thompson, 'The Registers of the Archdeaconry of Richmond, 1361–1442', *The Yorkshire Archaeological Journal*, xxv (1920).

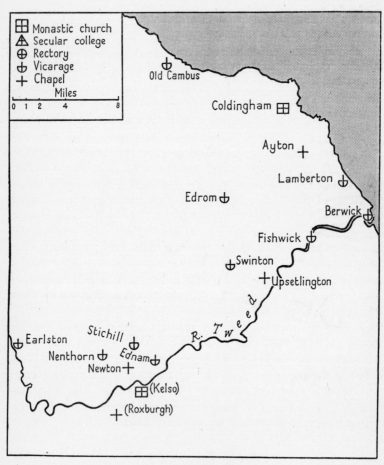

COLDINGHAMSHIRE

(The convent's churches)

III

THE LOTHIAN FRANCHISE
(COLDINGHAMSHIRE)

§ 1. *The Origin of the Franchise*

AT the end of the eleventh century the church of Durham acquired important estates in Lothian. The cultural ties of this area with Northumbria, of which it had once been part, and with the north of England in general, were strong; and occasionally in the eleventh and twelfth centuries, especially in 1107 when Earl David was given Cumbria and Lothian, and in 1195 when King Richard I planned the union of Lothian with Northumberland and Carlisle as an honour for his favourite nephew Otto of Brunswick, the future Emperor Otto IV,[1] it seemed that a buffer state, spanning the later border, might be established. But the Scottish monarchy, by depending increasingly on a Normanized Lothian, itself acquired some of the characteristics of a marcher power; and the chance long remained that it might detach from England the northern counties, and, perhaps in so doing, fall under the effective suzerainty of the Norman kings.[2]

Until the Norman conquest of England the Anglo-Saxon church had stood between the Celtic church of Scotland and the growing uniformity of western Christianity, and had weakened and absorbed the recurrent impulses from Rome and Gaul; but during the reign of Malcolm III (Canmore) (1057–93) the position was transformed. The English habits which Malcolm had learned as a youth at the court of Edward the Confessor were reinforced when he granted

---

[1] *Chronica R. de Houedene*, iii. 299, 308; cf. A. L. Poole, 'Die Welfen in der Verbannung' in *Deutsches Archiv für Geschichte des Mittelalters*, Heft 1, 2. Jahrgang 1938, pp. 145–6.

[2] For the historical background see Hume Brown, *History of Scotland* (1911); John Dowden, *The Medieval Church of Scotland* (1910) and *The Bishops of Scotland* (1912); Raymonde Foreville, *L'Église et la royauté en Angleterre sous Henri II Plantagenet* (1943), pp. 64–71. Cf. also Miss M. Morgan, 'The Organization of the Scottish Church in the Twelfth Century', *Trans. R. Hist. Soc.*, 4th ser., vol. xxix, p. 135.

asylum to Edgar Atheling and married his sister Margaret;
and the reformation of the English church under the guid-
ance of William and Lanfranc produced a situation in which
the reforming zeal of the new Anglo-Norman episcopate,
backed by the papacy, conspired with the political ambition
of the Norman kings to exert pressure on the northern
kingdom. Hence in the course of the next century the
Scottish state was re-established on the Anglo-Norman pattern and the Scottish church was reorganized on the common
western model. In this development Durham had its share.
Prior Turgot became the confessor of Queen Margaret, and
exercised an influence over her sons, three of whom were to
wear the crown.

Malcolm himself seems to have given no land to Durham;
but the circumstances in which his sons gained the throne
made them particularly indebted to their southern friends.
After Malcolm's death his brother Donald Ban seized the
crown during a reaction against English influence; and it
then became the policy of William Rufus to encourage and
the practice of Anglo-Norman adventurers to aid the cause
of the exiled princes. In 1094 Duncan (II), Malcolm's son
by his first marriage, who had lived long at the southern
court as a hostage, tried his chance, and during his brief
power granted estates by charter to Durham;[1] but the church
could hardly have taken possession before Donald Ban regained the throne. It was then the turn of Edgar, a son of
Malcolm and Margaret; and in 1095, while waiting in
England for an opportunity to invade, he gave by charter to
the bishop and monks of Durham two groups of vills, one
in East Lothian depending on Coldingham, and the other
in the Merse with Berwick at its head.[2] Two years later
Edgar Atheling with the connivance of William Rufus drove
Donald Ban from the throne, and set up his nephew Edgar.
The new king did not forget his promises to his friends.

In the eleventh century the population of the coastal plain
of East Lothian and the valley of the Tweed, which form a

---

[1] James Raine, *The History and Antiquities of North Durham*, &c. (1852) (henceforth *North Durham*), appendix, no. i.

[2] Ibid., no. vii; ibid., no. viii is a (?forged) variant. These two groups are clearly
examples of 'Northumbrian' shires. See J. E. A. Jolliffe, 'Northumbrian Institutions', *E.H.R.* xli (1926), 1–31.

crescent of rich land round the Lammermuirs, was reinforced by English settlers pushed north by the Danish and Norman invaders; and the country prospered.[1] Had the convent of Durham secured both the shires promised by Edgar in 1095, it would have been fortunate indeed. But the grant had been to the whole church of Durham; and when after Edgar's accession it was decided that the monks should re-colonize the ancient double monastery of Coldingham near St. Abbs Head, only that group of vills which depended on Coldingham was assigned for their maintenance, and even this was diminished temporarily by the withholding of Swinton.[2] Later, however, the endowment was increased; Swinton was given again by Edgar as dowry on the dedica-tion of the monastic church,[3] and a few vills from the Ber-wick group were also in time restored, Fishwick and Paxton before Edgar's death (1107)[4] and the two Lambertons before 1126.[5] These estates, known as the barony of Coldingham, or Coldinghamshire—although the ancient shire organiza-tion had been disrupted—were granted extensive feudal and public privileges by Edgar and his successors,[6] and must have been one of the most important possessions of the convent at this time. The priory of Coldingham was re-dedicated before its benefactor's death, and flourished. Although constitutionally it was completely dependent on Durham—a mere detached portion of the mother house, it alone of all the Durham cells developed a corporate life and tradition of its own. Its behaviour indeed was often unfilial.

It is unlikely that many parish churches were in existence at the beginning of Durham's rule in Lothian; but chapels were acquired or later built at Old Cambus, Ayton, Pren-derguest, Swinton, and Fishwick; and although the monks lost the vills of Berwick and Upsettlington, they kept the churches. The convent also benefited by private gifts. Thor Longus gave the church of Ednam before 1124,[7] and Gos-patrick II, earl of Dunbar, granted the vill of Edrom with

---

1 For evidence of colonial adventure cf. the case of Ednam (below, p. 125). Edgar granted Durham animals with which to stock Swinton (see below, p. 119, n. 3).

2 *North Durham*, no. ii; cf. also no. iii.   3 Ibid., no. iv; cf. also nos. x-xiii.

4 Ibid., nos. v and vi.   5 Ibid., nos. xv and xvi.

6 Ibid., nos. ii, iii, vii, ix, xv, xvi.   7 Ibid., nos. clxi, clxii; cf. no. cii.

its church before 1139.[1] With the acquisition of Ednam Durham influence reached deeply into the Merse, and clashed with the estates of the new abbey of Kelso, for a parochial system was but in formation, and the attachment of chapels was often hard to determine. Hence it was not until the second half of the century that Durham established its right to the chapels of Earlston, claimed for Ednam, and St. Lawrence, Berwick.[2] The chapel of St. Mary, Berwick, was acquired from King David I (1124–53) in exchange for the church of Melrose,[3] to which Durham had, apparently, acquired some title. From this summary it will be seen that the churches of the prior and chapter in Lothian fall historically into two groups, which will also have an ecclesiastical significance once the area is reorganized on the Roman model: the conventual church of Coldingham with its dependent chapels, and the other churches. The extent, however, to which Coldingham will be able to throw its shade over the churches on the annexed estates will depend not only on the development of those churches towards parochial status, but also on the relations between the priors of Durham and the bishops of St. Andrews.

The dominant influence on King Malcolm III and on his son Edgar had been English, and while English religious ideas had ruled at court little progress had been made with the reform of the Celtic church. After Edgar's death in 1107, however, there was a change in spirit. Edgar had decided that his brother Alexander should succeed him as king of Scots, but that the yet younger brother David should hold Cumbria and the greater part of Lothian with the title of earl. One of Alexander's first acts was to appoint Turgot, prior of Durham, as bishop of St. Andrews. This was the first breach in the line of Celtic bishops, and opened the way to the division of the kingdom into territorial dioceses. The reform, however, was hindered by the question of obedience. In 1072, as part of the compromise between Canterbury and York, Scotland had been placed within the province of the

---

[1] *North Durham*, no. cxi; cf. nos. xix, ciii, cv, dcxlii, xl, xli. For Gospatrick see *The Scots Peerage*, ed. Sir James Balfour Paul (1904, &c.), iii. 246–7.

[2] *North Durham*, nos. clxiv, cccclix, cccclx, cccclxi, dcxliii, clxv; nos. ccccliii, dcxliii, cccliv-cccclvi.

[3] Ibid., no. xviii.

northern metropolitan. The scheme was never popular in Scotland, and after Turgot's death in 1115 disputes over the profession of the bishops kept the see of St. Andrews vacant for more than ten years; so that not until a compromise was reached over the consecration of Robert, prior of Alexander's foundation at Scone, as bishop, could the fashioning of a new ecclesiastical system proceed apace. Hence David, not Alexander, was to be the real founder of the new monarchy and church in Scotland. David had surrounded himself with Normans and had built a feudal state in Lothian; and when in 1124 he succeeded his brother as king the reform of the church, which he had already started in his earldom, could be undertaken in the whole country.

No charter of Bishop Turgot to the convent of Durham is extant. In the absence of a diocesan system, of archdeaconries and rural deaneries and of a firm parochial organization, the priory must have had a free hand with its churches, and could have required no episcopal surrender in order to strengthen its rights as a proprietor. Thus even if Turgot had given the monks a charter its terms could have been of little value a few decades later. Shortly after Robert of Scone had at last been consecrated bishop, a church council was assembled at Roxburgh on 17 July 1127 under the presidency of King David to review the ecclesiastical position of the Durham estates in Lothian. Present at the synod were the archbishop of York, the bishops of St. Andrews, Glasgow, and Durham, and the abbot of St. Albans, and the prior and sub-prior of Durham who had been summoned to attend. There is no reason to think the principal members hostile to the convent. Although Robert of Scone was a regular canon, having migrated from Nostell in Yorkshire, he does not seem to have disliked Benedictines; and it is unlikely that the 'sore saint' wished harm to his brother's foundation. Nevertheless it is possible that king and bishop were intent on restoring order after the ecclesiastical anarchy of the last ten years, and on settling Coldingham's proper place in the new system they were devising.

Charters of the bishop of St. Andrews and of the king granted to Durham on this occasion have been preserved; but the former cannot be considered entirely authentic in its present form. King David says that the bishop freed the church of Coldingham from all episcopal custom and service saving episcopal obedience.[1] The episcopal charter is more elaborate. Robert says[2] that with the counsel of the king and the bishops present and for love of St. Cuthbert and fraternity with the Durham monks, he frees Coldingham from all claim, custom, *cana vel cuneveth*,[3] and all service. So far, except for the omission of the very important saving-clause, there is substantial agreement between the two charters. If we restore the omission, the privileges granted are reasonable and clearly authentic. The church of Coldingham was granted certain fiscal privileges; but, except in so far as it enjoyed the ordinary status of a convent, it was to be fully subject to the bishop. The episcopal charter then continues:

'Wherefore we wish, and by episcopal authority confirm, that the church of Coldingham, and all other churches or chapels which shall

[1] 'dicens et contestans se nullam consuetudinem, nichil iuris clamare super ecclesiam de Coldingham, sed velle et concedere ut ipsa ecclesia libera et quieta esset ab omni consuetudine et servitio, salva episcopali obedientia.' *North Durham*, no. xvii.

[2] 'ecclesiam de Collingham liberam et quietam inperpetuum tam a nobis quam a successoribus nostris ab omni calumpnia, consuetudine et Cana vel Cunevethe, atque ab omni servitio quod ad nos pertinet vel ad successores nostros', ibid. no. ccccxlvi.

[3] *Cana* and *cuneveth* have puzzled Scottish antiquarians, who, although seeing that they were some tribute or custom due to a superior lord, not necessarily ecclesiastical, were unable to discover the nature of the cess or its justification. See Cosmo Innes, *Lectures on Scotch Legal Antiquities* (1872), pp. 204–5, and John Dowden, *The Medieval Church in Scotland*, pp. 177–8. *Cáin* (plural *cána*) in Old Irish means 'law' or 'rule', and hence by extension the penalties incurred for infraction of the *cána*, and also the payments made to abbots of monastic churches as the heirs of the saints who had made the *cána*. See James F. Kenney, *Sources for the Early History of Ireland* (N.Y., Columbia Univ. Press, 1929), vol. i (ecclesiastical), p. 237. Thus there is a close resemblance between *cáin* and *consuetudo*. *Cáin* is clearly a generic term, and difficulty has been created by attempting to identify it with some specific burden. No comparison can be made with Irish usage in the eleventh and twelfth centuries, for the word is not used in the charters of the Book of Kells (cf. Kenney, op. cit., p. 754). According to Miss N. Neilson [*Customary Rents* (Oxford Studies in Social and Legal History, vol. ii. 1910), p. 15], both *cana* and *cuneveth* were food rents, the former a tribute due to important chieftains, the latter a purveyance right of princes and their households. It was, perhaps, because this franchise was secular that it alone escaped the wreckage of the convent's immunity. Besides obtaining freedom from these customs, the monks had plough-alms introduced in their favour. King Edgar with the assent of the men of Coldinghamshire established an annual payment of ½ mark of silver from each *carruca* (*North Durham*, no. iv).

henceforth canonically pertain to the church of St. Cuthbert, shall be free in perpetuity from all episcopal aid and *cana* and *cuneveth*, so that they shall be freer than any other churches of abbeys in Lothian. And we prohibit for the future any bishop, archdeacon or dean to exact any custom or aid whatsoever from them, unless they shall care to give gratuitously.'[1]

If this were completely genuine it would free all the convent's churches from any possible financial burden due at any time to any ecclesiastical official in the diocese. It is a surrender of the episcopal customs, and would create a franchisal jurisdiction. We have already seen that this charter has one unsatisfactory feature, and therefore more can be suspected. It will be noticed that if the phrase 'and all other churches and chapels which shall henceforth canonically pertain to the church of St. Cuthbert' were omitted and the grammar amended, the episcopal charter would be in harmony with the royal confirmation. If we infer that there has been an interpolation, it is easy to see why this should not have been made in both documents: the royal charter constituted no title to these rights in an ecclesiastical court.

Although charters referring to Lothian churches in the twelfth century are relatively common, it is difficult to discover the conditions which prevailed on the Durham estates, and discuss the charter of Robert in the light of them. The general situation in Lothian, however, is easy to establish. The reorganization of the church undertaken by King David was thorough; and, as it was achieved in so short a time, and on a ground so different that compromise could seldom be invited, anomalies and irregularities are rare. The surrender of episcopal customs, for instance, was most uncommon. The abbey founded by King David when earl at Selkirk in 1113, which moved to Kelso in 1126, was granted monastic

---

[1] 'Quare volumus et episcopali auctoritate confirmamus, quatinus ecclesia de Collingham et omnes ecclesie vel capelle, que amodo canonice ad ecclesiam S. Cuthberti pertinuerint, libere et quiete sint inperpetuum ab omni episcopali auxilio et Cana et Conevethe, ita ut liberiores et quietiores sint quam alique alie ecclesie abbatiarum que fuerint in Lothoneio. Et prohibemus ne aliquis amodo episcopus, archidiaconus vel decanus aliquam omnino ulterius consuetudinem vel auxilium ab eis exigat, nisi forte gratis dare voluerint', ibid. no. ccccxlvi.

liberties of the most extensive nature, and far greater than those allowed to Coldingham. Bishops John of Glasgow and Robert of St. Andrews freed the abbey from their control, so that any Scottish or Cumbrian bishop could be used for providing chrism and holy oil, ordaining the abbot and monks, and according any other sacrament.[1] The monastery depended directly on the pope,[2] and the abbot wore the mitre.[3] But this type of exemption has no bearing on jurisdiction over parishes,[4] and only one of Kelso's parishes is found to have large privileges. Bishop Joscelyn of Glasgow, in imitation of his predecessor Herbert (1147–64), freed the churches and schools of Roxburgh from all custom, 'that is to say from all synodals, and from all aids, hospitality and corrodies'.[5] The monastery of Scone also was privileged. Bishop Richard of St. Andrews, like his predecessors Ernald and Robert (1127–59), freed the monastery and its chapels from all exaction and episcopal custom,[6] which was later explained as freedom from synodals and aids.[7] Both these definitions omit the profits of jurisdiction, or the justice itself, which does not seem to have been granted in any case by the bishops of Glasgow and St. Andrews. The parish churches of Scone, however, were liable to the epi-

---

[1] Charter of Robert, *Liber S. Marie de Calchou*, ed. C. Innes (Bannatyne Club, 1846), p. 339; charter of King David, reciting the grant, ibid., p. 5; charter of same, mentioning John's grant, ibid., p. 9.

[2] See statement of Cardinal-legate John of Salerno, ibid., p. 329.

[3] Privilege granted by Pope Alexander III, ibid., p. 359.

[4] See Lemarignier, op. cit., pp. 131–7. The pleading in the Evesham-Worcester case (*Chronicon abbatiae de Evesham*) makes this abundantly clear; cf. also *Registrum Epistolarum fr. J. Peckham*, i. 74. For such exemptions, see Dom David Knowles, 'Essays in Monastic History; IV. The Growth of Exemption', *Downside Review* (1932), vol. 50, pp. 201–31, 396–436.

[5] 'ecclesias et scolas de Rokesb' burgo regis liberas et quietas ab omni consuetudine, scilicet ab omni redditu synodi, et ab omnibus auxiliis et hospiciis et conrediis, sicut bone memorie Herebertus, Glasg' episcopus, eisdem monachis carta sua confirmavit', *Liber S. Marie de Calchou*, pp. 318–19. For the other churches cf. the following charters which include reservations of the episcopal customs: ibid., pp. 61, 62, 326, 337, 345, and 346.

[6] 'excepta canonica de Scona et capellis ad eam pertinentibus, quas ab omni exactione et consuetudine episcopali volumus et concedimus esse exemptas', *Liber ecclesie de Scon*, ed. Wm. Smythe (Bannatyne Club, 1843), p. 31.

[7] Charter of Bishop William: 'ecclesiam suam de Scon, que hucusque a prestatione sinodalium et auxiliorum immunis fuit, quam decetero cum capellis suis et cum omnibus pertinentiis suis ab omnibus episcopalibus imperpetuum liberam volumus esse et immunem', ibid., p. 34.

scopal customs,[1] and so were those of Dryburgh[2] and Holy-rood.[3]

Throughout Lothian, then, only one parochial church has been found in the twelfth century undisputedly free from payment of customs to the bishop—Roxburgh; and it is always carefully distinguished from the rest of the Kelso churches. When seen against this background the charter of Bishop Robert to Durham appears quite exceptional.

Many of the original grants of the Durham churches together with confirmatory charters are extant. In the case of Fishwick, part of the benefaction of King Edgar, there is a separate quit-claim of Swaen, a priest, and probably the parson, who grants to Coldingham Fishwick with all its per-tinencies in land and water, half Prenderguest and other lands which he held.[4] King David granted St. Mary, Ber-wick, with the land, tithes, and all rights pertaining to it.[5] Edrom came with the vill and all its customs in churches, waters, and meadows.[6] Ednam was granted by the founder, Thor Longus, who states in his charters that King Edgar had granted him Ednam, then a waste, and that after he had settled it, he built a church from its foundations, which King Edgar dowered with one carucate of land, and had dedicated. This church with its carucate Thor granted to Durham.[7] The church of Earlston, in the twelfth century a chapel of Edrom, was originally granted with one carucate of land and all pertinencies to the abbey of Kelso by Walter de Lindsey.[8] It was later adjudicated to Durham by papal judges,[9] and so Walter's son, William, regranted the church to Durham, as far as he was competent *sicut dominus fundi*.[10]

It is clear that the grantors in all these cases were the

---

[1] Cf. episcopal charters in which the episcopal customs are reserved, ibid., pp. 26 and 31.

[2] Cf. charters of Bishops Robert and Richard, in which the episcopal customs are reserved, *Liber S. Marie de Dryburgh*, ed. John Spottiswoode (Bannatyne Club, 1847), pp. 9 and 174.

[3] Cf. charters of Bishop Robert, in one of which is included, 'salva dignitate et auctoritate episcopali', *Liber cartarum Sanctae Crucis*, ed. Lord Francis Egerton (Bannatyne Club, 1840), pp. 7, 10, 19, 207; 11; and charters of Bishop Richard in which the customs or episcopal jurisdiction are reserved, ibid., pp. 12, 15, 27, 209.

[4] *North Durham*, no. cvi.   [5] Ibid., no. xviii.   [6] Ibid., no. cxi.

[7] Ibid., nos. clxi, clxii, cii.   [8] Ibid., no. clxiv.

[9] Ibid., nos. cccclix-xi, dcxliii.   [10] Ibid., no. clxv.

founders or proprietors of the churches. As would be expected at the time the whole ownership of the church was transferred. The pertinencies and rights are, unfortunately, never defined in detail. Yet there is no mention of episcopal customs, and there is no evidence that the pertinencies went beyond the dowry, tithes, and all revenue normally appendent to churches.[1]

There are, however, references to the customs in some of the confirmations. According to Durham records Bishop Richard (1165–78) confirmed the chapel of St. Lawrence, Berwick, to Kelso free from all exaction and synodals.[2] Kelso surrendered it to Durham in 1171 with all things pertaining to it.[3] Richard then confirmed it to Durham. There are two versions of this sanction with identical witnesses, and one is said to have been granted in that synod of Edinburgh at which the convent secured episcopal approbation for many of its disputed titles. The first of these confirmations of St. Lawrence proclaims that Durham is to hold it in the same way as did the monks of Kelso;[4] the second confirms it as agreed between the two monasteries, free from all exaction and synodals.[5] From this it could be inferred that the freedom from exaction and synodals was among the *pertinentia* granted by Kelso and adhered to the church. There is no inherent improbability in there being two versions of the charter. The monks may have thought the first two vague, although they had secured the bishop's statement of Kelso's rights in the church, and asked for another. But there is also extant a third episcopal charter with the same witnesses, and given at the same synod, in which the convent's churches in Berwick, and this presumably included St. Lawrence, are confirmed, with lands, waters, tithes, and all other pertinencies *salvo iure episcopali et consuetudine.*[6] It is certainly difficult to harmonize these statements, and there appears to have been some tampering with the charters.

In some of the other confirmations bishops free the

---

[1] For these revenues and their lay ownership, see Paul Thomas, *Le droit de propriété des laïques sur les églises et le patronage laïque au moyen âge*, p. 25 and *passim*.

[2] 'liberam et quietam ab omni exactione et sinodalibus', *North Durham*, no. ccccliii.

[3] Ibid., no. dcxliii.

[4] Ibid., no. cccclv.

[5] Ibid., no. cccliv.

[6] Ibid., no. cccclvi.

churches from certain burdens. Bishop Robert (1127–59), who had settled the Coldingham privileges, confirmed in a synod at Berwick in 1150 Gospatrick's grant of Edrom, and also, at the prayer and counsel of various persons, recognized Durham's possession of Fishwick and Swinton.[1] The phrasing of the charter suggests reluctance, and neither are the churches accorded liberties nor are the episcopal rights reserved. One charter alone of Bishop Ernald (1160–2), a former abbot of Kelso, is extant, a confirmation of the church of Ednam with its chapels and rights, to be held as freely as under Bishop Robert, *salvo iure episcopali*.[2] Rather more charters of Bishop Richard (1165–78) have survived. Those referring to the Berwick churches have already been discussed. Two more, dated at the same Edinburgh synod, refer to Earlston. After the convent's title to this chapel had been vindicated before judges-delegate, Richard confirmed it to the monks, to be held as freely and quietly as other chapels in the diocese,[3] and, in the other confirmation, occurs the reservation *salvo iure episcopali et consuetudinibus nostris*.[4] He also confirmed Gospatrick's grant of Edrom, declaring that the monks were to hold the church free from all custom and exaction, *salvo iure episcopali*.[5]

The reservations *salvis episcopalibus* and *salvis consuetudinibus episcopalibus* appear to be interchangeable.[6] The variation *salvo iure episcopali*, by which the episcopal jurisdiction was safeguarded, seems to have been used when the recipient of the charter was not personally responsible for the payment of the customs. All three reservations meant

---

[1] Ibid., no. ccccxlix.   [2] Ibid., no. cccccli.   [3] Ibid., no. ccccclx.
[4] Ibid., no. ccccclxi.   [5] Ibid., no. cccclvii.
[6] Compare the following examples: Durham grant of a church in the diocese of St. Andrews, 1158×63, 'Et omnes episcopales consuetudines ipse [clericus] adquietabit' (ibid., no. dxxiii); Kelso concordat of 1201, 'Qui erunt vicarii perpetui, et suscipient curam animarum de manu episcopi, et respondebunt episcopis de episcopalibus; de procurationibus vero . . .'; the portion of the vicar must be sufficient 'ita tamen quod nullus sit defectus de episcopalibus' (*Liber S. Marie de Calchou*, pp. 327–8); Kelso presentation of a vicar to the bishop of Aberdeen, 1240, 'Et de omnibus episcopalibus, dictam ecclesiam contingentibus, [vicarius] plene respondebit' (ibid., p. 187); taxation of vicarages in the Holyrood churches by David, bishop of St. Andrews, 1251, 'vicarii vero dictarum ecclesiarum de honeribus ordinariis et consuetis, dictas ecclesias contingentibus, respondeant, exceptis procuracionibus nostris, de quibus dicti abbas et conventus nobis . . . respondebunt' (*Liber cartarum S. Crucis*, p. 63).

that the diocesan, or common law of the Church prevailed, and were fatal to a franchise.[1] It is incontrovertible, therefore, that the bishops of St. Andrews after Robert regarded the parishes of Ednam, Berwick, and Edrom as within the normal diocesan system; and from the evidence of the few administrative documents that have survived it can be proved that this was no idle claim. Bishop Richard safeguarded the episcopal customs when instituting a clerk to Edrom on Durham's presentation;[2] and Prior Thomas (1156–62) ensured that the clerk to whom he granted Ednam should be responsible for payment of all the customs and defray the expenses of the bishop should there be a dedication of the church.[3] As far as can be seen, then, the parish churches of Durham in Lothian were burdened with the episcopal customs in the middle of the twelfth century; but the liability fell on the rectors and not on the convent.

The position on the Coldingham estates, where several chapels come to notice in this period, including Old Cambus, which was to develop in the next century into a parish church, is not known. We may assume, however, that these chapels were still covered by the immunity of the priory church.

From the whole of this evidence it is clear that either the terms of Bishop Robert's charter of 1127 were disregarded, despite the solemnity of their promulgation, or the section which purports to give privileges to Coldingham and all

---

[1] In the reservations, *ius episcopale* can be understood as *jurisdictio episcopalis*. The counsel in the lawsuit between the abbey of Evesham and the bishop of Worcester, which concerned the exemption of the monastery and its franchisal jurisdiction over the churches of the Vale, used the terms indifferently when arguing the case before the pope in 1205–6 (*Chronicon abbatiae de Evesham*, cf. p. 185). That such a reservation was fatal to a franchise is amply proved by the settlement of the Evesham case by arbitrators in 1248–9. Cf. the terms concerning the church of Morton and the abbey's confirmation: ordinance—'ecclesiam de Mortone et ejusdem parochianos episcopo Wigornensi . . . decrevimus lege diocesana perpetuo subjacere . . . Et idem vicarius onera episcopalia et archidiaconalia que fuerint sustinebit . . . in ceteris autem ecclesiis et capellis villae et vallis Evesham et earum parochianis . . . nec ipse nec aliquis successorum suorum jurisdictionem sibi de cetero possit vendicare'; confirmation—'Concessimus etiam praefato episcopo et successoribus suis quod episcopali jurisdictione secundum tenorem ordinationis memoratae in ecclesia de Morton et ejusdem parochianis perpetuo possint libere uti' [T. Nash, *The History and Antiquities of Worcestershire* (1782), ii. 179].

[2] *North Durham*, no. cccclxxii.

[3] 'Et omnes episcopales consuetudines ipse adquietabit . . . Et si dedicatio contigerit de eisdem capellis despensam episcopalem inveniet', ibid., no. dxxiii.

the churches was entirely or in part an unwarranted insertion by Durham. The former hypothesis is not impossible, for some of Durham's acquisitions were remote, and the assertion of such privileges in respect of them may have been administratively inconvenient. Yet if the position be considered in its entirety—the disharmony between the episcopal and the royal charters, the rarity of such grants, and the inefficacy of the terms—the latter hypothesis is to be preferred. At the time of the reorganization of the Scottish church Durham secured no great privileges for its churches other than Coldingham, and in the first half of the twelfth century probably had little desire for them.

§ 2. *The Concordats with the Bishops of St. Andrews,* 1193–1204

By the first quarter of the twelfth century the ownership of *episcopalia* by immunists could have been profitable only in certain cases. If a church was remote and feudalized, the immunist obtained little more from the customs than payment for his administrative duties. In the middle of the twelfth century the rector of Ednam, besides having to render the episcopal customs to the bishop, was also made liable to give the prior and monks hospitality should they pass.[1] This probably represents the *albergaria* due to the owner of a church;[2] and with this the convent may hitherto have been content. Durham's interest in its franchisal rights and claims was, however, quickened when appropriation became its settled policy, for these would give the monastery a firmer hold on the temporalities of the churches. Moreover, when it became necessary to reallot the responsibility for the payment of the customs between vicar and appropriator, there was the temptation to repudiate the burden altogether so as to increase the value of the church. The fundamental urge which underlay these diverse attitudes was the desire of the proprietor of churches to change his ownership into new forms, so as to be able to withstand the increasing episcopal attacks on such corollaries of *Eigenkirchentum* as the private custody of vacant churches. This pattern of

---

[1] 'convenientia eis hospitia et necessaria inveniet', ibid., no. dxxiii.
[2] See Paul Thomas, op. cit., p. 68.

events, which shows so clearly in the history of the liberties within the diocese of Durham, is almost equally apparent in the history of the Lothian franchise. The churches of Earlston, Ednam, Swinton, Edrom, and Old Cambus were appropriated towards the end of the twelfth century,[1] and the process was preceded by an assertion of franchisal claims and accompanied by disputes over them.

All that was necessary in order to justify a franchise in Lothian was to extend the application of the privileges genuinely granted to Coldingham to all the parish churches. So an interpolation was made in Bishop Robert's charter of 1127.[2] The exhibition of this composite document took place apparently between 1157 and 1178. In 1157 Durham secured a comprehensive privilege from Pope Adrian IV, in which the position of the Lothian churches was reviewed. No episcopal charter is quoted. The privilege recognizes that the church of Coldingham and all other lands held beyond the Tweed should be free from the unjust exaction of *cuneveth* and other things by the king and other persons, as granted and confirmed by the kings of Scotland in their charters.[3] This reveals a desperate state of affairs. The amended privilege of Bishop Robert was, however, available by the pontificate of Alexander III (1159–81), from whom at least two confirmations of it were secured, neither of which can be dated exactly.[4] One of these confirmations was

---

[1] Bishop Roger de Beaumont recognized that some churches had been appropriated before 1198 (*North Durham*, no. ccclxvii). The exact dates of the individual appropriations are uncertain. Edrom was a vicarage under Prior Thomas (1156–62) (ibid., no. dxliii). Ednam, however, was still a rectory under that prior (ibid., no. dxxiii), and Earlston under Prior German (1162–86) (ibid., no. dxxiv). But the latter and also Swinton were vicarages at the time of Prior Bertram (1188–1212) (ibid., nos. dxxxiii and dxxvi). Old Cambus was a vicarage during the priorate of Ralph (1214–33) (ibid., no. dxli; cf. nos. cxcii, ccl, ccxcvi, ccxcvii, ccxcix, ccclxxi). Berwick was appropriated by 1253 (ibid., no. ccxxxviii), Lamberton by 1271 (ibid., nos. ccccxiii, ccccxxx), and Stichill by 1272 (ibid., no. ccxl).

[2] See above, pp. 121–3.

[3] 'Paci uero et tranquillitati ecclesie uestre in posterum prouidere uolentes decernimus, ut Collingamensem ecclesiam et totam terram, quam habetis ultra Tuedam, secundum quod in cartis donationis et confirmationum regum Scotie legitime continetur, sine regis uel quarumlibet personarum grauamine et exhactione iniusta in coneueth uel in aliis quietam et liberam habeatis', W. Holtzmann, *Papsturkunden*, ii, no. 94.

[4] 1160 × 78: 'Innotuit nobis ex scripto, quod nobis est presentatum, quod bone memorie Robertus quondam episcopus sancti Andree ecclesie uestre . . . ecclesiam

also reissued by Pope Urban III in 1186.[1] In this way Durham obtained papal recognition of the freedom of all its churches in the diocese of St. Andrews from all claim and custom, *cana* and *cuneveth*, and all service due to the bishop. In one of the privileges the immunity from the demands of the archdeacons and deans is also specifically mentioned. But papal privileges were of little value unless the charters they confirmed were accepted by the diocesans, and the bishops of St. Andrews seem either to have given no credence to the amended charter of Robert or to have maintained that it was inefficacious through disuse.

In Lothian towards the end of the twelfth century occurred a struggle between the convent and the bishops similar to that which took place in the diocese of Durham at the same time, except that it was waged with less acrimony in the north where the complications of prestige and domestic rivalry were absent. For our knowledge of these disputes we are almost entirely dependent on the agreements by which they were settled.[2] Two concordats were negotiated between Durham and St. Andrews, the first in 1193,[3] while Roger de

de Coldingham cum ecclesiis et capellis in eius episcopatu ad uos pertinentibus ab omni calumpnia et consuetudine, cana et cuneued et ab omni seruitio liberam et quietam prompta liberalitate concessit et scripto proprio roborauit' (ibid., no. 165). This is an extension of the first part of the charter (cf. p. 122, n. 2). 1159×81: 'Propositum est siquidem nobis ex parte uestra, quod bone memorie Robertus quondam episcopus sancti Andree ecclesie de Coldingham et aliis ecclesiis et capellis uestris, quas infra episcopatum sancti Andree habere noscimini in Lodoneio, huiusmodi contulit libertatem, ut a can et conuethe et ab omni exactione episcoporum et archidiaconorum uel decanorum libere sint omnimodis et quiete' (ibid., no. 202). Here we have a paraphrase of the middle and suspect portion of Robert's charter (cf. above, p. 123, n. 1).

It is noticeable that in none of the confirmations of the title to individual churches obtained from Pope Alexander III is there a reference to franchisal rights. Cf. ibid., nos. 203 (Berwick), 205 (Swinton), 206 (Ednam with chapel of Earlston), and 208 (Earlston).

[1] Ibid., no. 241—based on no. 165.

[2] *Ante* 1187 the abbots of Rievaulx, Melrose, and Byland and the prior of Newburgh attested the charters of liberties granted by Bishop Robert, King David, and Pope Alexander III [Holtzmann, no. 165] (*North Durham*, no. dviii), and *post* 1186 the abbot of Alnwick, the priors of Newburgh and Brinkburn and Bernard the bishop's clerk attested the same privileges with the addition of that of Pope Urban III [Holtzmann, no. 241] (*North Durham*, no. dix). In the former authentication the abbot of Melrose says that he has examined the documents privately and has also afterwards heard them recited before the judges-delegate. The latter transcript was sent to the pope 'in the case against the bishop of St. Andrews' (*North Durham*, no. dcix). [3] *North Durham*, no. cccclxii.

Beaumont was bishop-elect, the second in 1204,[1] two years
after the translation of his successor, William Malvoisine,
from Glasgow. We can also compare a settlement of similar
quarrels between the abbey of Kelso and the bishops of St.
Andrews and Glasgow secured by the papal legate, John of
Salerno, cardinal-priest of St. Stephen in Caelio Monte, in
1201, during the lifetime of Bishop Roger.[2] The prologue
to the first Durham concordat merely informs us that there
had been a long-standing controversy between the parties
over the liberties of the monks' churches in Lothian. The
heading of the royal confirmation refers to peace made over
Can and *Coneveth*.[3] The papal confirmation calls it an agreement over procurations.[4] The Kelso dispute is said to have
been *super institutionibus ecclesiarum*.[5] The prologue to the
second concordat is more explicit, and states that there had
been contention over *can* and *cuneveth*, procurations and
hospitality, custody and institution, and procession and visitation[6]—in fact over the episcopal customs and some other
matters.

From the terms of the concordats it is clear that the main
points at issue were the conditions under which the convent
could appropriate, the monks' right to have the custody of
their churches during vacancies, and the possession or incidence of the episcopal customs. As the two monasteries
were engaged in disputes with the episcopal authorities of
two Scottish dioceses at the same time, it appears that the
way in which monks were appropriating had provoked con-
certed opposition from the ordinaries. It may be surmised
that the bishops were claiming the superintendence of the
operation so as to ensure that the vicars were properly endowed and responsibility for payment of the customs was
not repudiated. In the case of Durham there were additional
grounds for dispute arising out of its production of the

---

[1] *North Durham*, no. cccclxxiii.

[2] *Liber S. Marie de Calchou*, p. 327; Wilkins, *Concilia*, i. 509.

[3] *North Durham*, no. lii.

[4] 1191 × 8, W. Holtzmann, *Papsturkunden*, no. 292.

[5] *Liber S. Marie de Calchou*, p. 329.

[6] 'Super Can et Coneveth et procurationibus et hospiciis et custodiis et institu-
tionibus ecclesiarum ad predictos priorem et conventum Dunelmens' in episcopatu
S. Andree pertinentium, et processione et visitatione earundem ecclesiarum',
North Durham, no. cccclxxiii. Cf. also royal confirmation, ibid., no. liii.

amended charter of Bishop Robert and its tenacious assertion
of archaic claims to the control of the temporalities of its
vacant churches. The quarrel between Kelso and the diocesans was *super institutionibus ecclesiarum*. There *institutio*
may mean position or arrangement, for *dispositio* and *institutio* are commonly paired;[1] but in the Durham case, as
institutio is coupled with *custodia*, it can hardly be understood otherwise than in the sense of induction—*institutio
corporalis*.

The monks were also engaged in great quarrels with the
bishops of Durham over custody and induction at this very
time; and were entirely unsuccessful.[2] Their prospects were
even worse in Scotland. Owing to the spread of reform in
the Church it was useless by the end of the twelfth century
to assert claims to these relics of proprietary rights, now
considered episcopal rights, unless the claimant possessed
a jurisdiction, ordinary or franchisal, for which they might
reasonably be claimed by special custom;[3] because it was
only in those circumstances that the true origin of the rights
could be overlooked, and the inherent rights of proprietors
be disguised as alienated *episcopalia*. In the diocese of St.
Andrews the convent was not in general possession of the
episcopal customs, although it was exhibiting a spurious
surrender of them, and it certainly had not created an archidiaconal franchise.

It cannot be without significance that here, as in the
diocese of Durham, the conflict over custody and induction
should have been associated with appropriation. Each stems
basically from the same conception of ownership. With custody the proprietor enjoys the fruits of his property during
a vacancy; with induction he invests the priest with the
temporalities; with appropriation he takes the larger part of
the property into his own hands. Custody gave the owner
a firm hold on the church, and allowed him to appropriate

---

[1] Cf. bull of Pope Alexander III to Durham, 1164, 'ut decedentibus personis
ecclesiarum uestrarum liberam . . . dispositionem et institutionem . . . habeatis'
(W. Holtzmann, *Papsturkunden*, ii, no. 119); charter of Bishop Hugh of Durham,
1188 × 95, 'Sciatis nos concessisse . . . liberam disposicionem et institucionem et
personatum omnium ecclesiarum' (*Durham Annals and Documents*, pp. 146–7).

[2] See above, pp. 22 seqq.

[3] Cf. the position in Howdenshire and Allertonshire; see above, pp. 108–9.

more easily. Indeed, appropriation carried out as an administrative act by the owner can be regarded as self-induction into possession of the parsonage of which the appropriator had had the custody since the avoidance of the church. If the bishop desired to strengthen his control over the temporalities of the parish churches, then he must try to destroy these vestigal proprietary functions.

It is clear that at the end of the twelfth century the bishops in northern England and southern Scotland were becoming conscious of their responsibilities towards the maintenance of a satisfactory parochial system. In 1198 Bishop Roger de Beaumont had obtained from Pope Innocent III a mandate to restrain monks and canons regular from appropriating to their own uses churches to which they had the presentation, unless such churches were exempt from his jurisdiction.[1] But in the next year he gave the monks of Durham permission to appropriate at will.[2] The convent had similar charters in respect of their churches in the diocese of Durham. Yet appropriation without the express consent of the ordinary was by this time contrary to the common law of the Church,[3] and Bishop William may have repudiated the privilege of his predecessor. If so, he made amends in 1204, for the terms of Roger's charter of 1199 are repeated in the concordat: churches may be freely appropriated, and the vicars are to be presented to the bishop for admission, and are to be subject to his jurisdiction, saving the immunities granted. Nothing is said in the concordats on the subject of custody and induction. We know that the convent did not possess these rights after the agreements; but we cannot tell to what extent the monks had possessed, or even claimed them in the preceding century.

The other matters at issue were settled without much heed to the convent's wider claims. The position of Coldingham was reviewed in both agreements. In 1193 the bishop granted that Coldingham and its chapels should be free in perpetuity from *can* and *cuneveth*, procurations and hospitality, synodals, aids, and all other exactions and payments due to the bishop

---

[1] *Calendar of Papal Letters*, i. 5. [2] *North Durham*, nos. cccclxvii, cccclxix.
[3] Cf. reply of Pope Innocent III to the bishop of Ely in 1204, Migne, *Patrologia latina*, vol. 215, coll. 481-2.

and his successors and to all the officials of the bishopric, saving only canonical justice and obedience.[1] This was repeated verbatim in the agreement of 1204,[2] and is quite unambiguous. The position of 1127 is maintained, the exemptions given in more detail, and the saving-clause strengthened without changing its nature. Coldingham was not to pay a penny to the bishop or to any inferior ecclesiastical official; but it was subject to the bishop, and enjoyed no jurisdictional rights. One other controversy was settled in 1204, the liability of the monks to welcome the bishop with a procession. It was characteristically agreed that the prior and monks of Coldingham were to receive the bishop *processionaliter* once after his consecration, and whenever he should return from across the sea, but that no procuration fee was to be paid.

There was, therefore, little change in the status of the cell during the twelfth century, nor, as will be seen, in the thirteenth. The parish churches received less favourable treatment. In 1193 they are freed from *can* and *cuneveth* and from episcopal procurations and hospitality.[3] Their relations with the officials of the bishopric are defined as the same as those of the parishes of the abbot of Kelso, or of any other abbot 'qui liberius et melius tenet in episcopatu S. Andree'. In a similar way it is stated that the monks shall answer to the bishops for their parish churches when a common aid is imposed on the whole bishopric in the same manner as other abbots or priors who freely hold churches in the bishopric.

The position of the Kelso churches within the diocese of St. Andrews up to the episcopate of Bishop Roger de Beaumont has already been indicated. From an examination of the terms of the episcopal confirmations their status seemed,

---

[1] 'quod ecclesia sua de Coudingham cum capellis ad eam pertinentibus libera sit et quieta imperpetuum a Can et Cuneveth et procurationibus et hospiciis, et omnibus aliis exactionibus et synodalibus et auxiliis et omnibus aliis tam a nobis quam a successoribus nostris, et ab omnibus officialibus episcopatus S. Andree, salva tantum canonica iusticia et obedientia', *North Durham*, no. cccclxii.

[2] Ibid., no. cccclxxiii.

[3] 'Similiter quod omnes alie ecclesie sue parrochiales, que sunt in episcopatu S. Andree, libere sint et quiete inperpetuum a Can et Cuneveth et procurationibus et hospiciis tam a nobis quam a successoribus nostris, nisi gratis facere voluerint', loc. cit.

as implied by the concordat, similar to that of the Durham churches: certainly for the most part bound to render the episcopal customs to the bishop, and, in consequence, probably within the ordinary administration of the diocese. The terms of a confirmatory charter of Bishop Roger to Kelso, however, leave no room for doubt. It is expressly stated therein that the churches are subject to archdeacons, officials, deans, and other servants of the bishop.[1] We do not know whether this instrument is earlier or later than the Kelso agreement of 1201; but they both express the same idea. In the concordat, affecting equally the bishoprics of St. Andrews and Glasgow, and settled in the presence of the papal legate to Scotland, it is agreed that Kelso may appropriate its churches, and that the vicars are to be burdened with the episcopal customs. They are to pay procurations on the Lateran Council scale when bishops, archdeacons, or deans visit them, and their share in the revenue of the church is to be adequate for the proper acquittal of these charges. But the tenure of the perpetual vicars already in possession is safeguarded, which suggests that previously in some cases the monks and not the vicars had paid the customs. The churches of Roxburgh, in the diocese of Glasgow, are expressly exempted from these terms, and remain free from the episcopal customs.[2] The impression gained from this agreement is that the incidence of the episcopal customs, rather than the ownership of them, was the cause of the strife, and that the general conditions behind the quarrel were the dislocations caused by appropriation.

The equation of the position of the Durham and Kelso churches in 1193 may have rendered the concordat void through uncertainty owing to the dispute between Kelso and the diocesan, and it is not surprising that the settlement of the Kelso dispute in 1201 should have been followed by a new concordat between Durham and St. Andrews in 1204. In this agreement the status of the parochial churches is defined in much greater detail than before. As in 1193 they

---

[1] 'Quare volumus et precipimus archidiaconis, officialibus, decanis et aliis ministris nostris, in quorum administracione predicte ecclesie predictorum monachorum sunt, . . .', *Liber S. Marie de Calchou*, p. 61.

[2] Ibid., pp. 327–8.

are to be exempt from *cana* and *cuneveth*, and from episcopal visitation fees. The liability of the monks to a common aid from their churches is still equated to that of any prior or abbot *qui liberius tenet in episcopatu*. For the first time the bishop states explicitly that he may visit both Coldingham and the parochial churches during a general visitation of the diocese, although from none of them will he exact any procuration fee or substitute whatsoever. Then comes the main change. It is decreed that when the episcopal officials shall pass through the parishes with three to five horses, once in a year the churches shall give them hospitality, and it may be assumed that the bishop's officials, or *officiales S. Andree episcopatus* as they are elsewhere termed, are the archdeacons and rural deans. However, to soften the blow, William exempted, for his lifetime only, three churches, Old Cambus, Lamberton, and Fishwick, from the necessity of paying procuration fees to officials. After his death the three were to revert to the position obtaining before his promotion, and, as a matter of fact, Old Cambus paid these procurations in the later thirteenth century.[1]

Even after the second attempt at definition some loose ends were left. Nevertheless a great deal had been settled. The principle clearly enunciated by the bishop was that the churches were subject to the ordinary jurisdiction of the diocese, and burdened with its expenses. But two concessions are made: the bishops will not demand procurations from any church, nor will the officials from three churches for a specified period. The bishop's grant, however, was paid for. In 1193 the convent granted to the church of St. Andrews in return for the concession the chapel of Nenthorn, and in 1204 another of Ednam's chapels, Newton. These chapels were to be appropriated on the death of the parsons, and, until Newton fell vacant, Durham was to pay the bishop fifteen marks annually.[2] It is certain that these chapels were granted expressly in return for the freedom from episcopal procurations, for in Boiamund de Vicci's valuation of 1275 the church of Nenthorn is listed as belonging to the bishop *pro procurationibus suis*, and is valued at £33. 6s. 8d., while the

---

[1] See below, p. 139.
[2] See the concordats, loc. cit.

vicarage was worth £10. Newton, still conserving its status of a chapel, does not occur.[1]

The temporary exemption of three churches from the procurations of the officials can be regarded as a compromise on the wider claims of Durham; and it will be appreciated that the convent obtained little in return for its surrender of Bishop Robert's charter. Old Cambus and Lamberton, as chapels of Coldingham, had originally been free from the financial claims of the bishops and their subordinates. The former was at the time of the agreements almost, if not quite, of parochial status. Fishwick was among the earliest endowments; but the reason for its selection in 1204 may have been geographical. The exempted area formed the coastal strip of East Lothian.

Thus after the concordats the only real franchise left to the parish churches was freedom from *cana* and *cuneveth*. If we add the still remaining chance of freedom from common aids, it will be seen that this was not an unfair statement of the true position. Little credence had been given to the unsatisfactory portion of Bishop Robert's charter of 1127; freedom from aids was the only item which later bishops could, and then with reservation, accept.

Between 1193 and 1204 the bishops of St. Andrews won a decisive victory over the monastery of Durham. The monks were left with no more privileges than they had originally been granted. At the same time they, like all proprietors of churches, had suffered diminution of their rights through modifications in the conception of ownership. Moreover, whereas at the beginning of the twelfth century the possibilities of aggrandizement were great, in 1204 the convent had no claims to a franchise as of right. It stood to lose rather than gain.

§ 3. *Coldinghamshire after the Concordats*

The Coldinghamshire franchise in 1204 was inconsiderable: freedom from *cana* and *cuneveth*, the temporary freedom of three churches from the financial claims of archdeacons and

---

[1] *The Priory of Coldingham*, ed. Jas. Raine (Surtees Soc., vol. 12), appendix, no. lxx. For this assessment, see *Concilia Scotiae*, 1225–1559, ed. Joseph Robertson (Bannatyne Club, 1866), vol. i, pp. lxv–lxvii. See also below, p. 139.

rural deans, and a purchased immunity from episcopal procurations. No administrative functions were left in Durham's hands.[1] It seems that the concordats were respected in the thirteenth century; but Durham's position deteriorated in the fourteenth.

It is probable that a fresh agreement was secured from each new bishop of St. Andrews,[2] but it is unlikely that there was much change in the terms. Few thirteenth-century documents with bearing on our problems are available, and there are not many illustrations of the working of the concordat. In 1204 three churches had been freed from the procurations of the officials for the bishop's lifetime on condition that they then reverted to the position obtaining at his accession. In one case at least this meant that the church was not permanently exempt. A valuation of the church of Old Cambus, presumably an example of Boiamund de Vicci's assessment of 1275, notes that the vicar is burdened with archidiaconal procurations and with synodals.[3] Another document shows the prior of Durham's duty of attending the synods of the diocese.[4] On the other hand, there are illustrations of the freedom from episcopal visitation fees. Bishop David de Bernham dedicated the chapel of St. Nicholas at Berwick in 1240,[5] and issued a certificate protesting that he had conserved the convent's rights intact, and that no prejudice was to arise from the dedication. The document is headed 'David's letter that nothing should be exacted from Coldingham for the dedication of a church.'[6]

---

[1] In 1221 the chapter of the Merse was held at Ednam, and in 1268 the vicar of Swinton is found acting as dean of Christianity of the Merse, which shows that the clergy of the monastery's patronage were performing their share of the ordinary diocesan duties (*Liber S. Marie de Calchou*, no. 254 and i. 236).

[2] An extract from a concordat which is not extant is quoted by Durham in 1260 (*Durham Annals and Documents*, p. 112). Bishop William Fraser confirmed the 1204 agreement in 1295 (*North Durham*, no. ccclxxxiv), and Bishop James Bennet confirmed an agreement 'super Cane et Coneweth, procurationibus, hospiciis, auxiliis &c.' in 1329 (ibid., no ccccxciii).

[3] 'De quibus oportet eum [*sc.* vicarium] solvere stipendium clerici, procura*tiones* archidia*coni* et sinodalia', ibid., no. cxciii.

[4] 1310, mandate of Bishop William de Lamberton to the official of the archdeacon of Lothian to cite the prior of Durham, who had failed to attend the synod of the church of St. Andrews, to appear before the said bishop, &c. (ibid., no. ccclxxxix).

[5] 'Hec sunt ecclesie quas dedicavit episcopus David', *Concilia Scotiae*, 1225–1559, p. ccxcviii.

[6] *North Durham*, no. ccclxxviii.

The inconvenient journey forced the bishop to seek hospitality at Coldingham, and in consequence he issued another certificate to the effect that he had been received of charity, and that it was not to prejudice the composition of 1204.[1] The same thing happened in 1242, when David had to visit Berwick to reconcile the parish church of St. Trinity,[2] and another letter of indemnity was granted to the cell.[3] There are also extant similar certificates of Bishop William Fraser dated 1286 and 1288.[4] These facts suggest that the concordat was working fairly satisfactorily; but at least one unjustified, and probably unsuccessful, attempt of a bishop to interfere in the internal affairs of the cell[5] is symptomatic of the trend of events.

Conditions grew worse in the fourteenth century. There is evidence of old controversies being revived, and of a movement to deprive the monks of the last privileges they possessed. With the wars between England and Scotland the position of Coldingham became most difficult. Scottish clerks were reputed to have been deprived of their English benefices, and all that Durham could have hoped for on the ecclesiastical side was to salvage its patronage.

About a decade after the turn of the century, William de Lamberton, the bishop of St. Andrews who had been imprisoned by King Edward I, visited Coldingham and reopened the question of the recompense he received for surrendering his procurations. Apparently the old arrangement had been modified, probably in a renewal of the concordat, to refer only to the churches of Earlston, Old Cambus, and Upsettlington; but the reward was the same: the chapels of Nenthorn and Newton. According to the monks of Coldingham the bishop swore that in twenty years he had barely received £40 from those chapels, whereas before he had obtained 40 marks a year. This, we know, was due to the impact of the war.[6] And so, in recompense for the

---

[1] *North Durham*, no. cccclxxix.   [2] *Concilia Scotiae*, 1225–1559, p. ccc.
[3] *North Durham*, no. cccclxxx.   [4] Ibid., nos. cccclxxxvi–cccclxxxvii.
[5] *Durham Annals and Documents*, nos. 42–6.

[6] In 1316 William de Lamberton exchanged the church of Nenthorn and the chapel of Newton, *ad mensam suam episcopalem spectantes*, with the abbey of Kelso for its church of Cranston. The bishop recognized that they were destroyed and devastated through the war, and agreed to pay Kelso 25 marks annually until they

loss from these three churches, he was insistent that Coldingham should pay him not less than £20 annually during the
truce. The monks made a settlement; but its terms are not
available.[1]

Even if episcopal visitation was unaccompanied by fees,
it was nevertheless in this period the occasion of great expense. In 1400 the sacristan of Coldingham accounted for
£10. 12s. 8d. spent at the visitation of the bishop, which
was the cost of wine bought for their visitor and of various
gifts to him and his officers.[2] The visitation of the parochial
churches also entailed feverish expenditure on repairs. In
1330 15s. 8d. were spent at Ednam and Earlston *in visi-
tacione episcopi*,[3] and, possibly as a result of the visit,
£12. 1s. 6d. on the repair of the chancel of Ednam.[4] In
1331–2 more money was spent *ante visitacionem episcopi*:
£1. 7s. 10d. on Ednam, 30s. 8d. on Earlston, and 76s. 8d. on
Edrom.[5] The visitations do not seem to have been unneces-
sary.

The liability of the convent's churches to common aids
had not been settled in detail in 1204. Perhaps it was not
then a burning question; but the growth of ecclesiastical
taxation in the thirteenth and fourteenth centuries forced it
into the front. Naturally the convent claimed no exemption
from papal burdens; it did, however, try to escape from some
of the financial concomitants of the growing centralization.
The clergy of the diocese of St. Andrews agreed to make
a common contribution to the expenses of nuncios going to
the General Council of Vienne in 1311. The Durham monks
claimed that they were not liable. Whereupon the bishop
wrote to his brother of Durham asking him to put pressure
on the monks. He evidently felt strongly on the point.
'For these monks', he declared, 'because of too great an
abundance of wordly goods, as we believe, are raised to such
pride that they will not reply obediently to their superiors;
and, although they act as part of the whole in the gathering
of profits, yet they do not care to co-operate with that whole

should reach that value. He also absolved the two churches from episcopal and
archidiaconal procurations, 'salvis episcopo et archidiacono iuribus episcopalibus
et archidiaconalibus in eisdem' (*Liber S. Marie de Calchou*, pp. 251–5.)

[1] *North Durham*, no. dlxxxiii.   [2] *Priory of Coldingham*, appendix, p. lxxx.
[3] Ibid., p. vii.   [4] Ibid., p. x.   [5] Ibid., pp. ix and xii.

in the attendant burdens.'[1] The outcome is unknown; but in the accounts of the cell for 1331–2 an item of episcopal taxation follows the papal,[2] and, although this may have been imposed *privilegialiter*, it would have been fully in accordance with the general trend if the parochial churches of Durham lost this immunity, which was based on the interpolated charter of Bishop Robert.

The liberties of the churches thus show a certain deterioration as far as the bishop was concerned. In those rights which touched his subordinates there was an entire collapse. The dean of Christianity of the Merse inducted priors into Coldingham,[3] and we have also the record of a fifteenth-century induction performed by the same official in the case of Berwick.[4] What is more surprising is to find the sacristan of Coldingham in 1364 and 1413 paying procurations to the archdeacon of Lothian in respect of the church of Coldingham and the chapel of Ayton,[5] and in 1365 paying the same official 12s. for synodal dues (*pro sengis*).[6] If the conventual church had come under the control of the archdeacon, we can safely infer that the parochial churches had also. The concordat of 1204 had prepared the way for the subjection of all the parish churches; but the subjection of Coldingham was an innovation, contrary to a series of indisputably genuine charters, and probably at variance with the common law of the Church.[7]

It is also clear that if the monks had at any time obtained a degree of ecclesiastical jurisdiction, this too had entirely

---

[1] *Priory of Coldingham*, no. ccxli, p. 243.   [2] Ibid., appendix, p. ix.

[3] In 1333 (*Priory of Coldingham*, no. xx); in 1341 (*North Durham*, no. ccccxciv); in 1362 (ibid., no. ccccxcvii); in 1419 (ibid., no. ccccxcix). In 1340, when the position of Coldingham was discussed in the royal courts of England, following the insubordination of one of the priors, Durham stated that the admission, institution, and induction of the priors of Coldingham pertained to the bishops of St. Andrews (*Reg. pal. Dun.* iv. 236).

[4] In 1423 (*North Durham*, no. d).

[5] *Priory of Coldingham*, appendix, pp. xliv and lxxxii.

[6] Ibid., p. xlviii.

[7] See Pope Innocent III on the duties of an archdeacon (*Decretales*, lib. II, tit. xxiii). The monastery of Scone, however, seems to have been subject to the archdeacon at quite an early date. In a charter of a William, bishop of St. Andrews, which confirms its freedom from episcopal customs, occurs the reservation, 'Salvo tamen in omnibus iure archidiaconi S. Andree' (*Liber ecclesie de Scon*, p. 35). Durham's cells of Jarrow and Wearmouth were also at times subject to the archdeacon (above, pp. 43 seqq.).

disappeared by the fourteenth century. The priory had trouble with the vicars of Edrom over their pensions, and in 1325 the expenses of the suit prosecuted in the synods and chapters are noted.[1] This case serves as a reminder of how valuable archidiaconal jurisdiction was to the owners of advowsons. In the Yorkshire franchise of the convent defaulting debtors got short shrift.

§ 4. *Retrospect*

When the Durham position in Coldinghamshire at the beginning of the twelfth century is considered, the failure of the convent to develop a satisfactory ecclesiastical franchise is rather surprising. The monks had a compact block of estates forming a secular franchise; they were themselves the builders or the refounders of several of their churches; and they had a flourishing cell at the head of the barony which simplified administration. It is most unlikely that the situation of the estates in another kingdom had any significance during the period of origins, and by the time that some sort of national consciousness affected the Durham position there was little left to lose. Indeed, there seem to have been no complications or special factors in the case. It is true that the acquisition of the barony was followed by a period of active and enlightened ecclesiastical reorganization; but this applies to some extent to the other dioceses in which the convent possessed churches.

It is the very absence of special factors which probably determined the fate of the franchise: the convent had no equitable claims to a share in the jurisdiction; the Lothian diocesans seem to have been opposed to monastic franchises of the type Durham acquired elsewhere, and when the monastery eventually advanced its claims they were of no use except as a bargaining weapon in the squabbles which attended the liquidation of their old proprietary rights and the establishment of the new. The bishops of St. Andrews clearly were good administrators, and in the face of episcopal vigilance the Durham monks were unable to usurp sufficient privileges to give much value to the forged charter of

[1] *Priory of Coldingham*, appendix, no. ii.

Bishop Robert. The explanation of the failure is simple and instructive: all things being equal the ordinary was bound to win, or, as Thomas de Marleberg judiciously observed, 'quia semper interpretandum est pro jure communi'.[1]

[1] *Chronicon abbatiae de Evesham*, p. 196.

CONCLUSIONS

A CHRISTIAN church is founded for the worship of God; and the purpose acts as a focus for property and rights. The intention is symbolized or materialized in the altar, which must be enclosed by a building, served by a priest, and supported by the faithful either willingly or under the compulsion of law. The basic endowments of most churches were the dowry of land and later the tithes of produce; but the revenue varied according to the status of the church and the wealth or generosity of the founder and of other benefactors. The complex of rights around the altar was not stable: its particles could be separated and reformed in countless permutations; and the master of the design was not the ecclesiastical authorities, but the founder or owner of the church; for the men who had seen the vision and provided the altar, and especially their heirs and descendants, naturally did not renounce interest in their creation. They provided the priest, and disposed of the revenue as seemed best to them. The property actually enjoyed by the server of the altar was thus a mutable part of the endowments of that shrine; and it was often not until the thirteenth century, when vicarages were taxed by the diocesan bishops, that their portion became stereotyped.[1]

The Church in England remembered fitfully the Roman system of government as recounted by its missionaries, and as introduced by Theodore of Tarsus; but the Gregorian plan for England remained unfulfilled, and even that little which had been achieved was at times in danger of destruction. Yet though churches from the bishopric to the field chapel could be regarded by laymen and clergy alike as only another form of property, so that they mostly followed the rules of law governing private estates, the purpose remained; and on that basis a reformed Church could create an ecclesiastical pattern which would in time for the most part replace the design formed by owners and their property.

[1] It is not implied that the vicarage was immutable. The taxations, were, of course, often revised by the diocesan. But changes could only be made by due process of law.

We have seen that the relationship of churches to their proprietors had a basic position in the history of franchises, because it was for the *Eigenkirchen* that privileges were claimed. In this connexion appropriation became of some importance. It translated *Eigenkirchentum* into the language of the thirteenth century: *ecclesiae propriae* became *ecclesiae in proprios usus*. But the rights of an owner, even of a monastic owner of churches, were not sufficient on their own to create a franchise in efficiently administered dioceses, as the history of Coldinghamshire shows. Claims based on ownership, such as the right to enjoy the fruits during a vacancy in the church (*custodia*), to invest the new priest with the temporalities (*institutio corporalis*), and to appropriate at will, received a check during that reaction against the feudal grip on the Church, which not only shook the hold of the king of England on his bishoprics and abbeys at the turn of the eleventh century, and affected the rights of all proprietors in the course of the twelfth, but also rooted out the hereditary parsons in the churches of their owners. For the dioceses of Durham and St. Andrews the crucial period seems to have been towards the end of the twelfth century, when the increasing power of the ordinary and the growing tradition of regular diocesan administration were sufficiently strong to extirpate almost all corollaries of an archaic conception of ownership which had perdured when the churches were in ecclesiastical hands. And at the same time, at least in the diocese of Durham, the convent had been less successful in freeing its churches from the hold of the parsons. This probably represents the inevitable deceleration in the impulse of reform as it passed down the hierarchy of the Church; and it meant that victory lay with the bishops.

The importance of the dispersal of episcopal rights and of their possession by the proprietors of churches has been well illustrated by these histories: in Coldinghamshire the monks were unable to acquire the more important episcopal customs and failed to develop a franchise; in the diocese of Durham possession of the episcopal customs of synodals, procurations, and aids was obtained, but was held to provide an immunity only against the financial demands of the bishop and not against his functions, and, moreover, was held as of little value against the claims of the archdeacons. In Yorkshire the customs, including the right of justice, were secured, and there an archidiaconal franchise was created. This seems to show that jurisdictional rights were the most important. Whoever possessed the jurisdiction which would normally have pertained to the archdeacon almost inevitably enjoyed an archidiaconal peculiar.

The original alienation was of episcopal rights. In the course of the twelfth century they changed into archidiaconal rights. This reflects the history of the archdeacons. Similar *episcopalia* had been entrusted to the archdeacons, and had been usurped and later retained by them as part of their ordinary jurisdiction. But the bishop had refused to accept a limitation of his powers, and had debased the alienated functions by creating new episcopal rights of visiting, holding synods, and dispensing justice superior to those usurped by the archdeacons. Hence the *episcopalia* in the hands of the immunists had depreciated in sympathy, and certain types of liberties were accordingly considered archdeaconries.

The Durham franchises were in the beginning to a large extent personal and, therefore, movable. They comprised the proprietary churches of the bishop and convent, and charters were designed so as to admit later acquisitions of the immunist into the favours granted. The durability of these characteristics depended greatly on the nature of the immunist and his relationship with the grantor of the liberties. They lasted longest with bishops. The acquisition of an estate by a bishop in the diocese of another even in the later Middle Ages might lead to an extension of the area of his franchise. Cathedral chapters, too, might hope at all times, though with far less confidence, to exploit their position within their own diocese. This personal conception of a franchise also had a limiting effect. Just as on lay baronies a distinction was made between 'lands held in demesne as of fee' and the rest of the fief, which is often of importance in the history of secular franchises,[1] so in connexion with ecclesiastical privileges a distinction was observed between

---

[1] Sidney Painter, *Studies in the History of the English Feudal Barony* (The Johns Hopkins University Studies in Historical and Political Science, ser. lxi, no. 3, 1943), pp. 73 seqq.

that area which was immediately subordinate to the franchisal authority and the rest of its estates; and only those parishes under his direct control were considered preeminently worthy of privilege. A good and ambitious lord would, of course, endeavour to bring all his mesne tenants within the scope of his franchise; but it was regarded as a separate undertaking. The early history of Durham's franchise in Yorkshire illustrates this restrictive factor: the liberties were accorded not to the Durham fiefs but to the proprietary churches and demesne manors of the bishopric.

It should be noticed that the appropriation of parish churches can also be viewed from this angle: appropriated churches can be regarded as the demesne churches of the monastery, and those granted to parsons as analogous to mesne fiefs. There is an obvious equity in this distinction. If a monastery is considered as enjoying its franchise because it is a favoured monastery, or because it is the bishop's chapter, then privileges should apply only where the monastery was directly concerned and obtained the full benefit. At the same time the monastery was interested in extending its franchise to the alienated portions of its estates in order to increase its revenue, its control, and, above all, its prestige. This distinction in matters of franchise between the appropriated churches and the rest is seen clearly in the history of the convent of Durham's peculiar in its own diocese.

While such personal ideas were dominant franchises remained to some extent fluid, although viscous is, perhaps, a more suitable description. It is clear, moreover, that the mobility of the franchise varied according to the period. After the Durham immunities had been maintained, extended, or created at the turn of the eleventh century there was little movement again until a hundred years later, when the convent's policy of appropriation reached its climax. But at this time the eagerness with which the monastery was seeking not only to extend but to transform and consolidate its privileges was matched by the zeal of the diocesans in questioning the legality and scope of the peculiars; and this rival activity led naturally to a series of concordats and to definition. In the process the franchises were limited and stabilized. In the diocese of Durham the settlement was not final; but in the diocese of St. Andrews far more was achieved, and in the diocese of York the liberties assumed the names of ancient shires and lasted unchanged until modern times. The movement towards definition at the end of the twelfth century was doubtless the result of a new administrative efficiency common to all governments.

In discussing the origin of these franchises it has not been considered enough simply to say that episcopal customs were alienated; we have had to consider why the episcopal jurisdiction should have been divided. In the case of each of these Durham franchises we were led to ask what equitable claims the convent had to a franchise or what external powers could have desired that the convent should be preferentially treated. In the case of Coldinghamshire Durham had no special claim except that it was a monastery with a cell and a barony in Lothian. In the diocese of Durham it was part of the cathedral body, the bishop's chapter, the inheritor of a joint tradition. And it was through this special position alone that the franchise was successful, for the claim to an archdeaconry, which was in the end admitted, came mainly from that position and not from possession of the episcopal customs. In Yorkshire the manors of the church of Durham were those of the most important diocesan bishop in the province, and it was natural for the archbishop to extend or tolerate an extension of privileges accorded to such a person by his predecessors. This necessity to look behind the alienation of the customs is probably to some extent a reflection of the lateness of the period of origins. At the end of the eleventh century the natural tendency towards the feudalization of bishoprics had lost momentum, and the episcopal customs were alienated only in the most exceptional circumstances.

In the history of each of the Durham franchises spurious charters play a part, but hardly the dramatic role often associated with forgeries. As the monastery of Durham was only founded in 1083, Anglo-Saxon charters could not be created; hence the documents that were forged could not be used until nearly the end of the twelfth century. The long dormancy thus imposed had its effect on the development of the liberties, for in consequence they had to be established and maintained through a critical period without documentary support; and this characteristic gives particular value to the history of the Durham peculiars: we can discern the interplay of different tendencies unhampered by adventitious elements. In the absence of written titles peaceful possession of the rights claimed was of primary importance; and this brings us back to the factor of special justification. Only where the privileges were considered reasonable by the diocesan could peaceful possession be established. The bishops of St. Andrews saw no cause to tolerate a franchise, and successfully withstood the convent's claims. The bishops of Durham often behaved as an outraged parent towards a rebellious and grasping son, denying in their anger privileges which otherwise would have been permitted; yet the relationship and its implications remained. The archbishops of York, faced with the traditional rights of the whole church of Durham, were usually complaisant.

Although the forgeries were of little practical importance during the twelfth century, they were at all times of value. The nature of the usefulness passed through three main stages. While the Durham charters matured they provided a programme of action. The leaders of the monks were never allowed to forget the policy which had been laid down by their predecessors. When the charters took on active life towards the close of the twelfth century they had a twofold value. They were a half-concealed threat which the diocesans had to consider; and, when accepted as true or as incapable of disproof, they acquired a positive, though limited, legal value. In no case in this middle period could they be used to obtain possession of rights where there had been no anterior physical possession. Where the discrepancy between legal claim and actual conditions was wide, the forgeries could be used only as something with a compensatory value, with the compensation in proportion to the reality of the claims which were dropped. In Lothian, for instance, the monks obtained little in return for abandoning their full legal claims; in Durham the convent did rather better. By the second half of the thirteenth century the forgeries had assumed an ornamental quality. They satisfied the craving for a long history and ancient titles; and they were convenient and suitably distinguished for exhibition when in the later Middle Ages episcopal visitations took on *quo warranto* characteristics, and claims to any special privilege had regularly to be proved. And yet, although they may often have appeared an obsolete and harmless muniment, a picturesque relic of olden times, they were still munitions of war. The history of the convent's Durham archdeaconry shows how their hostile character lay but concealed under an ageing respectability.

The origin of the franchises lay in a private grouping of churches and the fragmentation of the bishop's office and territorial see. Tradition and the inertia which is found when rights and revenues are associated with land, especially when the particular customs and dues are absorbed into the endowment of a religious corporation, secured the maintenance of the system. Monasteries, it is true, were not concerned with the parochial cure of souls, and bishops had no proper interest in the diocese of another greater than that which they should have in their own. But to break their franchise was to deprive them of revenue. A movement to divorce financial customs from jurisdiction is noticed towards the end of the twelfth century. This, however, ran contrary to the medieval principle that the duty should go with the reward, and it produced a solution attractive to neither party. To the ordinary it meant labour without due profit, and to the immunist an insecure financial right. It was, therefore, basically unstable.

The financial advantages obtained from these immunities varied with the period. When the episcopal customs were first alienated they were no doubt chiefly prized by the possessors for their negative aspect, the freedom from the demands of the bishop. The possession of the customs, however, always implied their exploitation by the immunist, although in the early days dues could doubtless be collected without performing much in return for them, and the profits of courts could be obtained without an active intervention in the process of justice. But, as administrative efficiency spread through the governments of Europe, the duties of the immunist were quickened, and clearly without the performance of the functions for which the financial rights were payments the immunity must collapse either through atrophy or through the interference of a reforming bishop. If the franchise consolidated into an archdeaconry the advantages were great. The immunist had the financial profits of visitation and of synods and of the justice done in them;[1] he had effective control over the temporalities of his churches and the clerks who held them; and the monastic immunist had an area in which it was its own master, where it could publish its excommunications and pursue its own schemes without immediate hindrance.[2] In the exclusion of the archdeacon from their parishes monasteries must have felt a real joy, such as the relief that a borough experienced when it escaped from the sheriff, or the elation of an abbot when he was freed from episcopal control. These privileged areas are described as franchises and liberties. Even in the most feudal period the words had overtones beyond their legal meaning.

[1] The profits of the jurisdiction do not appear to have been great, and were certainly insignificant compared with the other revenues derived from churches. In 1293 the convent obtained £1,466. 16s. 4d. from its appropriated churches. This had sunk to £353. 0s. 6d. in 1436 owing to inability to collect from Scotland, the effect of the wars on Northumberland, pestilence, and, especially, the conversion of arable to pasture which reduced the tithe of corn (*Scriptores tres*, pp. ccxlviii–cclii). To be added to this are the pensions from the rectors. Out of the profits of jurisdiction during the nineteen and a half years of Prior Wessington's rule (1416–46) £13. 17s. 8d. was spent on repairs: 'Item reparaciones factae per officiales prioris de pecuniis receptis de jurisdictione xiijˡ. xvijˢ viijᵈ' (*Scriptores tres*, p. cclxxv); and in the inventory of 1446 the profits of jurisdiction are omitted: 'Perquisita jurisdiccionis et sinodalium. De perquisitis jurisdiccionis et sinodalium pro majori parte nichil ultra feoda; ideo non onerantur hic, nec assessantur ad aliquam summam' (ibid., p. ccciii.) The *Rentale bursarii* of 1539 also has no entries under the headings 'Perquisita jurisdictionis de Houedenshiere' and 'Perquisita jurisdictionis et synodalium infra diocesim Dunelm' et Aluertoneshieram' (*F.P.D.*, p. 328). A memorial of John Wessington re Howdenshire and Allertonshire also suggests that jurisdictional profits merely covered the expenses: 'Item, contra rectores ecclesiarum de patronatu prioris et capituli Dunelm' in Hovedenshir et Alvertonshir, asserentes ecclesias suas oneratas esse annuis pensionibus dictis priori et capitulo persolvendis racione jurisdiccionis et ejus exercitio in dictis suis ecclesiis per ipsos rectores clero et populo eorundem exercendis, et non per priorem et capitulum antedictos (*Scriptores tres*, p. cclxxi).

[2] The importance which the convent attached to the right of excommunication is shown by the quarrels with the bishop over the prior's right to excommunicate *qua* dean in the period preceding 'Le convenit'. See 'Attestationes testium', *F.P.D.*, pp. 220 seqq.

APPENDIX

THE EARLIEST ARCHDEACONS OF DURHAM

THERE is no evidence that the title of archdeacon was used in the church of Durham before the Norman Conquest, when the dean of the cathedral chapter acted as the bishop's vice-gerent. The first 'Norman' bishop, Walcher, made no change; but it is significant that Symeon of Durham calls Dean Leobwine archdeacon.[1] When the clerks of St. Cuthbert were replaced by Benedictine monks in 1083 the dean accepted the new order, and may have continued to act as dean/archdeacon until Prior Turgot succeeded him in 1093, possibly on his death.[2] Le Neve and T. Duffus Hardy,[3] followed by the Rev. D. S. Boutflower,[4] list Aldwine, the first prior, as archdeacon of Durham. This is untenable. That Turgot should have been appointed archdeacon by Bishop William of Saint-Calais seven years after his succession to the office of prior on Aldwine's death, and, moreover, that Symeon should have remarked on Turgot's promotion that the bishop did not take the step without authority and precedent—for there was a precedent to be found in the Life of St. Cuthbert,[5] makes it abundantly clear that Aldwine had not been archdeacon. Turgot's appointment was the logical development of the conception of a monastic bishopric as held by William of Saint-Calais; but so closely was the new office associated with the old that Turgot too could be styled dean.[6] And Symeon's remarks on Turgot's elevation also are noticeably old-fashioned. He says that Turgot was put in charge of the Christianity of the see and was to discharge the function of preacher. There is little here of the new office of archdeacon.

William of Saint-Calais had envisaged a prior-archdeacon as a permanent part of the constitution of the church of Durham.[7] But the succession to the bishopric of Ranulf Flambard, a secular who was apparently soon displeased with the pretensions of his monastic chapter, put an end to that plan. Ranulf is said to have engineered Turgot's election to the bishopric of St. Andrews in 1107 in order to remove him from Durham, and there seems to have been no monkish archdeacon after Turgot.[8] The succession, however, of the secular archdeacons has not been satisfactorily established; nor has the date of the creation of a second archdeaconry in the church—that which later took its

[1] See above, p. 13, n. 8. [2] See above, pp. 13–14.
[3] *Fasti ecclesiae Anglicanae* (1854).
[4] *Fasti Dunelmenses* (Surtees Soc., vol. 139, 1926).
[5] *Symeonis H.D.E.*, i. 129. [6] See above, p. 3, n. 3 and p. 13, n. 2.
[7] See above, pp. 3–4. [8] See above, p. 13.

name from Northumberland—been fixed with any certainty. One of the difficulties encountered in compiling satisfactory series is that the archdeacons in this period did not use territorial designations. Lists, therefore, tend to become swollen through the inclusion of aliens and duplicates. A re-examination of the evidence, however, allows us to prune severely.

The *Fasti ecclesiae Anglicanae* offers as archdeacons 'of Durham' Michael (occ. 1099 × 1128), Robert (occ. 1129), Turstin (occ. *c*. 1143), and Wazo (occ. 1 Dec. 1147), and as archdeacons 'of Northumberland' Robert (occ. 1140), Ralph (occ. 1140 × 3 and 1153), and William (occ. 1160). Boutflower added Henry (occ. 1104) to the 'Durham' list and William (occ. 1104) to the 'Northumberland' list, and he revised the dates for Archdeacon Ralf (Ranulf) to 1131–53.

Boutflower's additions are erroneous. Archdeacons Henry and William Havegrim are noticed as present at the translation of St. Cuthbert in 1104. Several accounts of the disinterment have been preserved. That printed as *Capitula de miraculis et translationibus sancti Cuthberti* describes two inspections of the body in the autumn of 1104, the first by nine brethren of the chapter, the second, after a wave of scepticism and indignation at the secrecy, by a mixed commission.[1] In the *Reginaldi monachi Dunelmensis libellus* nine persons are named as participating in the disentombment, and these include the archdeacons Henry and William Havegrim.[2] From this coincidence of number arose the error, for Thomas Arnold identified the nine brethren with Reginald's seven brethren and two archdeacons.[3] But, as a reference to the presence of Ralf, abbot of Séez, proves, Reginald's nine were the principal assistants at the second and impartial ceremony. Hence the archdeacons were not necessarily Durham monks, nor in any way connected with the church of Durham. Turgot, the prior, was at the ceremonies of 1104, and there is no reason to suppose that he had ceased to be the one archdeacon.

Turgot's immediate successor seems to have been Michael.[4] Boutflower claims to have found him as early as 1108.[5] If this is correct Turgot must have resigned his archdeaconry on his election to St. Andrews, and before his consecration, although the accepted date for Algar's succession to Turgot as prior is 1109. Robert followed Michael before the death of Bishop Ranulf Flambard in 1128,[6] and occurs in 1131,[7] 1133 × 40,[8] and 1141.[9] He supported the unsuccessful can-

[1] *Symeonis opera*, i. 249, 258. [2] Ed. Jas Raine (Surtees Soc., vol. i), p. 84.
[3] *Symeonis opera*, i. 249 n. [4] *F.P.D.*, pp. lxi, lxiii.
[5] Op. cit., p. 88; but in the list p. 153 the entry is 'before 1128'. Occurs 1109 × 28 (W. Dugdale, *Monasticon Anglicanum*, ed. J. Caley, iv. 332).
[6] See below, p. 155, n. 4. [7] *F.P.D.*, p. 56 n. [8] Ibid., p. 205 n.
[9] *Symeonis Dunelmensis historiae continuatio prima*, i. 145.

didate of the Empress Matilda and King David of Scotland for the bishopric—William Cumin—in opposition to the choice of the monks, William of St. Barbe, whom King Stephen accepted, and we lose sight of him during the troubles. Wazo (Gwace) is found as the successor to Michael and Robert on 1 December 1147, when a dispute between him and Prior Roger over precedence was decided in the latter's favour.[1] Although there was an appeal to history, no mention is made of Archdeacon Turstin; indeed, he seems excluded by the language used: 'archidiaconos vero Michaelem et Rodbertum, qui Wazonem praecesserant'. There appears to be no evidence for Turstin's tenure besides the bare assertion of Le Neve and Hardy. He may have been a creature of William Cumin, if Robert died during the schism; but it does not seem that he still deserves a place in the list.

Two archdeacons are for the first time found indisputably together in 1131, during the vacancy of the see.[2] The second archdeacon was Ralf (Ranulfus), a nephew of the late bishop, Ranulf Flambard.[3] There can be little doubt, therefore, that it was Ranulf Flambard who created the archdeaconry 'of Northumberland'; but evidence for Ralf's tenure of the office under his uncle is not complete. It cannot be overlooked, however, that the four witnesses to Bishop Ranulf's act of restoration to the monks in 1128 are Archdeacon Robert, Ralf, Osbert, nephew of the bishop, and Roger Coigners.[4] The order of precedence suggests that Ralf was the second archdeacon; but the omission of his title, indeed of any description, is hard to explain. It is possible that his appointment was an innovation, and that the scribe was uncertain of the etiquette. Several men, however, with the name Ralf were in Ranulf Flambard's *familia*. St. Godric met the bishop accompanied by his son, Ralf the clerk, and by Ralf the priest.[5] Even if we think it likely that the son, the clerk, and the nephew, the archdeacon, were in fact the same person, there is no proof that it was this Ralf who witnessed the bishop's charter of 1128. Nevertheless the presumption remains that his archdeaconry dates from before Bishop Ranulf's death. Archdeacon Ralf is found several times during the episcopate of Geoffrey Rufus,[6] and he played a leading part during the schism in the church after the death of that bishop, receiving favourable notice for his staunch support of the monks and William of St.

---

[1] *F.P.D.*, pp. lx–lxiii.   [2] Ibid., p. 56 n.

[3] *Symeonis historia regum continuata per Joh. Hagustaldensem*, ii. 312.

[4] *Scriptores tres*, p. xxx.

[5] Reginald, *Libellus de vita et miraculis S. Godrici*, ed. J. Stevenson (Surtees Soc., vol. 20), p. 66.

[6] 1139 × 52 (*F.P.D.*, p. 103 n.), 1143 × 52 (ibid., p. 132 n.), 1147 (ibid., pp. lxi, lxiii), and 1149 × 52 (ibid., p. lxiv).

Barbe, the victorious candidate.[1] Ralf was still alive at the election of Hugh of le Puiset to the bishopric on 22 January 1153.[2] He had a nephew, Wibert, a knight, who was in the service of Bishop Geoffrey Rufus.[3]

Archdeacon Ralf's predecessor is given both in the *Fasti ecclesiae Anglicanae* and the *Fasti Dunelmenses* as Robert. Le Neve's Robert, however, occurred in 1140, and is therefore undoubtedly Robert, archdeacon 'of Durham'. Boutflower, who amplified Ralf's tenure of the archdeaconry so as to make this date impossible, retained the name, but discreetly suppressed the date, thus pushing Robert back into the shadowy past. The position is, then, that no predecessor to Archdeacon Ralf is known; and it may well be that none existed. Bishop Ranulf Flambard may have created the new office because he wanted to promote his nephew, or son, at a time when the one archdeaconry was already occupied.

If our reasoning is correct the lists of the early archdeacons become quite simple:

'Durham'	*'Northumberland'*
Turgot 1093—1107 (?)	Ralf *ante* 1128—*post* 1153
Michael 1108 (?)—*ante* 1128	
Robert *ante* 1128—*post* 1141	
Wazo *ante* Dec. 1147	

[1] *Symeonis contin. prima*, i. 144 seqq.; 'vir praeclarae probitatis', John of Hexham, loc. cit. ii. 312.

[2] John of Hexham, loc. cit. ii. 328.

[3] Reginald, *Libellus*, p. 106.

INDEX

Persons are indexed under Christian names

PRINTED IN GREAT BRITAIN
AT THE UNIVERSITY PRESS, OXFORD
BY CHARLES BATEY, PRINTER TO THE UNIVERSITY

WESTFIELD COLLEGE
LIBRARY
UNIVERSITY OF LONDON